CONSCIENCE AND MEMORY

CONSCIENCE AND MEMORY

Meditations in a Museum of the Holocaust

Harold Kaplan

•

The University of Chicago Press
Chicago and London

Harold Kaplan was professor of English at Northwestern University from 1972 to 1986. He is the author of *Democratic Humanism and American Literature* (1972) and *Power and Order: Henry Adams and the Naturalist Tradition in American Fiction* (1981).

The University of Chicago Press, Chicago 60637
The University of Chicago Press Ltd., London
© 1994 by The University of Chicago
All rights reserved. Published 1994
Printed in the United States of America
03 02 01 00 99 98 97 96 95 94   1 2 3 4 5

ISBN: 0-226-42416-2 (cloth)

Library of Congress Cataloging-in-Publication Data

Kaplan, Harold, 1916–
    Conscience and memory : meditations in a museum of the Holocaust / Harold Kaplan.
        p.   cm.
    Includes index.
    1. Holocaust, Jewish (1939–1945)—Moral and ethical aspects.
I. Title.
D804.3.K36   1994
940.53′18—dc20   93-15485
                                                                          CIP

I dedicate this book to Jean Améry and Primo Levi.

I further dedicate this work to the future of the new museum of the Holocaust in Washington, an American museum on American soil, which inevitably must search the American national conscience in the shadow of the Holocaust.

For my brothers

Contents

Introduction

"By Auschwitz everything is to be measured," said one German voice in a recent symposium. The reasoning for making so large a claim may or may not be sound, but it is inevitable in the face of the event which in itself, some would say, remains unmeasurable. The challenge cannot be avoided. The Holocaust has arrived in the category of great apocalyptic events which succeeding generations have used as their standard of measure for right and wrong, good and evil in the growth of moral civilization. The examples have classic origin in the Bible with the Fall, the Flood, the Crucifixion; in history with the Inquisition, with the French and Russian Revolutions; and today, with Hiroshima, the Gulag, and the Holocaust.

The problem is that the moral significance of the Holocaust seems either terribly obvious or terrible in mystery, and in either case inaccessible. A recent colloquium, gathering some of the most distinguished writers and students of the Holocaust who had given their lives to its report, ended astoundingly with the agreement that it defied comprehension, that one could not find "meaning" in it, that is, meaning in the sense demanded by an ordinary writing task of history or fiction.

They were saying, in effect, that the Holocaust breaks down the essential terms by which we think and communicate. We are at the margin where we begin our moral lives, but it is that very margin of incomprehensibility that outlines clarity for the assumptions we make for the human estate. For to say something is incomprehensible is only to suggest certain terms by which to circumscribe our nature and its limits, and beyond which lies what is unintelligible.

It is remarkable how many of those who have addressed the Holocaust with eloquence have almost simultaneously recommended silence and done penance for speaking. We understand what it is that commands silence, and the eternal criticism that interrupts us. In a sense, silence here is an effort to allow extinguished voices to be heard. It is the victims' silence that is a problem, not ours. If we speak, we bring them back out of chaos; they come back to human identity and bring us back as well, for the human identity, though enclosed by silence, is our one inheritance. Why do we write about the Holocaust? Elie Wiesel makes the point that we write to have continuity with the dead. It is a rebuff to meet their silence with our own. For that which extinguishes the bonded life and the mutuality of consciousness is the most meaningfully meaningless death, the one the Germans called *"Vernichtung."*

The Holocaust, at the edge of all moral boundaries, is where discourse stops as before the unspeakable, but also where it begins. The memory of the Holocaust comes in a glaring light that casts a shadow over everything in our moral and political lives that we can respect. It is not absolutely necessary to understand the motives and reasons of the Nazis. Any uncovering of them humiliates us, humiliates the mind. The accused at Nuremberg were more than slightly comic. The very size of their crimes reduced them and added a pain to memory that we hardly expected. This essentially is what Hannah Arendt must have meant in propounding the banality of evil. Against the background of the Holocaust, human motives, explanations, justifications, descend to idiocy. What is important in remembering the Holocaust is not the reasons of the Nazis but the reason in us that is shocked. Why are we shocked? To what does our confusion of pain point?

•

One effort of the following text is to follow a path through the confusion of an apocalyptic event to its "ethical testimony." The latter is a term used by Emmanuel Levinas in his view of the serial narratives of the Bible.[1] The moral imagination requires vivid testimony from actual or mythical events. Whether Noah's flood took place or not is a moot question when considered alongside its ancient role in human memory and conscience. Similarly, the literal actuality of the Crucifixion has little bearing on its historic effects in civilized consciousness.

Today, we do not have a standard narrative of the Holocaust made invulnerable to obsessed skeptics and the argument of variant political and philosophic prejudices; we have an immense and wounding truth, testified to by a great number of witnesses. And though the actual survivors may be disappearing, the act of witness continues, with memorials and museums, and an increasing flow of documents, texts of scholarship, and literary embodiments, as well as popular narratives in fiction and film with their typically ambiguous division between morbid enthrallment and instruction.

If this means that the Holocaust is gradually becoming a "myth," in the sense implied by Levinas in describing the large radiating ethical testimony of the Bible, so be it. But it is a difficult myth, not at all because it deviates from factual truth but the opposite, because its reality transgresses belief. When we enter the world of the Holocaust in renewed witness, it as if all lights were turned out and we grope in the dark, impelled only by flashes of insight that are the effects of moral shock. That shock can be creative; it points to something in human nature and civilization that demands our effort to understand. The intention in this book is to explore the basis of terror and latent despair as we review the story of the Holocaust, much as visitors to the new museum in Washington or Yad Vashem in Israel might make the attempt.

That would explain the method of this book. I write as if in soliloquy, in passages that may seem parallel rather than serial. Consecutive narrative is impossible for studies of the Holocaust which want intimacy with their actual effect upon a consciousness struggling for comprehension. It may be that only questions are possible, interrupted answers, abortive explanations, and yet, one hopes, there may be judgment, something that touches conscience as well as memory, but with sharpness, unclouded by abstraction and generalizing formulae. As for questions, here are two I shall not be able to answer with sufficiency, and yet they lead me to write. What is it in human nature and institutions that made the Holocaust possible? And what is it in human nature and institutions that could make its recurrence improbable?

The difficulty comes in the way the Nazi regime, in its commitment to total violence, undermined the basis of judgment. Who can give reasoned motivation to Hitler and Himmler, Eichmann and Hoess? Early, as the slaughter was beginning, Elias Canetti wrote, "We have no standard any more for anything, ever since human life is no longer the standard."[2] But that may be the clue for revival, to look back to that standard, to cling to it. The dead are hungry, Elie Wiesel wrote in one of his narratives, *Dawn*. And, said Canetti, they "are nourished by judgment."

Without the least pretension, when treating the Holocaust one deals with first and last things. Did the Holocaust signal a modern moral apocalypse? Then ordinary historical and geopolitical terms will not do in discussing it. We need to revive archaic language in the epic of a civilization contemplating destruction or barbaric descent. The Nazi regime was an extraordinary effort to reduce mankind to animalistic nature, its pure living principle being the power to survive and prey on others. That is why it remains a case of civilization being tested in apocalyptic terms. Theodor Adorno, who once proposed that poetry died at Auschwitz, could only have meant that poetry had been given an exorbitant task.

Our worst fears for the devaluation of life, rightly or wrongly applied to euthanasia, genetic engineering, and, for some, abortion, were made real by the Nazis. We will not forget their experiment with the desacralization of the body and the death of the soul. A reductive consciousness, like a demon, ruled the world. And that, unfortunately, must condition all moral philosophy, whether in retrospect for this event or in preparation for future devastation in the human systems that protect life.

If we philosophize at all, we should do it in response to the major events of our lives that really challenge philosophy. The first duty of all students of the Holocaust is to record what happened, as clearly and completely as possible, since so much interest is applied to evading or coloring what happened. The Holocaust was an event and thus lives in thought. To say that the Holocaust is beyond explanation and therefore meaningless is to reduce it to a nonevent.

The second duty of students, then, is to pursue meaning to its ultimate border with the void. To begin again at that point is to begin the moral life. Did Albert Camus think of the death camps when he wrote about suicide as the background for all thought? And did Primo Levi and Jean Améry, the most articulate and compelling of survivors, pronounce final judgment in their own suicides? The Holocaust was a mass drama of testing the will to live. Every memory of the Holocaust begins to strive for replacing what was lost and destroyed. Or to put it this way, we think of the Holocaust in order to deny murder and suicide a complete victory.

But though Améry, and like him Primo Levi, admit despair of thought, both were the first to contradict themselves and say they could not dismiss judgment. The primordial chaos may be unintelligible, but their fate was to acknowledge it and take again the first step that makes them human. Take it as an obsession, we must live as if we were survivors, as if in the twentieth century it was destined that civilization end and begin again. If there was a sacrifice, it was to give us an experience we could not otherwise have, and which leads or could lead to the place where Abba Kovner, soldier and survivor of the Vilna ghetto, spoke when he said, "The destruction that we, for the lack of a better word, call 'the Holocaust,' brings every rational one of us back to the basis of human existence."[3]

•

In this writing I make the legally problematic, half-understood formula used by the Nuremberg War Crimes Tribunal, a crime against humanity, a center of my text. Since the trials of 1946, the world has been mystified or made skeptical by that largest of indictments. Was all humanity injured by those criminal attacks on Jews, some Gypsies, some Russian prisoners of war, the mentally ill, the sexually perverse? The Nazis sincerely thought they were purging and redeeming humanity. How do we attest the opposite without calling on a viable concept of general humanity? What moral force is behind that abstraction?

Some have said that the view of general suffering blurs the crime and diminishes the fate of the actual victims. Many Jewish students of the Holocaust reject the effort to diffuse the specific anti-Semitic intent of the Holocaust. And they are right in the sense that the distinctive crime of the Nazis found its source in their gospel of racism. But that is exactly what defines their crime against humanity.

It is futile to keep the Holocaust strictly an issue between the Germans and the Jews, forbidding all palliations by analogy and example. Enough has been written to cite the passive or active complicity of other peoples, and the dimensions of the Holocaust itself forbids the particularist view of it; human nature is at risk, civilization is in judgment, all men a part of that judgment. The Jews who were victims appealed in vain for rescue or intercession. Now, out of a pride of suffering, should they reject the collaboration in memory? Anger is understandable when one sees the Holocaust made an ecumenical issue after much of its death was caused by the refusal of so many to take its ecumenical meaning and act upon it. But to build a wall now between non-Jews and the Holocaust is only to confirm the wall that the Nazis built and which much of the world then accepted.[4] Whatever we say of a great crime and its punishment, the true universality of the Holocaust lies in its legacy to conscience.

Disregarding the temptations to judge divine fallibility, or the cosmic mystery of evil, or the unreachable depth of motive in irrational violence, the study of the Holocaust must return to mundane issues as if we were arguing with Nazism, not during or after the moral apocalypse but before—when the political structures and moral indoctrination of Germany and Europe were first being tested. What are the themes of warning, of what should a people beware? They must suspect "problems" which have totalist range and whose "solution" determines society's fate. They should dread solutions which are "final" and conflicts which are "final," as in the Communist anthem. They must be warned against welcoming the redemptive apocalypse, a new purified world born out of wide destruction. Skeptics they must be against the idolatry of group self-worship and its cults and symbols. They must consider that the first heresy of worship is that of a vitalist nature, whether mystically or scientistically proposed. The second heresy is the superstition that accepts the tyrant laws of history and the megalomania that claims to embody them. Biology as fate, survivalist doctrines, and belief in the inevitable cycles of the rise and fall of civilizations lead to the chief political evil of our century, the ethos of power which subsumes all behavior and dictates or cancels all values. In conclusion one is led to say that intellectually melodramatic and monothematic interpetations of history and culture can be a threat to human life.

But even as we moralize we may be conscious that the danger is moral abstraction itself. As Simon Leys writes in an article on the Chinese student massacre of the summer of 1989, totalitarians will always sacrifice "man for mankind" in the abstraction of their political goals.[5] How shall all those millions of Chinese, Russians, and Jews dead in this century help recover a humanist autonomy, where individual lives keep intrinsic and independent value, transcending the bigotries we associate with international wars, civil wars, religious wars, and revolutions?

What is needed is a chance to overcome the image recorded by Primo Levi, now enhanced by his own suicide, the image of the cold flickering glance of an SS officer measuring the fat on the buttocks of those he judged and ordering death with an uplifted finger. Around him silence, before him the passive assent of those chosen for life or death. This reflects the moral descent I place as the chief injury of the Holocaust, a wound hard to overcome and one experienced by all humankind. Levi's calm description points to a kind of logic that pervades the event, accepted by murderers and victims alike, who had transcended or subscended the level of murder. They were dealing with extinction, the nearest parallel being that used by the Nazis—the extermination of insects and slaughter of microbes. There is in the Holocaust something that resists description in language, for language is penetrated by certain assumptions that give irreducible value to life and to the bond that life makes between those who share it. One can kill in rage and fear, for self-defense or in the name of justice against crime, in the interest of profit or personal happiness, and all these do not necessarily extinguish the "soul" or the testamentary being of the person killed. On the contrary, these acts might give transcendent valuation to life, as when executioner and victim both see the life at stake in terms of laws broken and justice reclaimed, or when rivals for happiness exchange violence in the name of that goal, no matter how defined or measured. We feel a special shame and violation when we hear of a murder committed for a few dollars and cheap possessions.

It is very hard to distinguish qualitatively among the many forms of death, and perhaps for the living it is always an insincere expression. But the Holocaust makes it easier. As André Neher sets the issue, Auschwitz introduced "a new kind of death in the history of humanity."[6] We know that ordinary death was surpassed by that imposed by the Nazis when they violated human personhood and finally destroyed it. This it is, I believe, that impels the unremitting study of the Holocaust, not in eternal accusation but as an eternal problem for human self-understanding. In that context Emmanuel Levinas was surely right in his lesson which implies that the mirror reverse image of murder is not love, or compassion, but "responsibility" for the life of the Other. There is, of course, a world of meaning to be extracted from that premise which becomes nothing less than the imperative for a reconstructed human ethic.

•

At that point speculation should be free, and so I propose this book as a set of meditations, held closely to actual witness and the considerable richness of the literature of the Holocaust. The first two chapters describe the perspective in which I see the Holocaust in its lessons for memory, which I take to be the purpose of the new museum in Washington as well as those which exist elsewhere in the world. Writing is memory in the process of creating itself. In this case memory is of a great shock or wound, and if I dwell on it it is because I wish to explore the sensibility—human, moral, formative, and affirmative—which received the wound. The primary theme in Chapter 2 is the search for the "human," as concept and existential reality attacked by the Nazis in a program we universally and simply describe as dehumanization.

Chapters 3, 4, and 5 deal with three major myths of modernity that formed the basis of the articulated and implicit ideology of Nazism and set the principles that sanctioned the Holocaust. They are, namely, the myths of history, nature, and power—or to describe them differently, a view of the historicism and post-Darwinian naturalism which supported the Nazi cult of power. The sixth chapter treats the effects of victimization in the bureaucratic state order of power; the victim, not the narcissistic hero or adventurist ego, must be confronted first in order to understand the moral dynamics of post-Holocaust humanism. This in turn is the subject of the two last chapters, proposing that "redemption" in the Holocaust, the "*tikkun*" or turn from it, remains a demanding and unfulfilled possibility. The last chapter on modern humanist democracy approaches the theme of an

American museum of the Holocaust, and examines what must be understood as the hypothetical political and cultural antithesis to the world of
the Holocaust.

The focus throughout the text is on a humanism summoned by Nazi
racism and aroused by it to become its opposing term. One of the weak-
nesses of modern antiracism has been the obscurity of its affirmative language. Under the Nazis the worship of race was the worship of a naturalist
truth beyond moral superstructures of any kind. Race was a vitalism, a
sanction from the competition for survival in the animal world, and the
logic of racism led to murder. The affirmation of exclusive biological identity pretended to be a metaphysics which denied others the metaphysical
right to exist. The racist ontology implies as its opposite the ontology of
humanism. Paradoxically, the grounding of existential humanism becomes
clear only in the contrast of the hallucinatory biological myth.

Finally, I would pay tribute and mention my indebtedness to survivors,
witnesses, scholars, and thinkers who formed my own consciousness and
led my thoughts to clarity. When I speak of cultural memory and its obtained treasure I think of them. I mention particularly Jean Améry and
Primo Levi, Elie Wiesel, Emmanuel Ringelblum and Chaim Kaplan, Emil
Fackenheim, Arthur Cohen, Elias Canetti, Emmanuel Levinas, Theodor
Adorno, Terrence Des Pres, and George Steiner. Evidence of their works
will be found throughout my text, but of course I take full responsibility
for the versions I give. In addition, the work of the historians Raul Hilberg,
Lucy Dawidowicz, Leon Poliakov, Saul Friedlander, among others, suggests the wealth of the last forty-five years of study. All the people I mention have in one sense or another fulfilled the address of Chaim Kaplan
as he wrote in his diary in the Warsaw ghetto. His command to himself
was, "Record!"

1

A Museum for Conscience
and Memory

A museum for the Holocaust is being built under partial sponsorship of the American government, to be placed in Washington, D.C., in view of the Lincoln and Jefferson monuments. This then will be another American monument, though placed as far from the original event as the mind of Lincoln is distant from that of Hitler. But is an American monument to the Holocaust obliged to express American values? What is the relevance of a memorial site in Washington, D.C., to Nazi criminality? To Jewish, Polish, and Russian suffering, and the dreadful burden of European history? Is it to be a monument to our guilt or our innocence? Some Jews object to a view of the American museum that blurs the singularity of Jewish fate and ascends to universalist pieties. But the genocidal singularity, the killing of Jews as Jews, is the basis for confronting a universal human tragedy in the Holocaust. A whole people, identified in the fate of their birth, was selected to die, and this defines the precedent for a teaching of people everywhere. In building a museum to the Holocaust in a great capital which aspires to universalist values and is a crossroads of peoples, we must ask the following: How does a visitor of any allegiance or identification concern himself with the Holocaust, and how does the Holocaust affect his understanding of himself in the human condition?

The victims of mass slaughter have already suffered from abstract identification. Is it possible that a memorial to them, catalogued in the long list of human tragedy and atrocity, would only perpetuate the anonymity of their fate? This, says Lucy Dawidowicz in *The Holocaust and the Historians,* attacks the effort to give "ecumenical" meaning to its evil, denies the historical reality of the specific intent to murder Jews. "[It] was the direct consequence of a specific and particular history of racist anti-Semitism." But racism as an evil almost by definition must have ecumenical meaning. It is not that Jews have an account to settle with Germans, with Christians, with the world, but world civilization has an account to settle with itself. Dawidowicz herself cannot avoid the inevitably long reach of the major moral catastrophe of our time. She writes, "The names of these death factories—and especially the name of Auschwitz—replaced Dante's Nine Circles of Hell as the quintessential epitome of evil, for they were located not in the reaches of the medieval religious imagination but in the political reality of twentieth century Europe."[1] The "political reality" of Europe, America, the world, must become the theme in any study of the Holocaust, and if we are facing the "epitome of evil" then all moral reality must be our study.

That has no inconsistency with the fact that the Holocaust inescapably belongs to Jewish history and the Jewish future. It has an existential meaning for Jews that cannot be exchanged with others, for they are the people who were once hunted to be killed wherever Nazi power spread, through Europe and the world. They must think of themselves as all having been under sentence of death. This cannot be equated with the other casualties of Nazi extermination policy. The Russian prisoners and Polish elites who were killed died as a fraction of their nation's armed and political strength, and, criminal though their treatment was, they were war casualties on the scale of atrocities that might extend to the victims of Dresden and Hiroshima. But the extermination of the Jews is beyond that scale. No Pole or Japanese need think he was under death sentence by virtue of being Polish or Japanese.[2]

The issue may be that of abstract generalization facing an experience that seems fated to be eternally problematic. Analogies proliferate, most of them in the mode of a *deus ex machina*, the Holocaust serving to advance or oppose a political interest. Jürgen Habermas has quarreled with German historian Ernst Nolte for pulling the Holocaust into the Cold War and forcing analogies between it and the Gulag. In part, what he and others wish to reject is a historic alibi for the Germans and Nazis, giving them moral shelter in the shadow of Stalin and the Gulag. Jean Améry, in making his own statement as a survivor, expressed an increasing bitterness in seeing "the absorption of the Nazi past in its singularity and irreductibility into a universal theory of Fascism and totalitarianism."[3] But, then, does the Holocaust transcend the politics of its origin? It is true that the greatest horrors resist analogy. But if the Holocaust is unique and unlike any other evil, what category of meaning can it have, and what does it warn against in the future?

Discrimination and judgment drown in the massive statistics of death during and after the Second World War, and atrocities such as those of Kampuchea or Bangladesh give more "banality" to political evil than we ever had the right to expect. Still, there are distinctions, even in mass murder. The key word remains genocide. Michael Marrus makes the point while sounding the long roll of Nazi victims. "Unlike the case with any other group, and unlike the massacres before or since, *every single one* of the millions of targeted Jews was to be murdered. Eradication was to be total . . ." In the comprehensive listing at Wannsee of all known Jews in Europe, the "compulsive hunt for Jews . . . included the two hundred Jews of Albania as well as the three million of Poland."[4] One must understand what it means to suffer a generic sentence of death, and to have murder press past physical extinction to the obscurely metaphysical claim to identity that all peoples know. Is it death that is the horror, or the sentence that judges one—father, mother, and child—to be not worthy of life, *nicht lebenswertig?*

That horror can never leave memory, and this in part explains the refusal of attempted analogies. In murders the victims cannot generalize, nor can those who identify closely with them. For historians who do generalize, this arouses protest. One of them, Geoffrey Eley, wrote, "To insist upon the uniqueness of the event is a short step to insisting on the exclusiveness of interpretation which asserts an empathetic privilege and even a Jewish proprietorship in the subject."[5] Some critics go further, as noticed by Michael Berenbaum, in attributing to Jews a feeling of "sacred particularity," or a new version of "chosenness," blackly absurd as that may be in the context of the Holocaust.[6]

From this it does not reach far to accuse Jews, and particularly Israelis, of exploiting the Holocaust for political advantage and even financial profit. But the actual thoughts of those Jews who have the credibility of witness mock such suspicions. From the beginning interpretation had no "case" for judgment, retribution, or reparation, no "ontology of the Jewish predicament," as Eley put it, and still has none, with Chaim Kaplan's words in Warsaw forming the start of most Jews' thoughts: "The worst part of this ugly kind of death is that you don't know the reason for it."[7]

Such bewilderment, far from the pleading of privilege or special grievance, characterizes most firsthand reports by victims of the Holocaust. Aharon Appelfeld, who joins Primo Levi and Elie Wiesel in writing the most sensitive records that we have, said to Philip Roth in a recent interview that "the Jewish experience in the Second World War was not 'historical.' We came in contact with archaic mythical forces, a kind of dark subconscious the meaning of which we did not know, nor do we know it to this day." And thus he turned to fiction, he said, for there "reality can permit itself to be unbelievable, inexplicable, out of all proportion."[8]

The "inexplicable" can be the beginning of faith as well as fiction, but in this respect, too, Jewish proprietorship is not the issue. A Jewish theologian, Arthur Cohen, writes of the Holocaust as the *tremendum,* an ultimacy in experience which ranks with the great religious revelations.

The tremendum as abysmal evil, as the ultimate negative historical configuration, is regarded by some as no less paradigm than the giving of Torah on Sinai. To make, however, the tremendum even the symbolic equivalent of Sinai is false. The claim of Sinai is that God spoke to Israel, revealing his name to this one among the seventy nations of the world. But did the tremendum speak only to Jews? If only to the Jews then is all the rest of mankind exempted from hearing its meaning? . . . the imperative of the tremendum is final solution for much more than Jews and Judaism.[9]

A great suffering cannot silence the instinct for prophecy. Quite the opposite. Jean Améry, as if rising from suicidal depression, addressed the moral future of mankind. "The Swastika, onto which the Jew had been nailed, not only dispelled the image of the Jewish deicide, but became the universal symbol of what is humanly and historically intolerable."[10] In any confrontation of the Holocaust, this great claim requires serious attention. So do the words of Elie Wiesel as he remembered himself in Auschwitz, at the margin of death. "That boy was convinced later that were he to survive, he would tell the tale; he was convinced that if he would tell the tale history would be redeemed. Man would undergo a total metamorphosis, something of the Messiah would appear in every man."[11]

To prophesy and speak redemptively is an understandable response to apocalyptic experience. Every Jew of European descent might know an interruption in history where a whole continent, Europe, is left to the dead forever. It is as if for them half the planet and half of history had been erased.

And so memory and prophecy join against silence. Whatever the individual grief or obsession, or the collective wound of Jews, the Holocaust will remain a focus of resolve and insight, of support or disintegration, of damnation or redemption for a world civilization. If the Holocaust is accessible at all to the lucid mind, it creates a universal issue of moral discourse. It may be, in latency, as the young Elie Wiesel thought, the basis of a moral unity of the species. As a survivor, Jean Améry writes,

Nothing will ever again be the way it once was. . . . One must reorient, just as the ghetto dwellers were forced to experience the world in a new way. The Christian ethic is no more adequate for this purpose than the Jewish ethic. A new philosophy of history would have to be written, or rather: it is already in the making. It was the people in the Ghetto who recorded its first sentences.[12]

How can scenes of outrage be made the focus of such inspiration? If we acknowledge the universal response of dread and guilt, where is the inspiration? It is rare that we personally know tragic humanity. And it is always glib to speak of shared suffering. Yet surely it is there that the moral sense has its birth. No one can enter the actual suffering of victims, but we can share consciousness with them, whether it is of terror, or pity, or fearful guilt, all grounded in ourselves. Aharon Appelfeld spoke for many when he said that "despite everything we continue living." And yet, he said, something more is expected of survivors:

[They] have undergone experience that no one else has undergone, and others expect some message from them, some key to understanding the human world— a human example. But they, of course, cannot begin to fulfill the great tasks imposed upon them, so theirs are clandestine lives of flight and hiding. . . . One has a feeling of guilt that grows from year to year and becomes, as in Kafka, an accusation.[13]

"Something more is expected of survivors." We write and we read as if under accusation.

•

One member of a recent symposium on the Holocaust said, "We may have reached a point of surfeit with respect to moral attention to the Holocaust."[14] But the command of Chaim Kaplan to himself in the last days of the Warsaw ghetto, "Record!" was not an effort merely to reach across to the living for sympathy, for revenge, or for the mingling of both the living and the dead in obliterating despair. It was a command for moral survival for which there is no surfeit, and where, as in Milan Kundera's words, "The struggle of man against power is the struggle of memory against forgetting."

A participant in the Eichmann trial was asked if he could discern a meaning in Auschwitz. "I hope I never do," he responded. "To understand Auschwitz would be even worse than not to understand it." But Elie Wiesel, who quotes this, also remembers the words of Yankel Wiernik, a *Sonderkommando* who escaped during the uprising at Treblinka. He was describing a group of children facing death: "Their eyes glowed with fear and still more, perhaps, with amazement. It seemed as if the questions, What is this? What for? and Why? were frozen on their lips."[15] That is the point

at which one struggles and where some reach for cosmic insight. Arthur
Cohen and Roy Eckardt, Jewish and Christian theologians, would agree
that this is where the history of man and God "comes up to a fatal water-
shed."[16] (They must resort to the languages of awe; Eckardt uses Greek,
"*metanoia,* the climactic turning around of the entire world," Cohen turns
to Latin, the *Tremendum,* Emil Fackenheim more intimately takes the He-
brew, *Tikkun,* again to describe a moral turning of the world.) But before
questioning God and history, to remember the eyes of those children of
suffering may be more than enough to warrant a "climactic" seriousness
on our part.

In that respect one wants more and more memory, more and more
power of response to fulfill the testimony expressed in Chaim Kaplan's
command to himself. But we find that those most able to fulfill Kaplan's
mission, like Aharon Appelfeld, regard it with the greatest dread. It is the
normative imagination, the positive, assertive moral impulse in those who
redeem experience in language that suffers the greatest block. Language
itself seems compromised, seems guilty. Jacques Derrida said something
noteworthy in this respect: "If we admit—and this concession seems to
me evident everywhere—that the thing remains unthinkable, that we do
not yet have discourse that can measure up to it," and he goes on to give
partial defense to Martin Heidegger, recently attacked not only for his early
commitment to Nazism but for his later silence on its crimes. But there
were penalties to be attached to too easy speech, and on this Derrida,
quoted in a published interview, spoke with unusual succinctness and as-
perity: "Of course silence on Auschwitz will never be justified, but neither
will the fact that people speak of it in such an instrumental way and to say
nothing, to say nothing that is not self-evident, trivial, and that does not
serve primarily to give themselves a good conscience, in order not to be
the last to accuse, to give lessons, to take positions or to show off."[17] This
may be a wholesome base of self-criticism for all who do engage in discourse, but the blockage must have a deeper ground than a revulsion from
intellectual or moral vanity.

Silence can have its pathos and its own great weight of meaning, de-
pending on the context of the event, as Elie Wiesel illustrates in his writing.
A notably eloquent voice, that of George Steiner, almost persuades himself
to withdraw into silence: "The world of Auschwitz lies outside speech as
it lies outside reason," and as for art, "In the presence of certain realities
art is trivial or impertinent." But as if in purposeful contradiction (as his

own writing and that of Wiesel's deeply contradict silence), Steiner quotes one of the last messages to the outside world from the Warsaw ghetto: "The world is silent; the world *knows* (it is inconceivable that it should not) and stays silent. God's vicar in the Vatican is silent; there is silence in London and Washington; the American Jews are silent. This silence is astonishing and horrifying."[18]

Silence did nothing for those victims while alive. Who is served by speaking now? Those who are sensitive to language know that the Holocaust stunned the values that structure language and make it possible. The Nazi violence had that typical effect. Their victims could not speak, and even their screams were delayed. To say that the Holocaust is beyond explanation in the area of chaos is a way of confirming the descent into chaos that the victims endured. It is to presuppose a meaningful world which had thus been shocked into silence. But to realize that what we took for granted, that basic assumptions at the root of existence were vulnerable and could be destroyed, is to be shocked back into language.

Who and what was silenced? The dim shades of an authentic nihilism cannot speak. There must be those who can reduce shock and horror to their base. And the base may be everything that supports speech and in turn everything that gives a hold on life. Theodor Adorno was the first to say that after Auschwitz writing poetry became impossible. Many have brooded over that remark and repeated it. It may be rather that now every poem must acknowledge Auschwitz in some implicit sense before it can become a poem. It is not that we have no speech but that it is inadequate to the call made on it. The call exists, it is stronger than ever, it is the unsilenced voice of conscience. And to say that the message of conscience before that horror is obvious and needs no interpretation doesn't help, because, if we study the history of the Holocaust, the great number of those who thought the news from Germany and East Europe incredible tells how dangerous it is to take the moral base for granted. Even the victims, almost to the end, thought the message of conscience was obvious, unquestioned and unaffirmed, and so could not believe what was happening to them.

Words that are inadequate seem offensive, but worse, they are terrifying in their failure of mission. Today we live more certainly than ever in the age of Babel and silence, with linguistic skepticism punctuating every written or spoken word. But if the Holocaust defeats the power of language, it also gives its unalterable command. To surrender to silence is to surrender to the Nazis' destructive intent. For the sake of death *they* mocked language with euphemism and bureaucratic jargon. *They* desired that the world collaborate in their secret. Today they would want the world to forget. But if they almost succeeded by the magnitude of crime in surpassing the power of indictment, possibly they bring us to the place of birth, not death, of the moral sense. That may be the referent we seek, where we might regain the most serious respect for the demand made on language.

It is true that explanations, meanings, seem to familiarize and humanize the evil-doer, and we do not wish to comprehend evil, which always traces the incomprehensible, on that basis.[19] But it is also true that refusing human membership, human agency to the killers and their actions can lead to a nihilism like theirs but turned against ourselves. The Holocaust must have interpretation—a grand-scale hermeneutics. Can it be a gospel of politics and public behavior? A doctrine of the state and its power? It can be that and much more, but it cannot be a single monothematic interpretation. The questions held before us are, How does this story instruct the future? How does it discover important values? How does it decide what is human?

There is a level of moral descent that puts ordinary moral commandments into irrelevance. "Thou shalt not kill" is terribly weak in the face of the Holocaust. And so we return to the command nevertheless. Is it possible to conclude that the Nazis were not men like ourselves? Yes, but they were men transformed—in them we see the figure of the human and inhuman. Therefore, the Holocaust must not be reduced to one more item in the long list of human atrocities. It was a powerfully concentrated exposure of choice and fate. It can define our institutions, it can define us, it can be the basis of what we wish to be and be a constant standard. The Holocaust is no abstraction, it is vivid testimony and can teach.

•

To think or write for long about the Holocaust can move toward obsession, and it is the fate of an obsession to become boring or incomprehensible. To resist it, one might pass the Holocaust off as a nightmare or, if actual, a horrible perversion of human nature, limited to one people, one place, one time. Was it a great natural catastrophe, like an earthquake or flood? Or were the dead casualties of war, people caught in the path of Moloch? Should we abstract this event so that it follows the laws of history, installed in the metaphysics of nature? (Thus it was that Hitler and Himmler rationalized evil.) Perhaps it was a pathological accident, the meeting between a madman and a stranger, both victims of pure chance.

The secret of murderous strength is its power to startle and mystify. This remains the problematic challenge of the Holocaust. It is inevitable that many will attempt to lower the problem or dismiss it, name it the banality of evil, of crime, or find in it the greater commonplace of mass neurosis and insanity. If it was crime, it was abysmal; far beneath tragedy, yet it surpassed the ability to comprehend the space and numbers of death. Where do tragic sympathy or vicarious religious feeling gain their entrance? The condemnation of crime is merely redundant.

There is a degree of evil in which humanity stands alone, in its own responsibility. The victim gives us entry into an experience that does not entail a religious faith, a government of laws, or even a bill of human rights. We do not ask him for such lessons, though that may be the obligation we have to ourselves. We do not wish to die with him, but we can experience something that does not insult his suffering or give us the *self*-comfort of compassion. This requires an identification with the victim simultaneously with the more difficult identification with the murderer. It comes to this. We imagine that there must be a confrontation between the victim and his murderer, who must both now stand for the rest of humanity. And that is the bond of memory. A true memorial to the Holocaust gives first an approximate, a distant sharing with the experience of the victims. It can give a stronger sharing with that shadow of potential humanity who occupies the body of his murderer. We are the heirs of that murderer's lost and betrayed conscience.

The Holocaust cannot be made cheap. It was a great cost to the world, and the world makes a great moral demand on itself in consequence. What is the demand? It is as limitless as the Holocaust was limitless in its shame and suffering. This, the true Original Sin, is a descent from which we aspire to rise, without limitation of any standard. We rise with the imagination, exercising the moral sensibility which has the faculty, luckily for civilization, to restore and recreate itself.

•

When people say "never again" as their chief lesson from the Holocaust, we are at a loss. What is to be never again? And then to treat the Holocaust as indecipherable horror and mystery (even at its religious level in Arthur Cohen's *mysterium tremendum*) is to put "never again" at a total impasse.

Those who say "never again" speak only of the *final* result, the "solution." That comes too late for such a vow. The question is, Where, at what point in the Nazi series of crimes, does the "never again" begin to apply?

The first sin was not the gas chambers, of course. The first sin came when the Germans cast the Jews out from moral equality. The rights to work, to vote, to study, to speak, to travel, to love, to marry, to practice a religion, claim a theory, teach a value—all these are basic to the right to exist, and when these were cut off for Jews it was preordained that six million should eventually die. We understand that all human rights are connected, that a Holocaust is only the last stage of their loss.

Jews for centuries have repeated the lessons of Passover, the liberation from Egypt. One dares to wish that the whole world would now repeat the lesson of the Holocaust, but not as the obsession of grief nor an exercise of rage and despair.[20] It is a lesson in inhumanity which defines the human, in oppression which defines freedom, in cruelty which instructs sympathy, in prejudice which illustrates equality. The story of the Holocaust in all its details cannot tell us who we are, or who we should be. But would it not be true that if the whole world accepted the clearest simplest message of the Holocaust, a light would be cast unlike any we have known over the field of conflict where nations, races, societies meet? It is in the nature of crime that its significance is not reserved for the victim. The Holocaust was not reserved for Jews. The moral imagination has no sectarian allegiance. And if we can use the word "tragedy" for this destruction, it is because its evil transcends such allegiance and is universal in significance. We say that to know the Holocaust intimately, completely, or as much as possible in the way the victims knew it, combined with the large view of historic retrospect, is to face two alternative results, to know what is equivalent to moral destruction or, on the other side, to reach an understanding of moral principle that is the veritable basis of civilization.

•

Death, single or multiple, is always extraordinary in relation to its cause. Death has no meaning, that is to say, every death is a death of meaning. And yet the dead have always taught the living. How many lessons are there in six million dead?

Some ask if slaughter isn't the everyday business of war. Were the victims not soldiers in the barbaric modern sense of total war? But war enters the field of moral conflict, even if on a primitive level, in the sense that the soldier risks his life as he kills and so faces a moral equal on that level. It is obvious that soldiers in battle kill in a fury that is as much fear as aggression. They kill to gain an advantage or merely to survive. Warring sides have a kind of equality, people in conflict share the fate of violence. People who are robbed share normal acquisitiveness with those who rob them. A woman who is raped shares in latent sexuality with the man who rapes her.

Is it conceivable that some people are murdered without advantage on the side of the murderer? Is there a hatred that is totally liberated from self-interest? Is there a craving for the abstract power to decide who shall live and who shall die?

It is true that mounds of rings, jewels, watches, gold teeth, gold spectacles filled the Auschwitz warehouses. But robbery was incidental. The German Nazis assumed the power to inflict death because, dearer than wealth, it was the proof of their power. They assumed the role of fate which does not discriminate in human terms. As Himmler seriously said, they were idealists in fact; they committed murder on an unselfish, disinterested basis. But that choice to act as fate gives them their place in historic anathema.

That is why the history of the Holocaust retains an ultimate mystery. There is no answering intelligence, no answering conscience to examine or accuse. Thus we resist giving those killers the respect implicit in our fear, and even the dignity of a moral indictment. In one perspective, to call them evil, despite their actions at the summit of evil, seems grandiose and false. Joachim C. Fest, one of the most discerning students of Nazism, writes, "The chronicler of this epoch stands almost helpless before the task of relating so much incapacity, so much mediocrity and insignificance of character, intelligibly to their extraordinary results."[21] As strong as horror, one response to the lives and works of Himmler, Heydrich, Hoess, and Eichmann is an overwhelming sense of shame.

The history of the Holocaust both mystifies and instructs, and it is necessary to cling to the instruction. Its lessons and warnings might focus on the favorite teaching phrases and slogans of the Nazis themselves.

"The Jewish problem," for instance. One might tell young political apprentices to beware of such monothematic problems which have all-embracing causes and effects. "The racial question gives the key not only to world history but to all human culture," said Hitler, whose "key" rapidly became his murdering weapon.[22]

And then, of course, "the final solution." Who can now respect ultimate solutions upon which the future depends? The historicist imagination is always dangerous when, in becoming politically active, it uses history as a ventriloquist's puppet. In any context it is a form of madness to equate one's will with necessity.

Again, in the light of madness, who would not demand the closest view of any political attribution that would name "the arch-conspirators of history." Conspiracy theories are rampant in modern politics; it is important to remember that they were the potent instrument of the Holocaust where intellectual paranoids became the teachers of assassins.

The Nazis were messianic in preaching "racial purity." Should we not be suspicious of every use of the words "corruption, purity, health, and sickness" as major normative terms? Hitler installed a vicious vocabulary: "Jewry is the racial tuberculosis of nations," and that was the succinct basis of anti-Semitism in *Mein Kampf.* Biology was fate, and genetic hatred and genetic rivalry served the Nazi eschatology with determinist themes and salvationary violence. The apocalypse was linked with a "final" conflict and a "final" solution, major events of major destruction, but surgically wholesome, sacrificially redemptive in proportion to their destruction.

The Holocaust is a warning to those who propose collectivities as essences, with race, nation, and class projected as agents, embodied in acts and persons. The hypostatized leader-savior implies the hypostatized victim, and vice versa. Those lumbering abstractions of the German philosophic tradition—Fichtean, Hegelian, Marxist, then Fascist—sought immanence and became deadly, perhaps because immanence could be found only in violent form. History mounted a stage and demanded sacrifice. Nature, in its own temple, asked for victims. Who was to give denial to power if power struggle was the "law of existence?"

•

The Nazis insisted on defining their victims as subhuman. Presumably they idealized the human in restricting its membership. It is a just irony that they should now receive the historic charge of "crimes against humanity." Under this heading the Nuremberg Trials were forced to install their own standard of judgment in proposing that even the coded or uncoded concepts of war crimes could not find a place to be cataloged in the Holocaust; they were out of reach intellectually and legally.

Article 6b of the *Statutes of International Military Tribunal,* Nuremberg, 1946, declared that a crime against humanity is constituted "by the acts inhuman and persecutions which in the name of a state practicing a politics of ideological hegemony, have been committed in a systematic fashion not only against persons in reason of their participation in a racial or religious collectivity, but also against adversaries of that politics whatever the form of their opposition." Article 6c tries for more focus in a definition which might include the everyday political violence between groups. Crimes against humanity were characterized "by the assassination, extermination, the reduction to slavery, the deportation and all other inhuman acts committed against a whole civil population, before or during a war, as well as by persecution for political motives, or racial or religious." This may have been adequate for the concrete purposes of law and judgment, but it still does not satisfy the large implications of a "crime against humanity." Perhaps no legal process or terminology could.

The implicit meaning of a crime against humanity takes it out of a suit of injury and grievance between parties and universalizes such crimes as those committed in the Holocaust. Humanity, all mankind, were injured in that crime. But how? Perhaps in the ethical premise of all human existence. The phrase gropes for something quintessential in crime where the future of civilized life becomes deeply endangered.

With their appetite for intellectual melodrama, the French debated "crimes against humanity" during the Barbie trial of 1987. In the midst of argument it was at least made clear how much the concept could be misused by demagogues and political factions to lump every atrocity under its heading, or to call any human persecution or abuse by that name. The cheapest political analogies, made by the defense, were with Deir Yassin in the Israeli war with the Arabs in 1948, My Lai in Vietnam, and French torture in Algeria. Wars, revolutions, and counterrevolutions have many motives, some of them noble, but the violence whose chief aim is extermination of a people belongs in a separate category.

There are obviously great political crimes like the Stalin policy against the Kulaks, or the Gulag itself in its stupendous suffering, but these express a war of political interests, however ruthless the means. The Holocaust features something else: where a regime decided abstractly, beyond its own self-interest, and indeed at some cost to its war program, that a whole people, branded by genetic origin and not by organized or unorganized political interest, had no right to live—not anywhere in Europe nor anywhere on the planet. A witness at the Barbie trial defined the actions of the

Nazis as "a violation of the fundamental rights of man, the right to equality without distinction of race, color, or nationality." But these are corollaries that rest on the right to exist. On this presumption all other human rights base themselves. Without it, humanity itself has no definition.

In another perspective, one lawyer at the Barbie trial reminded the court that the crimes of Barbie were committed in application of a doctrine of the state and with all its authority. (This happened to be the chief defense of Eichmann and other Nazi criminals.) It is important to remember the kind of crime that distinguishes itself here, the crime not of individuals or gangs but of an organized community with a law, a theory, a concept of values, and with the crime resting on those instruments of civilization. "A crime against humanity" must be invoked for crimes that violate a higher law than any contained in the individual state's code, the code itself being criminal in the case of the Holocaust and against humanity.

But once we propose that a crime against humanity was committed, we need to affirm a new understanding of what is meant by "humanity." How can it suffer a crime? What entity is it that endured suffering and injustice? The Jews were exiled from humanity before they were destroyed, with the passive or active consent of governing nations and peoples. Was this not the crime we mean?

Humanity, then, is not the mass collectivity of the species. It is a membership founded on a contract of faith, a principle of being. It can suffer a wound and be violated. It can endure crime. It can be destroyed entirely. We must not assume that "humanity" in this sense is an achieved community of interests and laws, of traditions and values. Not in the world we know. And yet we understand and appreciate an affinity of the species wherever we travel and under any condition of difference or strangeness. It is more than an affinity of intelligence or the rudiments of civilizations, such as language. It is a principle that works like an instinct, without the need of long training or preachment. It tells us that we *can* communicate and share interests and inhabit the same space in the universe. And these structures we have created and this space we inhabit is ours only by virtue of coexistence, our mutual allowance of being. We would know no reality of existence if this "first idea" (to use a term from Wallace Stevens) of the human were not universally present in us.

The argument over nuclear disarmament converges on this point. The one thing everyone understands, amid so much confusion, is that the nuclear weapon threatens humanity precisely in the sense of dependent coexistence on the planet. The Nazis anticipated the nuclear destruction. In a sense they unleashed it at Hiroshima by defining a war of extermination on their own terms. It is glib and false to make a *moral* correlation of Hiroshima with Auschwitz, though they opened up the same *physical* threat to the basis of humanity. The atom bomb was a war weapon, handled abstractly in military strategy, like all weapons. But with the Nazis, the bomb was inside their heads. They had acceded to the bomb in will and motive, and each member of the SS was a threat to human survival in the same sense as any bomb.

Therefore, we can say that one affirmation proceeding from the most nihilistic of eras was this new definition of a crime against humanity. Men have always been taught by the martyrs they have made. But if we have reinvented humanity, we also know a new species of the antihuman, more dreadful in effect than could ever have been imagined.

To speak of affirmations is to imply acceptance of the Holocaust as a great sacrifice, the burnt offering implied in the Greek term. Bruno Bettelheim finds this enraging:

To call these most wretched victims of a murderous delusion, of destructive drives run rampant, martyrs or a burnt offering is a distortion invented for our comfort, small as it may be. It pretends that this most vicious of mass murders had some deeper meaning; that in some fashion the victims either offered themselves or at least became sacrifices to a higher cause. It robs them of the last recognition which could be theirs, denies them the last dignity we could accord them: to face and accept what their death was all about, not embellishing it for the small psychological relief this may give us.[23]

It is not their dignity that needs restoring but our own, all who in the most basic sense are survivors. To say what their death was "all about," truthfully, is not to accept the terms imposed on their deaths by their executioners. It is a double injury to do so. Yes, they were not martyrs in the strict sense, and their suffering cannot be compensated by any "cause" that could be described by us. Their deaths were not *for* a cause and give profit to no one as *in* a cause. And yet we are linked to their deaths in a "meaning" that must define the continuity of our lives. They, the original victims, give the sharpest illumination of a bond broken under attack; they were alone, and as Bettelheim rightly says, this induced many of them to surrender and accept their fate as a form of suicide. We know from their written words how they asked for witness at the border of death. They asked for meaning above the meaningless; and even if all we can say is the dumbly despairing "never again" as the alternative to a self-respecting silence, even those words mean something. Every great "No" must mean something and searches for its corresponding "Yes."

•

Wars, including civil wars and revolutions, we assume, devote killing to the immediate purpose of gaining one's will with the enemy. The Nazis, with the help of modern historicist and naturalist thinking, made war the ultimate geopolitical instrument; they would govern with it, they would apportion the world's space, and they would apportion the right to live. They assumed the right to control the population of the world, eliminating parts of it on the basis of a racial "Utopia" that harmonized with the "laws of existence." If they seized power over existence with a ruthlessness that was unique, they were nevertheless products of modern totalitarian thought, and one might reasonably want to give partial responsibility for their arrival in history to Hegel, Nietzsche, Lenin, and a host of lesser figures who gave a basis to the modern secular gospel of power. We approach a central meaning here. It focuses on total victimization, not the equal or unequal battle between right and wrong. It focuses on the genius of the Nazis for the discipline of terror that crushed resistance before it could begin. It stresses the ability of their system to reduce their victims to survival levels of existence. And most frighteningly, it proclaims the power to extinguish not only life but memory, meaning, and the memory of meaning.

To challenge, then, the death of meaning, the memorial to the Holocaust must achieve the tone of tragedy and the style of ritual memory. The true death is the death of memory. The genius of the Nazis was to reinstate the purity of death, death as death in proof of nature's first and last indifference to the "human."

But death is always something else—the dead arise immediately in our affection, our guilt, our longing to be one with them, for them to be one with us. Memory always entails a form of martyrdom: life sacrificed to a thought, an emotion, to our spiritual substance. For the victims of the Holocaust the issue is no longer death, as death has claimed them, but the manner of it in memory, for in the manner of their dying we face toward the void.

Near the end of the great year of slaughter, 1942, the order came from Himmler to dig up and burn all bodies so as to leave no trace. In his order he mentions that the first scattered reports of the Holocaust were reaching the West.[24] The Nazis did not believe in memory, or perhaps they believed they could destroy it. They may have sensed that memory would be their nemesis, that it preserves and restores conscience, that it is stronger than physical decay. (Did they think that so many dead Jews, whose mark on existence was three thousand years old, could simply disappear?)

Jean Améry wrote that "the revolt against reality . . . is rational only as long as it is moral." Reality was the power-reality of the Nazi conquerors. To resist it could be as "real" as power and more rational. Resistance is continuous in remembrance, the acknowledgment of guilt, the refusal to repress truth or remain silent. Jean Améry spoke for the dead and for the survivors when he said that "in the midst of the world's silence, our resentment holds its finger raised" in order that "history become moral." That is a duty to achieve and a task of memory, that "history become moral." [25]

•

We are taught a radical insult to life in all those terrible images: the women running naked and shivering in the cold, protecting their nakedness, while fully armed and booted men looked on; the piles of clothing and valued objects, gold rings, bracelets, a child's toy and shoes, a trail of treasure leading to mounds of ashes. And men stooping to extract gold teeth from corpses—profiteers and sage economists who knew what was valuable in a heap of bones. For them the scene resembled a drab industrial factory, a clean efficient slaughterhouse. Counting profit and loss, this was the "final solution," practical to the limit, of the notorious "Jewish problem." Were those dying millions so singular a "problem"?

The massive statistics of death in the modern geopolitics of murder cannot conceal the name and nature of murder. A murder can never be taken for granted and classified with other murders. Our actual reactions in the face of murder must be studied. One act of violence has transformed a complete living being into something. What is it? What has disappeared? What has been lost? An entire system of meanings, all the sense there is in the world or can be. It isn't one person's life that is the issue. The crime is against all who have breath, sight, voice, language, memory in their interlacing complexity. Against the background of planetary waste and empty space, all Being has been threatened. Truly the Nazis were phenomenologists, Heideggerians of a sort. The crime against humanity is the crime against *all Being*.

The question becomes, What is a *human* being? The relativist critique of conventions, laws and morals, modern cultural revolutions in art, in lifestyles, in politics, link curiously with the destroying agents of the Holocaust. They were inhabited by a reductionist passion, a determination to strip away protective illusions, whether bourgeois facade or naive idealism, and find the animal underneath the clothes, and if racially pure or racially corrupt, historically chosen or historically condemned, it was in the naked-ness of nature that all were to be damned or saved. It is this, the created landscape, the humanscape of nakedness, which gives the Holocaust its unending significance. The sin against man is the sin of enforced na-kedness.

To name these dead against their namelessness, the world redeems itself, not the victims, from the crime the Germans called *Vernichtung*. Death as we normally know it and treat it is not *Vernichtung*, the infliction of nothingness. *Vernichtung* is as absolute as zero; it denies life first and then it denies all record of existence. The camp commanders stripped their vic-tims of everything—of names, loves, allegiances, thoughts, hopes, prayers. In their own way those Nazis were philosophers preaching naturalist re-duction, vivid empiricists and experimenters of that sort. Their victims would become the known unknown in the anonymity of matter. For them death ruled absolutely, nature had declared it, and their killers, having made themselves the instruments of nature, knew the joy of survival as beasts in combat might know it. But their victims, Whom do they accuse? What do they teach? At the very least, they ask for a surrogate conscious-ness, they demand a justification of existence, and they confront us in both future and past.

The catastrophe of the Holocaust renounces like Job all reasons, all ex-planations. And Job's mood haunts all protests and laments. Thus George Steiner greets a moral apocalypse: "The house of classic humanism, the dream of reason which animated Western society, have largely broken down." He points to "the paradox that modern barbarism sprang, in some intimate, perhaps necessary way, from the very core and locale of humanis-tic civilization."[26] The support given the Holocaust by the German intel-lectual and professional elite was direct, not passive or covert. The inter-views conducted by Robert Jay Lifton with Nazi doctors who presided over the death camp selections have spirit-shaking effect. Gordon Craig cites statistics that show three thousand lawyers and doctors enlisted in the SS.[27] We don't know exactly how many teachers, professors, and journalists, but these were Himmler's favorite fields of recruitment. And the question Steiner asks remains pertinent: "It is not only the case that the established media of civilization—the universities, the arts, the book world—failed to offer adequate resistance to political bestiality; they often rose to welcome it and to give it ceremony and apologia. Why?"[28]

Again and again, Why? What was the source of that betrayal? What were its nurturing ideas? What was its inspiration? It is useless to repeat the basic moral commandments (in the twentieth-century context "Thou shalt not kill" has the effect of a primitive taboo) until we gain the ears of the guardians and creators of humanist culture, the teachers and preachers, the spokesmen for values in civilization. Did not Julien Benda prophesy this greatest "treason of the clerks?"[29] "No poetry after Auschwitz," said Theodor Adorno. Nor any poetry before it, one might say, unless it can answer for itself and disclaim responsibility.

Jean Améry in *At the Mind's Limits* describes how the intellectual prisoners in the camps (usually educated in culture of German dominance) endured their suffering less well than the nonintellectual, though not for the usual reason of physical endurance. It was implicitly a morale factor.

Were not those who were preparing to destroy him in the right, owing to the undeniable fact that they were the stronger ones? . . . Yes, the SS could carry on just as it did: there are no natural rights, and moral categories come and go like the fashions. A Germany existed that drove Jews and political opponents to their death, since it believed that only in this way could it become a full reality.

Did that "realism" make Améry's campmates collaborators in their own doom?

That is the way history was and that is the way it is. One had fallen under its wheel and doffed one's cap when a murderer came along. . . . More than his unintellectual mates the intellectual in the camp was lamed by his historically and sociologically explicable deeper respect for power. . . . The power structure of the SS state towered up before the prisoner monstrously and indomitably, a reality that could not be escaped and therefore finally seemed *reasonable*. No matter what his thinking may have been on the outside, in this sense here he became a Hegelian.[30]

Those words of Jean Améry are more than a mourning epitaph. They are a warning message to the living, and they reflect an intellectual guilt that crosses the border between victims and oppressors. Read and reread, they command all the soul of attention. Améry wrote of the swastika as that terrible new cross onto which the Jew had been nailed. But what is the redemption and where is the message of resurrection? A gospel, a text, needs to survive as the New Testament survived the obscure death of Christ. The voices from within the Holocaust are mostly silent now. If there is to be a gospel it is yet to be written. But we need some first assumptions, the hypotheses of belief, just as the early Christians possessed them. The only ones we have at hand are secular and find their centrality in what we obscurely name human rights, which, in turn, has to be a doctrine so deep that it leaves ideology and politics behind and touches the premises of existence. The Holocaust must propound itself and add its weight to all moral and political judgments and yet not be cheapened by false analogies, not be allowed to become a mere epithet of indictment in the mutual abuse of quarreling factions.

Thus we know that to explain the Holocaust becomes an impossible task where all explanations seem reductive and demeaning. Explanations, as from Job's comforters, attack the dignity of grief, though grief here is so much more than grief that it definitely surpasses the expressible. And yet such mourning resists the effort to turn it back to a lesser level. It fights to maintain itself as if it forecasts its own brief span, its intensity dissolved in the generalizing intelligence and its categories. We are inclined to say that, as in a religious mystery, the Holocaust should remain unexplained or should be declared holy in its transcendent meaning.

But as Améry also suggests, the great negative of the Holocaust returned upon its perpetrators and became the negation of a negation. Its grief and terror defined the "antiman" who violated and extinguished himself. In the "no" of the Holocaust we are forced to begin to say "yes." But "yes" to what? For this we study it, thinking that in the mirror image of Hitler's creed, like a counterdaimon he set free, we may discover our true beliefs.

Our rebuttal may refer to the institutions of a liberal humanist democracy but without intensity or passion. Do we meet a historic tragedy with the commonplaces of everyday political life, its hypocrisies and evasions? A town hall meeting, a free election, a free press as the answer and the cure for Auschwitz? But it was Fascism that did not find democracy heroic enough. In this country the profound ethical impulse of democracy in its first century—that of Jefferson, Lincoln, Emerson, and Whitman—seems in general view to have been replaced by a pragmatic laissez-faire that reflects only the democracy of the marketplace, of group interest measured by the pollster. Against this the Holocaust is a stern standard. Immense destruction hinges on the nineteenth-century thought that removed the moral rationale of politics or hid it behind other codes of language-historic process, racial conflict, class conflict, biological and economic competition, the rule and rivalry of power, all forms of determinism that undermined the ground of conscious value, conscious choice. The religion which once supplied us with metaphor, with principle, should tell us that politics today must have a conscience and aim for universality in human discourse. But the argument is not to reinstate metaphysics; the scientism of the nineteenth century was metaphysics enough. In our modern catastrophes, we have learned that we cannot use natural law or metaphysical edict as the ground for moral action. It is fatal to do so.

Human rights, as we understand them, are not a code for the happiness of mankind. Their starting point is far more serious, more lucidly apparent than the future of happiness. They begin, are born, with the misery of evil, with human acts against humanity. The Holocaust implies a definition of the antiman, and what we call human rights are a code for the civilized state. It is in this sense that the Holocaust can have an existential ending and beginning. On these terms the helpless victims give testimony to the reality of what they suffered. Confronting the strangest of murders, purposeless, disinterested, colder than cold, they received a moral shock from which all judgment flies. We imagine that for themselves they could only curse the earth and the beings who inhabited it.

Yet we live and take profit from their deaths. With everything else taken from them, we can also treasure their reproach, the world's guilt. We may understand that it is remorse, not aspiration nor hope of salvation, that is the strongest spring for a moral resolve. And if we speak of remorse and guilt, it is not a debt owed to Jews and other victims as a group. It is obscene to trade compensation for the Holocaust. The moral contract is not compensation or debt, though it acknowledges a deep remorse toward mankind. The guilt is in us and universal; we are the victims and the oppressors, we have humanity everywhere. But in fact there is only one victim, the one individual in his own time and place. And if the oppressor is large in number, abstract in his identity, he is also one, in singular conscience.

2

Crimes against Humanity

The Holocaust's bitterest lesson does not concern death on its own great scale of numbers but death qualitatively understood, that is, in the manner of one's dying. Dying is, of course, the most private of all experiences, and we respect it for that. But this death in the millions was an abstraction of numbers, imposed as such upon those who died. The people who struggled in the gas chambers hardly had single or separate bodies. They fell into a pit of dying flesh, unable to distinguish the screams of neighboring victims from their own. This, too, was part of the Nazi design. Everything they did was meant to dismiss the personality and singularity of death, for the victim as well as the executioner.[1]

We know about men in war going to their deaths singing. Leaving private existence, they might feel their deaths as the sublime abstract. But the collective scream of the Jews was the most reductive possible; in their group consciousness it may have been the sound of protoplasm collapsing. It was the logical expression of racist doctrine. Men and women were waste organisms, the detritus of a biological mass.

Universally people have clothed death with custom, and universally we sympathize with the form. But for the Nazis and their victims, dying was a ritual of extreme reduction, violating and inverting the habits of every civilized or savage people. The victims were stripped naked before they died. In a symbolic act of limitless contempt they were asked to leave their money, their jewelry, their shoes, dresses, and underwear as the dramatic badges of their own intrinsic worthlessness. If they could be immortal in their hatred, it would be this that they would recall, how the gold was extracted from their mouths, the hair from their heads, how their ultimate value was weighed in the great pile of used and torn clothing that accumulated in Auschwitz warehouses.

One effect noted in several narratives of the Holocaust is the speed with which the executioners worked, allowing barely a few minutes for the victims to understand what was happening to them. Subject to cunning deceptions and their own need to disbelieve the incredible, they were not, most of them, prepared for the ultimate act. The practical motive for speed was to avoid a bad scene of panic, possibly resistance, though so much had been done to them that destroyed their strength to resist. Conceivably, some of the Germans, in perversion of feeling, would have thought this a mercy, knowledgeable as they were in the ways of death.

But in retrospect one sees it as a culminating insult against the victims. They were deprived of full consciousness, or the ability to see and judge their lives and fates. *Vernichtung* is what the Nazis designed for them, and indeed it was annihilation in the most complete meaning of the term. It is this that emphasizes acts of memorial, embodied in the impulse to build Holocaust monuments and museums.

"We had been deprived of the right to an ordinary fate in suffering." This was said by a witness at the Barbie trial of May and June 1987, in Lyon, France. The point is one to remember throughout the terrible narrative. It was a deprivation in which Jewish leaders sometimes cooperated. Leo Baeck was apparently informed of the Holocaust plan and process some time in 1943 and was asked if the Jews of Germany and elsewhere should be told. He spoke against it, not wishing to add this terror to their suffering.[2] Obviously, he thought nothing could be done to save them. Perhaps in this Baeck was the victim of terror psychology. He was not the only leader who chose silence in the face of an unmanageable horror. And if some Nazis claimed it merciful to lead the Jews unknowing to their deaths, we should remember that the perverted model in their heads was not massacre but euthanasia.

Surely this was no "ordinary fate in suffering." The Nazis led their victims to their deaths with false promises and abrupt betrayals. They mocked the gravity of suffering with signs urging duty, obedience, "*arbeit macht frei*," over their heads, as, with a piece of soap and a towel in their hands, the victims filed into the passageway that led to the death chamber. The Jews lived on hope, they knew that despair confirmed only death, and so we imagine how the nerve shocks of such daily cycles of hope and despair did as much as anything else to wear down the human character of their victims. We know that the Nazis liked to use the term "subhuman" for their victims and were determined to prove their victims were that indeed. Naturalists to the edge of doom that they were in their reductive understanding of life, they performed a great moral experiment in defining the distinction between the human and the nonhuman. That laboratory at Auschwitz was meant to grind men down to their component cells, to demonstrate their uses as skin, hair, teeth, ash, and fat. The full human consciousness begins with this witness.

•

In his sober dispassionate record of a man in agony, Adam Czerniakow wrote the most enigmatic statement of his diary: "When I am awake I read *Don Quixote*" and "How much we need you, errant knight, today!"[3] Of all books, why Cervantes? In the midst of a dreadful, ignoble slaughter, why the errant knight? The question may not answer itself, but it gives a subtle and rare dignity to Czerniakow's mind as leader of the Warsaw Ghetto responsible for a community that lived at the extreme edge of survival. On his desk he kept a model of a Jewish gravestone.

Don Quixote may dream in that blasphemed existence called the ghetto; such insanities become parallel. The ghetto was, of course, only a way station to the camps, a process in dying. Jean Améry emphasizes how the victims were reduced to the state of the "unalive," to know death before they were killed:

The victims were not only made into a "series" by their oppressor; since they constantly saw, smelled, and touched one another, they were physically de-individualized and made into an opaque mass of flesh. . . . The ghetto was a malignant tumor of humanity. Every single one of those crammed into it understood it as such and felt himself to be the sick cell of an organism, which objectively he really was. Therefore he could love himself as little as he could the next person. For one another . . . we were nothing but disgust.[4]

It is instructive to place in this portrait the figures of Nazi officers and SS men, militarily erect, booted, well-uniformed, relaxed in a swagger while in the midst of their dazed, disheveled victims. Was it not their motive to thus feed themselves with more life and strength? Were not the camps tonic for German morale? A race theory has its own methods of proof, and murder is only the last of its demonstrations.

We are given a vision of Jewish women with their heads shaved, waiting for the gas chamber. To be stripped naked was an exercise in naturalist reduction, a philosophy put to work. Was this a revenge against nature or a defense—which? For what proof did the cold twentieth-century mind of Europe, of Germany, so wish to reduce life to flesh and then bone and ash? In our century, when the human animal learned to recognize and hate its animality, monsters of complex description were born.

For contrast, we think of the special circumstance when lovers reveal their nakedness to each other. It is as if they drop an enclosure of self in anticipation of the deepest acceptance of self. In being loved they transcend physical being even while disclosing and affirming it. Primo Levi writes of "the useless cruelty of violated modesty," and he offers a sobering context for speculation on the meaning of modesty. "One entered the Lager naked: indeed, more than naked, deprived not only of clothing and shoes . . . but of one's head of hair and all other hair." . . . "A naked and barefoot man feels that all his nerves and tendons are severed: he is helpless prey." As for clothes, "anyone who does not have them no longer perceives himself a human being but rather as a worm: naked, slow, ignoble, prone on the ground."[5] Elias Canetti adds insight with a note in his journal made during the war. It is not the naked who kill the naked. "If you all had to face one another naked, you would have a hard time slaughtering. The murderous uniforms."[6]

•

At perhaps his lowest point of despair, Chaim Kaplan wrote in his diary, "We have turned into animals, some of us into domestic animals and some of us into carnivorous animals."[7] But that other diarist of the Warsaw ghetto, Emmanuel Ringelblum, heard how descent could be deeper. A rabbi, taken to work in a garage, was told, "You're not human, you're not animal, you're Jew." It is fearful to think how often the Nazis may have succeeded in convincing their victims of this. Ringelblum writes, "In a refugee center an eight-year-old child went mad. Screamed, 'I want to steal, I want to rob, I want to eat, I want to be a German.' In his hunger, he hated being Jewish." But Ringelblum could sense that it was more than hunger. "The power and bearing of the Others [his code word for the Germans] is impressive. People [of the Ghetto] are trying to rise above the general mass of mankind and make an impression wearing the same high shoes as the Others."[8]

This is the pathology of victims at the moral apocalypse. For some to hate and abuse Jews was to eliminate the Jew in themselves. Ringelblum was present at the *Umschlagplatz* in late 1942 with the mass deportations from the Warsaw Ghetto, and he writes: "For the most part, the Jewish police showed an incomprehensible brutality. Where did Jews get such murderous violence? When in our history did we ever before raise so many hundreds of killers?" And he remarks with the greatest significance, "They weren't content simply to overcome the resistance, but with the utmost severity punished the 'criminals' who refused to go to their deaths voluntarily."[9] Ringelblum understood, and the Jewish police were made to understand, that in the Nazi regime the Jewish crime was their existence and their refusal to die.

In naming the Jews subhuman the Nazis understood the prohibitions and reserves on behavior that "human" suggests. In June 1935, Goebbels in his newspaper *Der Angriff* attacked the "stupid and foolish phrase-making by bourgeois intellectuals to the effect that the Jew was also human."[10] Indeed, those "intellectuals" had to carry that burden of an argument. Wasn't it old anti-Semitism that defined the Jew as somehow outside the human race? When did Shylock forfeit his humanity? But add to that the style of those who trade in atrocities during wars and revolutions. Were the Kulaks human to Stalin or were they just Kulaks, an abstract class term addressed in the cruel sociology of our time and its politics? But then according to this vein of thought, if we subtract the attitudinal concept of the "human" from these relationships of death-dealing violence, we come upon a positive, normative understanding of the "human"; the species belongs to a moral category, not biological.

Jean Améry writes, affirming a perception of Georges Bataille, that sadism is not sexual pathology but (as in existential philosophy) "the radical negation of the other . . . the denial of the social principle as well as the reality principle." This, Améry observes, was the stamp of National Socialism, a better definition than totalitarianism. The Nazi "hated the word 'humanity' like the pious man hates sin." "By negating his fellow man . . . he wants to realize his own total sovereignty."[11] The definitions are not quite clear, the subhuman could really mean human, and both terms subordinated themselves to the ruling *Ubermensch* who were a race apart.

It is in this sense that the Nazis leave us with verification of that debated legal concept of Nuremberg, "the crime against humanity." The Nazis gained peculiar conviction for themselves in reducing the Jews of Warsaw to beggary, theft, black market activities, and assault on each other, and, finally, not only to starvation and plague but to the status of the germs of disease themselves. In this, by logical paradox, those Germans were defining the "human" as an ontological concept. And that made their crime generic, an attack upon the condition of being human.

The threat in all death is metaphysical, extinction that goes to the base, and for the Nazis, as biological racists, the death of the species was the ultimate loss to be imposed on their victims. The Holocaust death of the Jew carried out a verdict of the universe against them. They were to be rejected totally, not merely in a pause or period as of one life ended but in the premise for all life in nature and on the planet. We strive ordinarily to give the life facing death an immortality of meaning. Men wish to die with their honors collected, their value recorded. Thus they wish to die with friends and relatives at their side, wish to leave an estate, and want a memorial. More specifically, in the deadly wars between groups, one might distinguish between the death of a Communist, say, at the hands of the Nazis, and that of an unmartyred Jew, that is, a Jew who was killed on a racial basis and not in ideological or religious persecution. The Communist might die knowing the significant value for which he died. The biological Jew, so-called, dies into the void, leaves nothing behind, not even his biological kin or survivors. He is not a martyr of his faith. He is merely a symbol of protoplasm and of a defined deficiency. This can be the basis of a reactive obsession, as in our wish to memorialize the Holocaust victims. They were reduced to unmeaning and to meaning we would restore them. They might become, in the imagination of the ages, the protagonists of human value at its base.

Therefore, the "crime against humanity" gains cosmic sweep in its definition. It must be a profound sin which points not only to the barrier between the criminal and his victim but to a form of self-alienation. The perpetrators' crime was against the collective nature of mankind, against its collective self in being. The Nazis mutilated the communal identity of man, and so they laid waste to themselves.

It is with this in mind that thinkers like Emil Fackenheim write of the Holocaust as a divesting of mind and spirit. We are in a moral void where judgment has no place to rest. "In an earlier exploration we concluded that thought cannot overcome the Holocaust, that where the Holocaust is overcoming thought is not, and that where overcoming thought is the Holocaust cannot be. . . . must we not conclude that where the Holocaust is, no thought can be, and that where there is thought it is in flight from the event?"[12] That is extreme, but it points to the difficulty. For instance, in dealing with the German Nazis we feel divorced from a common language of reference. Who are they, and of what kinship with ourselves? They could be a race from another planet. A crime against humanity? All language is estranged from that reality.

•

It tells us much to know that the Holocaust occupied an area of dead language, cold, bureaucratic, the language of industry and technocratic science. One camp commander habitually referred to the bodies of victims as "pieces." Some of the camp doctors studied by Robert Jay Lifton described themselves as thinking of the people disembarking from cattle cars as moribund, terminal cases, with the death camps simply considered as burial grounds, and with the train cars, the ramp selections, the gas chambers, the ovens fusing to become a single process in their minds. "Medicine" was now enlisted for the disposing of human waste.[13] The success of the Germans in reaching that level of technical abstraction in the administration of death suggests a skill beyond the reach of ordinary executioners and undertakers. Convinced that to cleanse Europe of the Jews was a sanitizing operation on the grand scale, they had the callous goodwill of excellent surgeons. Abstractions wear no flesh and are easier to kill.

One significant trait of the Nazi movement was to attach symbols of identification to themselves *and* their victims. Weapons were handed to men wearing armbands, death was dealt out to people wearing the Star of David. In a nation of uniforms, the uniforms came first, before the street riots, the assaults, the invasion of the Rhineland, Austria, Czechoslovakia. Behind the uniforms and insignia were the language of bureaucracy, the slogans of politics, the jargon of social science, the codes of philosophic abstraction, and the military festivals, songs, flags, parades that prepare for human sacrifice. Did these depersonalized, dehumanized, and abstract vocabularies invite destruction per se?[14] What is more abstract than a corpse, and, on the other hand, what tempts the hunger for clarifying, existential immediacy more than the exchange of violence? What Hitler and Himmler thought they saw or knew when they used the word "Jew" is to us an unsolvable mystery. Political abstractions are like blank spaces in the brain, immediately filled by shadows called up from dreams and nightmares, monsters of virtue and monsters of maleficence.

It seems strange that we don't have a word for the agents in atrocities. "Victimizer" is weak; "perpetrator" is a word from the police blotter. What can you call the agents at Himmler's side, or those who took the führer's *befehl* from his lips? Murderer is inadequate, since in that case we search for passions, urgencies of appetite and fear, direct confrontations. The Holocaust was an action that resists generalization and yet, on its scale of effects, can only receive large empty words for description. The inclination is to assume an act of pure natural violence like an earthquake. But we know the efficient mass organization and the so-practical technology with which murder was conducted. After the war the world could not find a better direct agent of mass murder than Eichmann, a third-level bureaucrat in charge of transportation. Students of the Holocaust pore over shipment orders and train schedules to find documentary proof for the greatest crime yet to challenge the human imagination.

Murder for the sake of murder has been normally treated as a perversion, even in fact an accident in nature. It was Nazism that turned murder into industrial production. Murder should be, we think, the most personal of acts, though that may be a limited understanding of the murderer's psychology. In the Holocaust murder was murder with no agent and no victim. That is why we hear a desperate call from those who died; restore us to humanity, they say, even as victims. One understands perfectly the compulsion behind the work of Nazi hunters like Simon Wiesenthal or Serge Karsfeld. They wish to pursue agents as if to restore or rediscover the valid existential truth of a murder.

On the other hand, dealing dispassionately with the Germans of the Holocaust, analyzing motives, etc., seems almost impossible. To do that requires a minimum capacity for identification with the subject. We resist the assumption that they lie within the field of human possibilities, and this is what we mean by the self-alienating act of the Nazi murderers. The refusal of many Jews to believe the rumors and reports of their impending destruction was not fear in the face of death so much as the resistance of the organism, the whole person, to reality in that form. It was the universe that would become intolerable, not their own existence. And there is a difference in the quality of despair between those two judgments.

•

One would like to imagine that hatred respects what it hates, that even this violence of spirit endows humanity with distinctiveness in nature. But that is not an easy conclusion for the Nazi phenomenon. Himmler had this to say for the people he destroyed:

We have . . . taken the question of blood as our starting point . . . by problem of blood, we of course do not mean anti-semitism. Anti-semitism is exactly the same as delousing. Getting rid of lice is not a question of ideology. It is a matter of cleanliness.

. . . We shall soon be deloused. We have only 20,000 lice left, and then the matter is finished within the whole of Germany.[15]

This was doctrine not only for the SS but for much of the German army. Ringelblum writes about women in Warsaw seized for labor early in the German occupation: "And, it just so happened, women in fur coats. They're ordered to wash the pavement with their panties, then put them on again wet." [16] The scene expresses a thuggish and vulgar hatred, as grotesque as it is terrible. Yet the Nazis showed themselves supreme experts in designing a program of humiliation for their victims. It may be argued that it was a secondary form of suffering when placed in the context of starvation, sickness, and death. But I would reverse the argument; in the context of humiliation, death is the bitterest death, and murder the most atrocious. It was a long exercise in punishment, beginning perhaps most overtly with the *Kristallnacht,* an event which Peter Loewenberg describes as a "ritual of degradation." [17] The Holocaust in general, and for its full span, should have the same attribution. We do not discount wholesale slaughter if today we dwell on this source of outrage. If I feel pain or shame, why do I assume that the observer inevitably feels some portion of it? And when he does not, why not? We live under an illusion that as we appreciate our own value in existence so others will or must. We are right to feel deeply that they should. There is this fragment of wisdom from the sages: "If any man shames his fellow man in public," declared the rabbis, "he forfeits his share in the next world." [18] One may more easily believe that the Nazis surely forfeited their share in this world, whatever way we define it as something worth prizing. And there is this for comfort, those scenes of humiliation help us to a definition. Emil Fackenheim and Terrence Des Pres join in using the term "excremental assault" to characterize that weapon of insult in the Nazi attack on humanity. The strict rules for work and life in the barracks combined with the effects of diet and dysentery to make "the demands of the bowels . . . absolute" [19] Imagine a world under the rule of that absolute. What could not one do with victims so subjugated? But as Fackenheim points out, more was intended.

Clearly, excremental assault was *designed* to produce in the victim a "self-disgust" to the point of leading them to collaborate in their own deaths. Nothing less was the essential goal, though it is one of the horrors of the Holocaust most difficult to accept. The Nazi logic of destruction was aimed, ultimately, at the victim's *self-destruction* . . . preceded by self-transformation into the loathsome creature which, according to Nazi doctrine, he has been since birth.[20]

This surely was to be "deprived of the right to an ordinary fate in suffering" and helps to explain the curious and challenging formulation. What is that right, and under what conditions is one forced to claim it? It comes from the reduction of the victim as a moral agent in his own fate. It comes from "excremental assault," subjugating the victim as if his own body were his enemy. The dramatic parallel is with inflicted torture in its last stages, when the victim is reduced below the level of any human engagement.

The essential crime to focus on is not annihilation as the final result but preannihilation, which concentrates on the absolute denial of moral equality. One does not ask for sympathy from a murderer. But "ordinary suffering" demands something quite different from the expressed attitudes of several Nazi doctors in the selection process at Auschwitz, as described by Robert Jay Lifton. The sufferer expects the world to share a minimal recognition of the terms of his suffering. The last prerogative of the dying is that death should be acknowledged as death, and in that respect even the expression of limitless hatred can serve the right to "ordinary suffering."

In writing of torture and beatings, Jean Améry refuses to use the words "human dignity." Too much and then too little is meant by it. He prefers to say that a person beaten by (Nazi) police "loses something we will temporarily call 'trust in the world.'" This includes a belief in causal predictability in human behavior. But more important, and fundamentally, it "is the certainty that by reason of written or unwritten social contracts the other person will spare me—more precisely stated, that he will respect my physical, and with it also my metaphysical, being. The boundaries of my body are also the boundaries of myself." The experience of pain almost always involves the "expectation of help" from others, even if not forthcoming. Torture and the blows of camp guards, SS men, etc., not only cut off that possibility but transformed it to its opposite. Améry may be touching here upon the real terror of this suffering. A necessary link with the outside world is broken. "A part of our life ends and it can never again be revived."[21]

Améry suggests that all violence has insult implicit in it. A moral education demands to know what it is that feels the insult. Can the will to live survive a certain degree of insult? If torture is insult as much as it is pain, then pain becomes a special sort of pain because of the insult. The outrage of the Holocaust is not the fact that millions died, though the Nazis tried to mask themselves behind the natural and universal law of death. Death is the enemy of the good faith with which we ordinarily receive life. But it is not outrage and insult until living beings challenge and deny the life in others disinterestedly. One may take a man's life from several motives—the burden of his existence, the envy of his possessions—as the obstacles to a political or personal will. All these bring less insult than the cold metaphysical motive that focuses on the right to live. Or is there an assumption that no one has the right to live? If people are commodities, their use value and future value are all that one must consider. Did naturalist thought proceed that far with the Nazis? To be murdered in hatred or fear is even a life-affirming climax, absurd to say, by contrast with the cold calculation of a naturalist purpose. Apparently, everything begins in Hitler's case with the euthanasia program. Do we mistake his "banality" and vulgarity and miss the imagination of the German Faust?

To reproach evil in outrage is one thing; but to condemn evil with contempt is still another. There are people who are against Hitler on moral grounds, yet who conceive of him as a great figure in the world's appraisal. In post-Nietzschean spirit, patronizing even in this case our own moral responses, we pay respect to the life force in a supremely dominant will. But this man and the others—Himmler, Heydrich, etc.—were assassins in the dark, destroying the weakest, most helpless of victims. Neither Faust nor devil, they express the absolute antithesis of a conquering spirit. Nietzsche would be the first to acknowledge this pathos in the career of the *Ubermensch.*

•

Primo Levi describes how at the end he with other survivors were left behind in the hospital, sick, starving, cold, the Germans in flight and the Russians not yet arrived: "We lay in a world of death and phantoms. The last trace of civilization had vanished around and inside us. The work of bestial degradation, begun by the victorious Germans, had been carried to its conclusion by the Germans in defeat." He observed the stronger waiting eagerly for the death of someone weaker. "Whoever waits for his neighbour to die in order to take his piece of bread is, albeit guiltless, further from the model of thinking man than the most primitive pigmy or the most vicious sadist."[22]

Earlier he describes the hanging of one last resister which the camp survivors were made to watch. The SS leader asked in his harsh voice if they understood the example before them, to which they all answered "*Jawohl.*" When the man about to be hanged cried "*Kameraden, ich bin der Letzt!*" not one voice or murmur of assent arose. He was hung, and they were made to pass in file before his quivering body. Levi writes:

At the foot of the gallows, the SS watch us pass with indifferent eyes: their work is finished, and well finished. The Russians can come now: there are no longer any strong men among us, the last one is now hanging above our heads, and as for the others, a few halters had been enough. The Russians can come now: they will only find us, the slaves, the worn-out, worthy of the unarmed death which awaits us.

To destroy a man is difficult, almost as difficult as to create one: it has not been easy, nor quick, but you Germans have succeeded. Here we are, docile under your gaze; from our side you have nothing more to fear; no acts of violence, no words of defiance, not even a look of judgment.[23]

"To destroy a man." We shall never understand what Nazism represents until the full burden of Levi's meaning is received. Emmanuel Ringelblum was witness also in writing the following in his journal during the last days of the Warsaw Ghetto:

This is a tragic paradox. Only those Jews have the right to live who work to supply the German army. . . . Never in history has there been a national tragedy of these dimensions. A people that hates the Germans with every fiber of its being can purchase its life only at the price of helping its foe to victory—the very victory that means the complete annihilation of Jewry from the face of Europe, if not of the whole world.[24]

When the Germans built the camps they used local labor and transported Jewish technicians, artisans, carpenters, electricians. Then as the camps were constructed these were the first to be gassed. When the camps operated, Jews were used to help work the ovens and gas chambers. They dug the ditches in which their people were to lie dead, and where they would eventually join them. They shaved the heads of their women; pulled the gold teeth from the mouths of corpses; stacked the clothes, eyeglasses, rings, books, wallets, diaries, letters, keys, toys, souvenirs; stealing what was valuable, eating what was edible, if by chance anything had been left by the official scavengers. They were in general the servants and keepers of a monstrous charnel house. They learned an intimacy with the details of their own deaths and were in effect forced to participate in their own execution. In this the Germans were committing a crime against the primary sensibility that defines life. Primo Levi understood their motive in assigning Jews to duty in the Special Squads.

One is stunned by this paroxysm of perfidy and hatred: it must be the Jews who put the Jews into the ovens; it must be shown that the Jews, the subrace, the submen, bow to any and all humiliation, even to destroying themselves.[25]

The Nazis were not nihilists themselves, not at their own expense, but they imposed an active nihilism of condition upon their victims. In this they had diabolical imaginations. Indeed, the *Ubermensch* could reach dimensions of outrage never imagined before, impelled as they were to know themselves by reflection from the *Untermensch*.

•

The greatest part of the Nazi "crime against humanity" was to drag others into inhumanity with themselves, a forewarning of the moral apocalypse. In all murder there is a humiliation of existence that may dominate more than we know those last terrible moments of consciousness in the victim. But the killing by the Nazis was exceedingly slow and began with the first insults of their racial propaganda and became more and more specific with the laws of restriction and separation and the ultimate transport to the camps. When death finally came, all the gradations of humiliation the Nazis had imposed on their victims were in place. It is clear that racism, a biological sentencing, implicitly means murder in its culmination. The Nazis were exercised by an unearthly and terrible logic.

Ringelblum describes the random, periodic shooting of Jews in the Warsaw Ghetto. "This shooting of people in the streets has become a deliberate tactic since April. The aim: to terrify the populace, to terrorize them."[26] Terror, an extreme and usually successful effort to paralyze the will of opponents or resisters, became a dominant political tactic of the twentieth century. That is a historic truism and has defined totalitarianism for us, and much of the tactics and countertactics of war. And if we speak of fear, we must add that the greater part of fear was in the taking of hostages. That, too, was a successful Nazi precedent. Every able-bodied man and woman among the Jews knew that the fate of the children, the old, the sick and feeble, hinged upon their acts and choices.

Why didn't the Jews do more to resist? That tiresome, inhumane question hardly needs an answer, though it reflects something innate in a consideration of death, the need to salvage self-respect in the face of annihilation. This may be the reason why the Holocaust continues to affront us with a destructive effect on judgment.

To contemplate what is needed for heroism, one cannot imagine two more crippling effects than hunger and the chronic state of fear. The Nazis understood this as a scientific basis of their practical rule. A continuously hungry man, under continuous threat to his existence, can shovel the bodies of his brothers into fire or ditch without protest, even with what Colonel Hoess called "eager obedience."[27] And then within terror and hunger, there was the deeper paralysis of hope. One SS (according to Kurt Gerstein's report) spoke with the voice of a pastor at the door of the gas chamber, the men, women, and children, all naked, filing past him. "Nothing terrible is going to happen to you. All you have to do is to breathe in deeply. That strengthens the lungs. Inhaling is a means of preventing infectious diseases. It is a good method of disinfection." When they questioned him as to the future: "The men will have to build roads and houses. But the women won't be obliged to do so; they'll do housework or help in the kitchen." [28] That "pastor" understood irony; perhaps he was a metaphysician at heart.

The strategy usually worked, the record says. Many went tranquilly and with hope to their deaths. Gerstein's report recreates for us the peculiar character of the Nazi crime. What is that strange sense of honor that tells us that a murderer must face his victim with the truth, what is their "being in the world" that takes double destruction from a lie? In close examination, the slaughter of the Holocaust was no fury of destruction, and the sort of fury it arouses, in later witness, can be justly that of contempt directed at the killers. One is almost reluctant to see them as little men, whose Wagnerian megalomania was vanity, and who, when viewed apart from the devastation they caused, were something like a buffoon devil out of Dostoevsky's pages. But some were cynics, too, like our "pastor." This is the chief obstacle to understanding the Holocaust as tragedy.

•

"God . . . has disappointed us," Chaim Kaplan wrote, and we have disappointed ourselves, he could have added. "The conqueror has surrounded himself with spies, traitors, and talebearers, some of whom are found even among our Jewish brethren. . . . In all ages and in every generation we have had destroyers from our own midst" [29] Evil, then, is a disappointment in the heart of being; and yet Kaplan's is a noble disappointment. One feels strangely encouraged by his remark.

It is troubling to have rage descend as deep as grief, but this is the case for it. We speak of a great hatred, and feel it ourselves, because we are at a loss to account otherwise for a cruelty magnified and translated into the dread statistics of the Holocaust. Grief that becomes rage, hatred that endows hatred—these are the features of the moral abyss to which we add contempt, the profound thirst for insult both given and received, the victim acting as surrogate for human self-hatred. That is why the large issue is no longer the destruction of the Jews as Jews. The large issue becomes the threat of all against all. That summons a response that has the highest moral latitude and cannot limit itself to the issue between Jews and their oppressors.

A problem in the modern world has been how to know evil, or call anything by that name. Surely the Nazi Germans supplied an answer. The usual terms are not helpful; there was cruelty to a degree that one can hardly comprehend, but cruelty is not a word that is adequate here. Brutality is even less available. Violence ruled everywhere, was a constant recourse. Violence is an instrument not in itself evil, we think. What was transparent in Nazi motivation was that they wanted the Jews dead, this first, and despite the opinion of nations, the laws of God, and even the conduct and success of the war. If this strikes us as pure evil, it is because the purest evil is the wholesale and unselfish commitment to the death of others. Every legal system judges murder in that way, distinguishing between calculated murder and crimes of passion. To deny life is only the maximum of entailed evils. Life has a scale of attributes: it means freedom to move, to work, to think, to talk, to love, to hope, to engage on some essential level of equality with other people. And that may be the second point to make, that evil in its essence and genesis arises from a motive to deny equality in the right of existence to others. Perhaps all this is so basic that we need not attend to it for long.

The characteristic Nazi evil, then, most imaginatively used, was the motive to impose drastic reduction of the human estate, the latter a term now historic, once generated by a human pride. But from that point we can reverse order and reexamine the *rights* that pertain to a claim on the human estate. Physical suffering is easy to inflict, easily arousing compassion, readily inviting the emotions of rescue. The motive to inflict pain, witness it, enjoy it, is a form of pornography, arousing disgust but hardly worth investigating. The infliction of indignity is a more complex matter. The injury is to spirit, as we say, to character, to self-image, to one's "being in the world." Difficult as it is to identify, that state of achieved being is what most laws and moral acts are meant to defend. Character, or personal being, is always known against the background of nonentity. Beyond character there is a void, though it may be inhabited by animal sounds and smells. To have being is a poignant condition, filled with pathos.

The rage people feel against crime cannot be explained simply as a reaction to violence, or to the specifics of theft, rape, and murder. The essential ingredient in criminal acts is a violation, intangible but profound, that reaches into one's state in being, that is, one's claim on it, *one's right* to it. Even those who have not suffered personal assault but who have had a home burglarized may understand this. The shock and anger seem to have less to do with the value lost of gadgets, jewelry, or money. One feels a violation of one's being through one's home. We say sometimes glibly that a criminal who is punished has forfeited his place in society, but that is true, at least transiently, not only for himself but for his victim. In the experience of crime the criminal and his victim both inhabit isolated space, outside society, beyond community. The criminal has violated the contract that engages equality in moral being, a much deeper level of equality than that associated with wealth or power. Imprisonments and even executions are an effort to symbolize that forfeiture. It is really hard to say that executions fail in this purpose, or that a society does not feel its convention of moral equality restored by the ritual act of punishment. When the criminal goes free, or is punished on a relative scale far below the dimensions of his crime, assuming his guilt, we all feel shaken in our moral security, which depends on the social contract.

René Girard thinks of acts of social violence as acts of ritual sacrifice that are supportive to the social order in its inception as well as in its continuation.[30] He and others of psychoanthropological orientation tend to think of a purging that gives deeper unity to those who witness and survive. He also suggests that what they may purge is not the mere instinct for violence but rather a universal impulse that is deeply subversive and would destroy the social order as such. The Nazis were perhaps doing this, projecting onto the Jews the alien and dangerous force they felt in themselves. Note that they used to say *all* our misfortunes come from the Jews. Hitler invented a massive ceremony of sacrifice; his passion for unity, his totalitarian spirit, required unceasing murder. Racial purity was the highest good for him, above all moral terms and at the same time "truly" scientific. The value terms he understood were sickness and health, weakness and strength, and capping these for his people, a passion for order. Being an absolute moralist in that vein he was capable of limitless destruction. And to order his people to kill in the way they did and to the degree they did, he succeeded in "criminalizing" the Jews and his other enemies. That would be the paradoxical alternative to saying that he converted a whole nation and part of a continent to great crime.

•

How did the Nazis understand the slogans in favor of life with which they covered the walls of the death camps? On the road to extinction, the Auschwitz gate read,"*Arbeit Macht Frei*." Who put that up, a cynic or one of the unimpassioned bureaucrats of death? One would prefer to believe it was someone who in these words expressed a bitterness with which he would poison the world. But those executioners were more mundane creatures, perfectly at home in the world. We have the record of one official who wrote in his journal the details of a day's "action" and followed it with the greater detail, warmly reported, of what he had for lunch. This normalcy may seem proof of its opposite, a true insanity. Chaim Kaplan can be witness for that:

We are conscious that the creators and enactors of these cruel decrees are psychopaths. In every one of them one can find signs of madness, of a psychopathy affecting an entire community in the form of a monomania. A poison of diseased hatred permeates the blood of the Nazis and therefore all their stupid decrees, the fruit of this hatred are doomed to failure. . . . Anything founded upon insanity must not last long.[31]

But Kaplan, though he saw and felt more than we can share, did not know all that we know of the Holocaust. If he did he would find it hard to see it classified as an instance of psychopathy, even on the mass scale. Psychopathy needs a context, a form of acceptable and universal existence which marks out the deviance. But here the world had been seized in a convulsion of evil that wiped out its contrast, and wiped out the basis of judgment which defines either insanity or crime. Here evil was itself purely in the void it had created.

The moral life of humanity might be improved if the dead could return in order to judge their own deaths. Is it too fanciful to imagine and compare the testimony of those who died at Hiroshima and those who died in the Holocaust? There might be a point in saying to a man dying of cancer on the ramp at Birkenau that the difference between dying in his bed and dying in the gas chamber was ultimately of minor importance, but that I think is to evade the issue. All of us die, yes, but to think in those terms is to say that lives are cut off in varying measure—a month, a year, ten, twenty, forty years. But the time span is not the crucial issue and death itself is not the crucial moral issue. To mark the Holocaust we focus on death as *inflicted;* we focus on the relationship between murderer and victim.

Indeed, it is better to die in one's bed than in the gas chamber, so much so that all of our values may hinge on the difference. The war naturalist who accepts the rule of death, who submerges himself in its "law of nature," as Hitler, Himmler, and their executioners no doubt did, adds a force to murder that it otherwise does not have. He has abdicated the humanist ontology that arranges and supports life on terms other than those of nature. The Nazis knew what they were saying or claiming when they called their victims subhuman. To kill is subhuman, the victim is made subhuman, and the killer becomes subhuman in the process.

•

Nazi anti-Semitism, generally representing a modern secular anti-Semitism, was demoralizing in a special way for most Jews. They were not hated for that which was their own foundation of right, their religion, or their own self-valued identities. There is after all a proud tradition of martyrdom in Jewish legend and history. On such terms even death has a comfort. But under the German power they were given only the void to inhabit. Even a murderer offers some form of moral identity to his victim. But the Nazis almost succeeded in installing a naturalist fatalism that took moral agency from their own hands and moral identity from their victims. "Who is doing this to me and why?" was the unanswerable question echoing above the ramps, the cattle cars, and the gas chambers.

The brilliance of the "final solution" lay in this masking of moral agency, this impersonation of abstract destiny. Vasily Grossman, whose imagination in fiction approaches the unbearable truth, writes that at the end Jews shoved each other in order to be the first in line to meet death.[32] For some, even if their fortunes improved, the world was no longer acceptable. But who could then feel such general judgments? For the most part they were in the condition of those in intolerable pain, where to stop consciousness is the most urgent thing. And there were the "Musulmen" as example, who had stopped living before they died, as if bare survival required a superior act of will, an impossible reserve of strength.[33] At another extreme to which they were pushed, there were many who thought only of staying alive. And if some of these disgraced all standards, they had been thrust beyond the exercise of judgment. They, too, died in advance, like the "Musulmen."

To destroy the visible human bond, as at Lodz and Warsaw, was important for the Nazis perhaps because there was a perverted need to prove their own racial purity by killing what they could call the "racial" feeling in others. More deeply, obsessed with the reductive naturalist imperative, they sought to destroy the superficies of a moral community in others. That may be the basis of the conflict between Jew and Nazi that led to the Holocaust's absolute effort at "solution."

But the problem is no longer the "Jewish problem." That Hitler almost solved, on his terms, but it is the German Nazi problem, the racist chauvinist problem, the bigot nationalist and religionist problem, the one problem that bases a group identity on the need to deface it in others. In this respect all men have become "jews" (with the small "j" in Jean-Francois Lyotard's usage) and must adopt that suffering in Lodz and Warsaw as the gentiles of old adopted that of Christ. Hitler and his followers were the anti-Christ because, as vulgar Nietzscheans, they would overthrow a traditional "morality of the weak" for its presumption against nature's law. But if they made their blood and violence speak natural truth, we know now the value of that truth. We have paid much for the bitter, enraged thought of this century, but above all for that vitalist earth creed which would liberate any cruelty so long as it promised relief from repression, satisfied power, and conquered living space.

And yet Hitler and his cohorts defined evil too; they called it the "Jew." It is the worst of all possible paradoxes that pagans should moralize. The Nazis were not true pagans; their violence was abstract, its instrument a bureaucracy, its soldiers technocrats, their theory a vulgar and false science. In the twentieth century it is not passion or instinct that kills, but mind, enslaved by abstraction, by method, by collectivized action and thought. Hitler called the Jews a cancer for which the only cure was their surgical removal from the world. They were in effect a force of nature, to be treated with radical counterforce. The cruel irony is that they were anything but a force of *nature*, even in the form of disease. The Jews were powerless by any view, but their weakness was multiplied radically by their inability to conceive of a human agency in their oppressors, a moral agency, that is. I may be speaking of the situation of war and, of course, war was the essence of Hitler's own creed. In war enemies deal with each other in terms of blank force, whether exterminating sword or exterminating plague, and that is the generating sin of war from which all its evils flow. But the deepest evil was to propose a metaphysics of war as rule and context for both nature and human existence.

•

Czerniakow, the head of the Warsaw Jewish Council, committed suicide after the deportations to the death camps began, and when he learned that ten thousand Jews rather than six thousand would be the first quota. Katznelson, a Jewish resistance leader, condemned him for this marginal judgment. Why the difference between ten and six, he asked. Czerniakow must have realized at the time that the plan was to kill *all* Jews, and his death marks the dramatic failure of the survivalist principle aimed at "saving the remnant." His suicide is emblem of the fatal cost of collaborating with the Germans by the Jewish Councils. An agonizing debate of this sort goes on among Jews, trading levels of complicity, marking the humiliation of passivity, and the sense of deep betrayal in the behavior of the Jewish ghetto police and the Kapos in the camps. And all this is the post-facto reasoning of suicide.

Some prisoners in the camps, like hostages in a plane hijacking, developed a dependency relationship with their masters and captors, in instances even to the extent of imitating their manners, their values, their cruelty. On the opposite side, the "Musulmen," the terminal victims in the camps who reached total enervation, were following the pattern of children suffering from extreme abuse, and who act as if rejecting life by external command. The point is that as the camps prescribed mortally dependent relationships, the treatment exactly reversed the nurturing role of parents. Thus the condition for suicide was deeply implanted in the minds of the victims. Suicide can mean rejection of the world, but equally and perhaps more often it can mean conformity to the world's rejection of one's self. Nazis were saying in multiple brutal ways "we want you to die," and the suicide ultimately answers that command.

To make the extreme point, What is the alternative to suicide for the survivor and for all men who as vicarious survivors must climb out of the abyss of the Holocaust? The bravest in their thought, the most articulate of survivors, Jean Améry and Primo Levi, both committed suicide three and four decades after their return from the camps into life. Perhaps it was an act postponed, a promise fulfilled. What was taken from them that could not be restored? Améry called it "trust in the world." The darkest victory of the Nazis was in their discovery that they could kill something indispensable for living in the world.[34]

Bruno Bettelheim wrote that the energy of resistance, even hatred, was necessary to support the will to live.[35] Améry, in his earlier writing about his own experience, agreed. But that requires that the option of resistance be present, or else the effective choice is suicide. When resistance is made hopeless, then the vital force fades and the victims accept in one form or another the death in which they now collaborate, so to speak. Revolutionary theorists like Frantz Fanon also say that in resisting oppression one is exercising a vital force in oneself and so restoring mental health and redeeming life. And Hitler himself somehow knew, with his natural cruelty, that the will to live of his people was connected with the persecution and murder of others.

Primo Levi understood the cost of this vitalist spirit of violence. Writing a year or so before his own death and contemplating Jean Améry's suicide, he describes their correspondence during the years when both were writing about their experiences at Auschwitz, and how Améry's belief in "returning the blow" and achieving some dignity in resistance differed from his. Accepting confrontation, Améry suffered a ruthless beating from a camp criminal and described himself as deeply satisfied. Levi suggests that his later suicide (which took place in 1978, almost ten years before his own), followed from this. "I must point out that this choice, protracted throughout his post-Auschwitz existence, led him to positions of such severity and intransigeance as to make him incapable of finding joy in life, indeed of living."[36] Levi says that he himself had never known how to "return the blow" and could not believe in it—even in the politics of resistance.[37]

Levi is cryptic, but presumably he meant that an unpurged violence, trading blows with the world, turns finally against oneself. It becomes the rule of life and death. Earlier in his text he makes a more directly instructive but parallel interpretation of Améry's death, and he takes it quoting Améry's own words. "Anyone who has been tortured remains tortured. . . . Anyone who has suffered torture never again will be able to be at ease in the world, the abomination of the annihilation is never extinguished. Faith in humanity, already cracked by the first slap in the face, then demolished by torture, is never acquired again."[38] What it comes to and what may help account for Levi's own suicide is that the radical alienation enforced by the Auschwitz experience is subject to eternal question and recurrence.

Where then is the vital force for survival—in resistance, or in "faith in humanity?" Ultimately, one only knows the impulse to argue against suicide, whether that of Jean Améry or Primo Levi or Paul Celan, and even of those who committed moral or literal suicide while still in the camps. We can believe that intimate experience of the Holocaust finds a nihilism at its center that cannot be resisted when the vital forces are low. The crisis comes certainly and proposes either the equivalent of suicide, or a will to live that summons violent resistance to the outside world. Must that either-or be so desperate? Terrence Des Pres writes as if to say that the natural instinct toward survival adapts to a collective will to survive, and this in turn has its consequence in mutual aid and support, for which he found evidence in the camps.[39] That may be so, but then we must allow the opposite, as when in a weakened state nature dictates the preference for death as the alternative to the survival struggle. It seems better to say that the higher will to survive is not natural instinct but requires faith in humanity, that is, it becomes a moral obligation that arises from recognizing who we are, where we live and with whom, and what makes our lives possible. We might also remember that nature can dictate Hitler's chief premise as well as that of Des Pres. Nature can say that the group life is foremost, demanding sacrifice of individuals, ordaining deadly conflict with other groups, and always for the sake of survival. Survival is not then the chief issue, and when it becomes that we have already descended below a humanity we can accept.

In the moral universe created by the Nazis, subject to the laws of power and conflict, resistance was absolutely dictated, and even the barest continuance of breath was a form of that resistance, but it was ordered by all that prompts the moral sense as the negation of a negation. If the Holocaust teaches many things, one of its lessons is against suicide. So one would have wished to say to those men of martyred consciousness, to Jean Améry and Primo Levi.

•

To dishonor the Jew, the Nazis tried to force him to reject his humanity and his life. In a true sense and in witness, we contemplate the terms for our own survival. Reaction to the Holocaust has to be other than mere horror and revulsion. It has to be more than empathy with the victims, sharing their fear and some part of their actual suffering. We forbid ourselves any tendency to think of the Nazis with the awe hidden in terror, to involve them with the demonic, the satanic, or even to call them criminal and insane. They used the word "subhuman" against their victims; it would be worth much to know what they meant by it. But we describe them in their own terms when we dictate a judgment that all their efforts made them descend to the "subhuman's" lowest definition. Should we not offer them the credit for redefining a modern humanism? So it seems would be the answer from one survivor and witness, Pelagia Lewinska, who is quoted with deserved high respect by Emil Fackenheim and others.

At the outset [of her camp experience] the living places, the ditches, the mud, the piles of excrement behind the blocks, had appalled me with their horrible filth. . . . And then I saw the light! I saw that it was not a question of disorder or lack of organization but that, on the contrary, a very thoroughly considered conscious idea was in the back of the camp's existence. They had condemned us to die in our own filth, to drown in mud, in our own excrement. They wished to abase us, to destroy our human dignity, to efface every vestige of humanity, to return us to the level of wild animals, to fill us with horror and contempt toward ourselves and our fellows. . . .

But from the instant I grasped the motivating principle . . . it was as if I had been awakened from a dream. I felt under orders to live. . . . And if I did die in Auschwitz it would be as a human being . . . I was not going to become the contemptible, disgusting brute my enemy wished me to be. . . . And a terrible struggle began which went on day and night.[40]

That struggle continues in the striving of memory, the need to record, which still characterizes Holocaust witness and seems never to cease or dwindle, not even as the actual survivors begin to disappear. As Lewinska says, primarily, and in their names, we are "under orders to live." The actual scenes of the Holocaust defeat the imagination. Therefore, they seem unreal and the Holocaust a fiction for some. The most interesting questions comes up when we ask why the story of the Holocaust received initial incredulity and still does in some quarters. Disbelief was justified, for to discover its reduction of human beings from all existential assumptions is to undermine reality. As Jean Améry wrote, "Reality is rational only as long as it is moral."[41] In the gas chambers, a struggling mass of bodies had descended to a level of being which consciousness cannot invade, much less conscience. In this the Nazis made themselves expert. They proved themselves supermen by feeding on scenes such as these. They had the need of great negations. The slave exists in order to affirm a master. The dead are dead in order to give murderers life. Invariably, it seems that racism suggests and invites a crime against humanity. Humanism, which has been validly defined as the antithesis of racism, assumes a mutuality of wounds, an empathy within violence for a humanity so civilized that it considers all blows as directed against its collective self.

The Nazis almost succeeded in remaking the world in their own image of it. How many victims finally believed that they deserved to die? We dare not imagine how many, though Vasily Grossman refers to Jews of the Holocaust who declared in their final moments that their extinction would benefit the human race. A novelist like Grossman might know, it takes a brave imagination to recognize a total defeat of spirit. But it is on those terms, acknowledging a moral abyss, that the records and archives of the Holocaust should be kept and read.

3

Three Myths of Modernity:
The God in History

"Who is doing this to us and why?"

It is true that the Nazis were hardly significant thinkers or political theorists, but that makes it all the more certain that they were ideologists in the modern sense. That is, ideas for them were not reflections of reality but instruments for changing it, expressing the will to power in the crudest, simplest meaning of Nietzsche's doom-haunted phrase.

For example, and despite the respect paid him by Trevor-Roper and others as the rare intellectual among the Nazis, the terms of thought in Goebbels's diary cannot be distinguished from his official propaganda. Perhaps his mind could not move in any other way. Perhaps he and his leader lived in their ideological myth and its hallucinations, which they would impose upon the world as reality. They would rule the world while being estranged from it. One thinks, in comparison, of the alienated humanity of Dostoevsky's characters, say, Svidrigailov or Stavrogin, but there a void within combined with a despair which comes from awareness of that void. The truly inhuman must express an absence of self-reviewing consciousness whose closest parallel would be the "thought" of a robot. In Goebbels, a robot consciousness was inhabited by a shrewdness searching for advantage, a resentment searching for its source, a pride searching for its occasion. He had a soul within him that became the perfect receptacle and perfect messenger of propaganda. He is our subject if we wish to contemplate how the collective consciousness, the *public* consciousness of our time, can degenerate. All his ideas, all his notions of fact, were designed for the conclusion he wanted to reach. The era of totalitarian politics installed many forms of insecurity in people's moral lives, but the greatest may have been the anxiety bred by a regime of lies.

How does one know and judge the reality in which this man Goebbels lived and died, with his family, in the inferno of the Bunker? Was he, that man of poisoned language, capable of authentic being? And if he killed his children, by measure of what devotion? One would think that there could

45

be no felt intimacy or personality in the Nazi way of death. Was it *vernichtung* for Goebbels's children and his wife, or something else? The Nazis applied death in its most alienated forms, that of abstract numbers with abstract goals delivered by a technically abstract industrial process. Beyond abstraction, death itself was purely reductive, a biological process with no more implication than the routine death of subordinate living cells. The Nazis were scientistic with a vengeance, engineers of survival and extinction. It was activist biology for them, as if their work could best be expressed in the images of a statistical chart and a slaughterhouse. This is what causes consternation in those who would write their record. And yet, in that world of quantified death, the Wagnerian intoxication of a political myth reigned supreme. The modern dualities of alienated consciousness joined in destructive climax, and abstract murder, nature's *Diktat,* came to the service of national chauvinism and racial self-love. This was the field of work for the myth maker, the fiction maker, Goebbels, who could mix passion and lies with complete conviction.[1]

Today the word "ideology" suggests an instrumental truth, a belief not of fact but of power that would impose itself on reality. At the time when he was enacting Hitler's order to create murder battalions, the *Einsatzgruppen,* Heydrich spoke to his subordinates and explained the deadly use of ideology. In "this war [with the Soviets], which represented the final, violent clash of two irreconcilably opposed *Weltanschauungen,* the Führer has expressed his resolve to find simultaneously a solution to the Jewish problem."[2] The German word, *Weltanschauung,* summarizing a large and positive view of life and ultimately contracted into a weapon, carries the threat left behind by the Holocaust. It swears to the conflict of autonomously intact value systems fated to attempt to eliminate each other. How could there be more than one *Anschauung* for the single world? And it blends with that equally fateful German word, *Kultur.* This is a language of knives and hammers, with such monolithic terms as *Volk* and *Rasse,* all with their irresistible tendency to be used as weapons.

It may some day astonish readers of history to note this century's political practice of committing truth entirely to the service of power. The Moscow purge trials, the Czech trials of Rudolf Slansky and others—these all record the amazing willingness of the victims to lie and collaborate in lies against themselves. Apart from the considerable effect of torture, many students agree that the confessions had a strong degree of ideological assent from the victims. Still believers, they accepted the principle that the lie against justice was the last service they could perform for the party and the future of the revolution. Conceivably, even Stalin, if he had been over-thrown and treated similarly, might have agreed to lie to the degree neces-sary to achieve a politically valuable result for his own trial. If the thesis is valid (and Robert Conquest and others mark its support in the evidence), the point is that these victims were not conditioned to believe in their indi-vidual rights and fates, were not conditioned in favor of either truth or justice. Their values were all subsumed in the interest of the revolution, the process of history, the power of the party. In the end, they were visited by the fatal passivity of those who lose in the conflicts of modern history, those who accept the verdict of force, the *Diktat* of victory, as superseding the mere ideas of right and wrong.

When the politics of ideologies reigned supreme, as they did in the thir-ties and forties of this century, the propaganda of the lie was used to unlim-ited excess. Is this not a contradiction? A politics founded on theory was in action most apt to debase theory by using ideas as weapons, as manipu-lative propaganda. But Stalinist ideology and the Nazi ideology in particu-lar, always more weapon than thought, were designed to serve power. And power was effective truth, or that *Daseins-Willen,* the Will to Be, which Heidegger hopefully said inhabited the führer and his people. A theory of force and fatality which reigns supreme over other ideas turns them all into lies, that is, one or another fiction at the service of power.

Engaged in war, truth comes only at the behest of the victors. If one hears the outcry of suffering and danger, or the sounds of moral protest, these are as likely to be tactical propaganda, or be treated as such in any case. It was considered beforehand that men lived and fought in the realm of the lie, that the claim on truth was a brandished lie, that truths were never nonpartisan, as for instance in the history written by the victors. In that realm of the lie, affecting both sides, it was then easy to dismiss the early reports of the Holocaust not as atrocious truth but as atrocity mon-gering.

In December 1943, Goebbels referred in a conference with his aides to the first reports of the Holocaust coming out among the Allies. He ordered his people to create a counteroffensive of atrocity stories, a "hullabaloo," he said, to get away from the "embarrassing" (his word) subject of the Jews.[3] (This was actually a year after public announcement had been made in the West on the subject of the death camps and how they operated, but the fact was that the Allies did almost nothing to exploit the presumable propaganda advantage.) "All this kind of unfavorable publicity was known as atrocity mongering." said Eichmann, under interrogation. The propaganda of the enemy gave bad currency to all propaganda. The democracies could not retaliate with the truth when the excess of cruelty sounded like lies. But more ironically, the fact that the Allies restrained their own propaganda of atrocity gave currency to Goebbels's thought that they shared the Nazi hatred of the Jews. In his notes Goebbels refers to the shedding of crocodile tears, assuming as Nazi leaders always did that each side hated the Jews in the same way, with hypocrisy the only difference.

For students of language and culture these bizarre expressions of linguistic skepticism have an interesting effect. On the one hand, the rhetoric of persecution and atrocity had become compromised by tactical exploitation. On the other, the reality-truth of the Holocaust still capable of shock had to be concealed in bureaucratic euphemism, the strange language the Nazis used to communicate with each other over the screams of their victims and the smoke of the furnaces. Eichmann, in his interrogation, spoke as follows: "When questions were asked, the answer was: For labor service in the East. . . . to avoid the misuse of such information for purposes of atrocity-mongering, no mention was to be made of evacuation or deportation."[4] But "evacuation" and "deportation" were themselves the language of concealment for the slaughter, as were terms like "selection," "special action," and "special treatment." In general, we can say that the Holocaust reached its extreme level of a horror beyond the power of language exactly because it was allowed to take place in a realm unreachable by language, and that the language surrounding its reality had absconded from its role; hardly any at this juncture believed that it could treat truth or reality at all, and almost all believed that it was only another weapon in the tactics of war and the struggle for power. When the confidence in truth-speaking language breaks down, it is only a seeming paradox that the regime of lies is accepted under the protection of a fanatic gospel of faith. Truth becomes equated with authority, and so the issue comes to accepting authority in the strongest lie, armed with power, which has the monopoly of truth. Thus cynics and bigots unite as they do so often in modern political conflict. The cynic and the bigot, aided by the endemic skepticism directed against language, create a void at the center of discourse, a void filled by the monopolists of power. This may be one more major lesson of the Holocaust, that it was in its nature to be a carnival of totalitarian crime.

•

The argument for anti-ideological politics is in favor of letting "reality" in—that multiple, pluralist, distantly decipherable truth, that possible truth which protects us from becoming the creatures of someone else's fiction, another group's myth. For fictions can remake us, even to ourselves. A fiction imposed by others is pure oppression. On the other hand, a skepticism that perceives all truths as fictions makes way for the same oppression. One message from that "low, dishonest decade" of European modern history is this: be very careful what doctrine you believe for it is certain you will try to bring it to reality. Declare that you have an enemy and he will become that enemy. Declare a people to be of inferior race and you will soon write the scenarios that will fulfill your theory. This was Hitler's effort and his success. He defined Jews and made them become, through methodic abuse and torment, the proof of his definition. That is the poison; prejudice, given any degree of power, is never merely subjective prejudice: it acts upon the victim, imposes corroboration and receives it, sometimes flimsy, sometimes drastic, as in the terrible degeneration suffered by Jews in the Polish ghettos under German rule.

What did Hitler believe? He believed in his "Will," for which he thought he had warrant from the German philosophers. He was certainly the chief of half-educated men, but whether or not he had read Hegel, Schopenhauer, and Nietzsche, they were his environment. The astounding fact is that Himmler recruited the higher SS chiefly from the ranks of academics, lawyers, doctors, and journalists. George Steiner mentions what must have been the main point of the attraction to Nazism for Heidegger, and he quotes Heidegger's words, "The *Volk* [under the Nazis] has won back the 'truth' of its 'will to be,' of its *Daseins-willen.*" [5]

As Hitler could have known or understood it, Heideggerian thought would translate itself with ruthless cruelty. If we assume that he was some sort of second- or third-degree disciple of Heidegger's thought (for which we have no evidence), he might have believed that "truth" was in the dedication of warriors who express that which "wills-to-be." Was not sacredly authentic "Being" the prize to be won by the strongest? Perhaps it followed that those committed to "non-Being" invite a great and licensed slaughter. But Hitler thought more simply. "There is no such thing as truth," he said to Rauschning, "either in the moral or in the scientific sense." [6] This was the belief of the most powerful politician of his time, one whose conquests would have been envied by Alexander, Napoleon, or Genghis Khan. What are the consequences of such a belief when combined with great power? If there is scandal in a great modern philosopher's sympathy for Nazism, it might focus here, on Heidegger's reductive *Daseinswillen,* a mysticism of the will which in vulgar perspective could respect pure violence. And borrowing with animal instinct from Nietszche, of whom he may have had a more detailed report, Hitler did believe power was all the truth he needed, power through which he could dictate the "truths" of others. This radical insight, insidiously undercurrent in the early decades of the century, may account for the moral paralysis of his early opponents and many of his victims. Two forces acted with terrible effect: on one side a megalomania of power, and on the other a void of moral purpose, a void of meaning, which de-energized resistance to power.

It cannot be doubted that Hitler was the intellectually aborted offspring of apocalyptic modernism, one by-product in the use of the powerful weapons of reduction and demystification against traditional values, the superstructure above the base. The struggle was mask against mask, weapon against weapon, until it reached the level of primary truth—biological race, economic class interest, levels of "reality." Then, as in war, it was base against base, the differences among peoples resolved through class war and revolution, or race war and genocide. On this basis of reduction, the superstructure is put in the hands of Goebbels, propagandist, to be reinvented. Ideas are propaganda. Conscience has no independent validity, and conscience cannot debate conscience except in forms of manipulation and deceit. There is nothing left but atrocity and outrage to awaken the bare elements of conscience. So, for example, each side in war vies for the news of atrocities committed by the other. So moral response is cheapened, made a blunt and heavy instrument, reduced to demagogy. The force of conscience has not been eliminated. Rather it has been put completely at the service of group power and survival. The Nazis had a racial conscience, an imperial conscience, which worked on the side of war and genocide. Communists, in their historic struggle on a higher, warrantable level of value, mobilized themselves for the survival interest of a class and something subliminally strong in faith, the historic destiny of the whole species. Power becomes fate; power is reality. Conscience is myth, to be manipulated, destroyed, recreated. Terror and propaganda are then developed to refinements of great craft as the primary means of political rule.

All this is too simple a summary for the greater "holocaust" of lives that extended through most of the first half of this century. Can we reduce to propaganda those narrowly intense, cosmically confident beliefs—abstractions reduced to slogans—that drove the engines of destruction? To see Nazi behavior beyond the level of atrocity or criminal pathology is to travel in a maze of abstractions. The operators of the camps could not have been seized day after day by bloodlust. There was a mental habitation, an environment of fantasy and belief that impelled their actions and made them possible, if only in the fetish words of war discipline and Teutonic obedience, the defense that was usually made in postwar military tribunals. The record shows that quite possibly many were in their own fashion, on their own terms, idealists who believed in what they were doing and the ultimate good it would achieve, though it was in the nature of their faith that they could at the same time appear to be nihilists and act as opportunists seizing power.

It is natural to ask what abstractions of belief could conduct mass murder on the scale of the Holocaust. One thinks first of *Ordnung* as the alternative to chaos. The killing was the resolution of a "problem" of disorder. But order for these Nazis was not a mere war problem under simple military discipline; expressed in cultural and racial uniformity, it was in fact equated with the order-making process of nature. In the death camps they thought of themselves as surgeons and sanitation experts. Politically they were pathologists and healers devoted to a drastic cure. The chief enemy (perhaps we should say their chief victim) was not Bolshevism, the ideological rival in cults of order.[7] At its most heartfelt base, the Nazi attack was against all forms of pluralism—racial, ethnic, religious, political, and cultural. Democracy, internationalism, egalitarianism, freedom—these formed the precise antithesis. (If Americans, as such, wish to build a museum of the Holocaust, they can only do so believing that the instruction is for themselves, not in moral boast but renewed dedication.)

The Teutonic faith in discipline conceivably made it possible to transfer all motive and reason to the mind of Hitler alone. Many historians and writers seem to accept the plain German devotion to wartime unity as a primary force, as if unity were a kind of god offering absolute commands from an intelligent source. Certainly the German generals seemed helpless against Hitler at the end, and the war lasted longer than it conceivably would with a different regime. But viewed in the context of the Holocaust, the theme of Prussian discipline seems grotesque as explanation. "I obeyed, I obeyed," was the major defense of such as Eichmann and Ohlendorf, but the fact that the Eichmann and his cohorts were terribly eager to complete the extermination of the Jews, even at the last turn of the war into defeat, at a time when Himmler himself was already trying to close down the gas chambers, disproves the notion of automatic obedience. These people were zealots for a cause, and if they had the opportunity would have continued without the leadership of Himmler and Hitler himself. Eichmann's quoted remark, that he would go to his grave happy for the deaths of six million Jews, deserves credence.

Widespread killing, extended over time, would demand the support of abstract thought. Only a devotion to principle could maintain such bloodthirst. The war abstraction, first of all, links all violent acts to self-defense. Otto Ohlendorf, the most savage of *Einzatsgruppe* leaders, explained the Holocaust's greatest dimension of atrocity by saying that every Jewish child was a future danger to the Reich if he survived to revenge his parents. Thus the most long-range rationalization linked with the immediate urgencies of war; violence was both purposeful and inbred, with the biological battlefield supporting the reasons of the state.

Race was the inflammatory abstraction, the most deadly that the Nazis possessed and distributed, and yet the most realizable to the average German when translated from the term *Volk*. *Volk* meant more than Darwinian principles, esoteric theories of genetic transmission; it was myself and my people, here and now, the only collectivity I trust in a world of tribal war. All familiarities, all genialities that make the world a home are in the word *Volk*. Yet at the same time race is an esoteric mystery. Mysteries of race imply and enjoin an abstract foreign identity that grows like a hydra monster to be cut off again and again. Race delimits humanity, puts a barrier beyond which nothing is forbidden. The racially subhuman has lost the justification of his existence. In confrontation, murdering violence becomes normal and part of everyday life.

In the cause of race, the Nazi ideology took even more violence from the political cult of revolution. This was explicit in the early talks of Hitler with Rauschning and Wagener. Revolutionism conceives of destroying an old order and establishing a new one, cleansed and purged of the poison of decadence, the bacilli of disease (familiar metaphors treated literally by the Nazis) that had afflicted a civilization. The decay of the old order was attributed to bourgeois democracy itself, represented by the Weimar Republic and the traitors of Versailles. But revolution was also counterrevolution opposed to Bolshevism on the other side. Those enemies on the two fronts can explain what led the German soldiers and Nazi leaders to endure to the very end. They were fighting the true apocalypse; stepping between a dying civilization and revolutionary chaos and anarchy, they believed they had civilization on their side and also the purging renewing force of the chosen revolution. They had the advantage in ideological politics of being reactionary and revolutionary at the same time. And the incredible cruelty of their war, and, in fact, of both World Wars in this century, may be partly explained on this apocalyptic basis. Even peace had an apocalyptic message for the Allies in the First World War, "the war to end wars."

The Nazis recognized an evil that had to be swept away, and in their scientistic faith it was an evil to be dealt with by nature's best remedy: extinction. Their age was an age that did not believe in conversion or redemption. Torquemada had more human compassion than either Hitler or Stalin. These had rather to believe in absolute force directing epochs of change, overturnings, and destruction. Destruction itself, as Goebbels made it out by process of sublimation, became equated with revolution.

Such versions of the political apocalypse had been preached for two hundred years, since the French Revolution recorded itself in the human imagination as blessed by historic fate. History became the god in fate, to be served, placated, worshipped, and, most dangerously, to be co-opted in the interest of race, nation, class, empire, and ideology. History was necessity, a force ultimately beyond direct control in which all people are swept. But individuals and groups, reaching into their deepest intuitions, their deepest violent needs and motives, could find themselves acting on its behalf. In the Marxist sense, their freedom became equal to necessity. And if they could prophesy for history, they could lead and govern the world, acting with a force which in proportion to its ruthless violence could certify its historic authority. This was the cruel paradox (cruel for their victims), that they could see their moral justification only in the extreme of force they could summon.

•

It may be imagined that two forms of fatalism met to make catastrophe in the Holocaust. As reported by Emmanuel Ringelblum, the Warsaw Jews waited for a miracle to save them. Most reports of the passivity of the victims tend to underplay their actual helplessness. Nevertheless, an outward passivity and obedience to the orders of their tormentors was the rule.[8] To account for this is a greatly complex matter, but one may speculate that the fatalism of Orthodox Jews had some effect; the Messiah will or will not come and, as some sects even in Israel today proclaim, to act as savior in his place was a sin. But that was met by the aggressive biological fatalism of the Nazis where races and species were in a contest of destruction.

In general, we know that a political fatalism dominates modern history, whether it calls itself racial destiny, an imperial glory marked by geopolitical exigency, or redemption in the class struggle. Eventually, only the latter faith, plus a Russian nationalism as tribalist as that of the Nazis, could be a match for Hitler's intoxicated horde. Those who dislike all forms of ideological megalomania must remember that strength is on its side. Irony of vision and intellectual humility will not champion a cause or conquer a people. There is a fatalism of defeat and a fatalism of victory, and both mask the effective will that determines events. History itself warns us to beware of those who pretend to have absolute confidence in the future they would create.

It came to pass, in this century, that historic agents believed in their role in history more devoutly than any programmatic historian and aimed all their actions accordingly. It was to be history in command, and commanded. Like Spengler, Hitler was fascinated by the rise and fall of civilizations—of empires and their collapse. Europe must be saved from the Jewish Bolshevik ideology by the Nazi ideology of the racial elite. He said to Rauschning, "Europe is for us. Whoever conquers it will press his seal on the coming age. We are the chosen. If we fail, we shall die out, as all Europe's nations will degenerate." [9] Alan Bullock points out Hitler's interest in the Roman Empire, "in which Christianity—the invention of the Jew, Saul of Tarsus—had played the same disintegrative role as Bolshevism—the invention of the Jew, Marx—in the Europe of his own time." [10] The coupling of the Jew Paul and the Jew Marx suggests how much Hitler's hatred of the Jew was based on rivalry, striving in maniacal competition to found a cultural-historical empire, in fact to be the god-creator or, in the Roman sense, the imperial god himself.

On this ground Hegel could have given him the important image of himself as one of the "World Historical Individuals" chosen to embody the "World Historical Process." [11] Accordingly, like many dictators before and after him, he invoked Providence constantly and told his people that this was the source of his strength as well as his justification. In a speech at Wuerzburg in 1937, he said, "However weak the individual may be when compared with the omnipotence and will of Providence, yet at the moment when he acts as Providence would have him act he becomes immeasurably strong." [12] So his followers were convinced and the faith hardened them to atrocity.

Reading Goebbels's diary, we listen to the exercises of the abstract political mind, invoking "history" at a time when German cities were being bombed to ashes and thousands of his "racial" partners were being killed.

The war was close to its end. Years of suffering imposed on his own people as well as their victims might have weighed on his mind, and yet Goebbels's chief concerns were, first, his rivalry and hatred for Goering and Himmler; second, his bitterness toward the German generals on the various fronts; and third, his dream of splitting the Allies and turning the West against the Communists. Only this kept him and his chief in the fight, that and their belief, even at the end, that "history" was on their side. If not, then they were doomed by history, and so they continued the exterminating struggle without trying to mediate the sentence. In fact, they would confirm it (Albert Speer reported at the end), as if a complete historicism culminates in madness, as if in the hands of fate there is no need for sanity. And how could the Allies not know that their interest was in making a separate peace and keeping Hitler armed against the Bolsheviks? The logic of history carries a merciless sword.

Political historicism, used as a political weapon, invokes a large web of causality as the agency of sure destruction. Can anything arouse more force of retaliation than the threat to put an end to a community, a civilization, a race? And surely those who use that threat must feel it rebound against themselves. To understand that vengeful consciousness, witness Goebbels's diary. These finalities of destruction in the minds of its agents help explain how the Holocaust came close to absolute success in the goal of destroying all of Europe's Jews. Genocide is a modern nightmare which follows from a metaphysics of conflict between nations, races, or classes, and it follows from installing history as prophecy and threat.

To measure a political culture, we might ask how people prophesy for each other. How do they conceive progress and change? Who uses a supervening force of fate for confidence and a threat? What is made of warnings of decline and decay, and who threatens extinction for a species, biological or political? The Nazis always meant *Vernichtung,* annihilation, but they used the term "final solution" as an objectively minded euphemism. It even sounded like a moral appeal. Now it rings like a scream from the Birkenau ramp. Nevertheless we contemplate the term: a "final solution" of any "problem" threatens devastating behavior; it is a phrase for apocalyptic violence. In the time and history of its use, its parallel, perhaps its model, was "the final conflict" springing from *The Communist Manifesto* of 1848 and used in the Communist anthem. Such prophecies are weapons to be used.

Hitler's ideology, insofar as he had one, was largely determined as a counterforce to Marxist Bolshevism, as he conceived it, the other alternative to a "New World Order." On their side Marxist Socialists and Communists in Germany believed that Hitler was merely the last voice of dying capitalism, doomed even in gaining power. It was a matter of two revolutions at each other's throats, both imagining that they expressed the sentence of history, and both realizing that their testing battle was with each other. These were premises first laid by the Marxists themselves.

In any case, apocalypticism of that sort was universal in the germinating period for German Nazism. It was a strong aspect of literary and artistic modernism; as one example, Berthold Brecht could proclaim that Communism was the only alternative to the end of the world. Weimar was the chief image, repeated until believed, for political and cultural decadence.[13] It was understood that all authentic revolutions manifested ruthlessness. The historic dialectic required great destruction in order to give proof to redemption and renewal. It is remarkable how the cult of apocalyptic revolution carried itself forward into the twentieth century when, as with sundry "Weathermen" and "Red Brigades," and their ideological mentors of the sixties and seventies, it was proposed that a whole system needed to be wiped out, according to the laws of historical necessity, to build a new order. It was forbidden to ask too closely what the terms and character of that order would be, inscribed as they were in the future. But these were minor battles, aftershocks to illustrate that the god worshipped in history is an ugly god, the same god of historic struggle and revolutionary violence that Lenin preached, and which was transformed, beheaded of intelligence, so to speak, in the practice of Stalin and Hitler.

A political determinism is thus the grand opportunity for megalomania. Wars come of necessity; one lives, fights, murders, and dies through necessity and to fulfill a fate larger than judgment or personal choice. And yet the hero can choose to be the instrument; "necessity" becomes his alibi, and for the rest there is passive obedience, that is, a submission to violence in the hands of violent history.[14]

Again one asks, What was the role of Judaic fatalism in all this? The largest percentage of Eastern Jews were Orthodox, all of them retaining at least the memory of orthodoxy. Religious Jews were conditioned to think that their misfortunes were destinarian, that divine fate had given them periodic affliction, and those misfortunes could be linked with equally fated salvation. God's will acted in place of "the laws of existence" and so paralleled the modern deities of biological fate and economic laws. The best authority on Jewish response to the crisis they faced in the early period of the Holocaust, Isaiah Trunk, writes as follows, "In this time of dreadful ordeals, many deeply religious Jews became more pious, detecting the hand of God punishing the Jews for their sins." Some saw their suffering as preceding the coming of the Messiah, a purifying ordeal of fire. They could say we are a nation that has "greater ethical demands made upon it than other nations and hence we are punished harder than other nations."[15]

Ironically, the same fatalism, from a matching perspective, affected much of the world's witness. In *Shoah*, a naive anti-Semitic Pole tells the story of a village rabbi who calls his people together at their ultimate ordeal and tells them that this is the fulfillment of their historic punishment for the Crucifixion. Did this commonplace fantasy gain the concurrence of those Christians who stood by or helped during the slaughter? The habit of giving at least passive consent to the persecution of Jews has venerable standing in Christian history. The keynote is the conviction of destinarian punishment. The vicious parallel is the destinarianism of modern militant politics, like that of the Nazis.

Himmler did not say he was God's sword; he was nature's sword in acting for the Thousand Year Reich and redemption in history. But for pious Jews, Jews of endurance, there was not much to distinguish the two swords of fate. For other Jews it still was true that all power was on the other side, and the other side might be bribed, placated, circumvented in the strategy of enduring one more historic ordeal, one more punishment, but never opposed by the confidence to challenge fate's judgment. The exceptions in acts of resistance and escape—among Bundists, Communists, and Zionists—outline the more general pattern of compliance that Raul Hilberg reports but do not challenge its prevailing effect.

•

The führer principle and determinism in general may seem at odds, but not in the German philosophic tradition. Speaking of historic "heroes"— Alexander, Caesar, Napoleon—Hegel writes, "It was theirs to know this nascent principle; the necessary, directly sequent step in progress, which their world was to take; to make this their aim, and to expend their energy in promoting it."[16]

How beguiling this grand effort to reconcile freedom and necessity was to the German mind is reflected by Heidegger at the time he was most

tempted by Nazism. In November 1933 he gave this advice to the German
people in support of the plebescite confirming Hitler's power:

The German people are called to the voting places by the Führer. But the Führer
asks nothing of the people; quite the contrary, he gives the people the most immediate possibility of the highest kind of free choice: the people in their entirety will
decide if they want their own Dasein or if they do not want it. Tomorrow, the
people will choose nothing less than their own future.[17]

One asks, What choice was that when "their own *Dasein*" or affirmation
of Being was at stake? We are struck by the unity of thinking between a
major philosopher and a political theory and practice armed for apocalyptic
violence. In our time men conditioned themselves to act as if by historic
necessity and then blamed necessity for the ruthlessness of their own natures. One reason the Holocaust can shock as it does (and could reach its
extreme of mass murder) is that it was conducted as if divorced from human agency, as if human agents could hide behind the force of an earthquake or some natural and historical catastrophe, predetermined, set in a
pattern of growth or conflict, like a break in evolution, or more plausibly
by the effect of an iron law of evolution, as in the annihilation of an ancient
species, dinosaurs or other. The shock comes in the meeting between one
perspective of that sort with another which finds the malignant motives of
actual agents on the actual scene of murder. But we still have difficulty
placing them behind the gigantic machine of slaughter.

Politics had become war, war was a form of natural violence, killing was
more like fatal accident than murder. Perhaps that was politics at its fur-
thest development into itself away from ethics and conscience. What is difficult to ponder is that the effect had philosophical backing. George Steiner
makes this important judgment of a message in Heidegger on language
and meaning. There is in Heidegger, he says, the supposition

that it is not man who speaks where language is most fully effective, but "language
itself through man," an ominous hint of Hitler's brand of inspiration, of the Nazi
use of the human voice as a trumpet played upon by immense, numinous agencies
beyond the puny will or judgment of rational man. This motif of dehumanization
is key. Nazism comes upon Heidegger precisely at that moment in his thinking
when the human person is being edged away from the center of meaning and of
being. The idiom of the purely ontological blends with that of the inhuman.[18]

In the background there are the voices of Fichte and Hegel. Fichte
spoke for generations of Germans and, essentially, for the Nazis when he
gave metaphysical right to the fulfillment of national destiny. Germany is

"the *Volk*," he wrote, "metaphysically destined, which has the moral right to fulfill its destiny by *every* means of cunning and force."[19] Metaphysical destiny had the power to overwhelm "moral right," transcend it, replace it, and the strongest German moral institutions gave way. Early in the rule of the Nazis, an archbishop of the church found a defense for their racist program. Archbishop Grober of Freiburg wrote in 1935, "Every people bears responsibility for the success of its existence, and the absorption of entirely alien blood will always constitute a risk for a nation which has proved its historic worth. Consequently, the right to safeguard the purity of the race, and to devise measures necessary to that end, can be denied to no one. The Christian religion simply demands that the means used shall not be contrary to moral law and natural justice." But in this phrasing all ambiguity and equivocation were left on the side of the moral law and justice.[20]

Naturalists by profession were not behind the bishop in this respect, as Robert J. Lifton reports from his study of Nazi doctors employed in the death camps. To judge what was going on, one doctor said, was useless; "whether one condemned it or not was not really so much the issue." The issue was that "Auschwitz was an existing fact. One couldn't . . . really be against it, you see, one had to go along with it whether it was good or bad." Lifton adds, ". . . that is, mass killing was the unyielding fact of life to which everyone was expected to adapt." This appropriately enough was naturalist fatalism. But adaptation to a "natural phenomenon" (*Naturereignis*) was merely neutral; most of Lifton's doctors went further to share Himmler's dream of eugenic control and mastery, the Holocaust as brave experiment.[21]

The Nazis carried the confidence of men who had *assumed* the role of natural destiny, and that was the secret of their power over others. It was a form of self-hypnosis, and to see this intellectual deformity is to feel the profound disgust which has expression in these words of Elias Canetti: "Each man finds his weapons in this arsenal (history), . . . " "Every historian has an old weapon on which he dotes, and which he makes the center of his history. There it stands now, erect, proud, as though it were a symbol of fertility, and in reality it is a cold murderer turned to stone." Canetti rightly sees that the deity is power. "I hate the respect of historians for Anything merely because it happened, their falsified, retrospective standards, their impotence, their kowtowing to any form of power." Let us, he says, judge men "by whether they accept history or are ashamed of it."[22] Men meet the judgment of history, the determinists say. Is it possible to renew the confidence that history must meet the judgment of men?

Czeslaw Milosz viewed historicist thinking in politics this way: "Dialectics: I predict the house will burn; then I pour gasoline over the stove. The house burns; my prediction is fulfilled. Dialectics."[23] Elias Canetti and Milosz were men who suffered from the armed god of history. In contrast, there is Heidegger to consider. Jean-Francois Lyotard, as a philosopher with close connection to Heidegger's thought, is well-equipped to summarize the relevant theme in *Being and Time (Sein und Zeit)*. "Being-there (*Dasein*) and only there" but choosing it, throws itself before the possible, projects itself beyond the powerlessness of the Being there, and achieves "the authentic relationship of *Dasein* to time."[24] This is Heideggerian language which needs a lucid second translation, for which one can go to George Steiner: "To accept one's *Dasein* in the full sense is to enter on one's true historical inheritance . . . [and] to accept actively . . . the individual's afterlife in the destiny of the group. Destiny is fate made authentic on the national or ethnic level. History . . . is the dynamic embedding of individual fate in communal destiny."

What is inauthentic fate, one wishes to ask? The "authentic" seems to mean the collective agreement that is irresistible, and it means force. And what is wrong with the worship of *Dasein* which seems to mean fatal reality, the existential absolute? *Dasein* can be seen as Moloch, god of overwhelming force. *Dasein* can be the enemy of judgment, the enemy of responsibility; it can mean the submergence of individual conscience (inauthentic?) in a superior collective will, or in compulsions of loyalty, terror, passion. Reason and freedom surely require a higher allegiance to uncertainty, the undefined and debatable choice, to judgment and the consideration of collective judgment. Steiner says that for Heidegger *Dasein* is "to be there" and "there" is the world. But the world, unfortunately, is specific in its violence. Steiner then quotes this remarkable but consistent public statement made by Heidegger in 1933: "The Führer himself is the only present embodiment and future embodiment of German nation and its law. . . . To oppose him would be treason against Being."[25]

Did ordinary Germans need this instruction from their greatest modern philosopher? One would like to say with a certain amount of unphilosophic impatience that there is no *Dasein* to betray, no tyranny of "Being," and what moves us most insofar as "Being" is concerned is its open invitation to judgment and freedom. Nothing confronts us in the Holocaust that is not within our power to condemn and reject. And that is what was true for the masters and functionaries of that event in history. "Being" was a divinity, like that of History, which had its cult of priests and worshipers, who found, as Canetti said, their "weapons."

The obsession with history, whatever philosophic or ideological form it takes, tends to become the alibi of actors and agents. It was easy for Eichmann and the extermination camp commanders to reduce their agency to function, structure, and process. "Obedience," Eichmann repeatedly announced, was his own. Even Hitler and Himmler must have felt that the decision to murder all Jews was taken out of their hands by evolutionary racial biology as well as by the immutable machine of war as it began grinding. Culture critics speak much of bureaucratization and technology as problems of civilization but forget to trace their essence to the dominant neoscientific intellectual modes they represent. Bureaucratization could be defined as any social process which dissolves and destroys the moral immediacy of social relationships. However, it is not inconsistent or a paradox to say that a bureaucracy devoted to an abstract principle, an ideological cause even voiced as the highest morality, can be and has been the most destructive force working against authentic moral response. To judge a civilization one should ask what allowance is given immediacy of perception, individuality of choice, as opposed to the rule of abstraction. What we mean by freedom can be understood as action controlled by a maximum degree of moral immediacy, by which is meant action that is governed by values that know and exchange knowledge of persons. It is not that freedom requires reconcilement with necessity, in the old-fashioned Marxist-Hegelian form of resolution, but as Emmanuel Levinas would put it, with responsibility.

The enormous power built by the Nazis was guided at no point either by moral abstraction or moral immediacy. Rather they had ascended to another level according to Hegel who was one of their tutors: "The History of the World occupies a higher ground than that on which morality is properly its position, which is personal character—the conscience of individuals—their particular will and mode of action. . . . Moral claims that are irrelevant must not be brought into collision with world-historical deeds and their accomplishment."[26] Are we still shocked to learn how much dominant German intellectuality did to divorce "world-historical deeds" from moral claims? One might pardon Hegel for speaking the truth for actual leaders in actual history but not for claiming "higher ground" for them. This was more than allowance, it was justification, perhaps partly able to explain the horrors Germans of middle and higher culture were later capable of inflicting.

It was certainly a justification that Hitler seized early in his career when he conducted intellectual discourse with Rauschning. He had only one guide or standard for his movement, and he said, "I do not follow General Ludendorff nor anyone else; I follow only the iron law of our historical development."[27] Historic destiny was iron necessity which inculcates the iron of will, a force and ruthlessness to match the weight of determinism. "We must be ruthless. We must regain our clear conscience as to ruthlessness. . . . We must compel our people to greatness if they are to fulfill their historic mission."[28]

In this respect he knew where his true rival existed. ". . . there is more that binds us to Bolshevism than separates us from it. . . . The *petit-bourgeois* Social-Democrat and the trade union boss will never make a National Socialist, but the Communist always will." It is customary to stress the importance of ideological anti-Communism as a force in Fascism or Nazism, beyond its purely propagandistic use, but the record indicates an affinity as well as competition on a deeper level. Particularly in the early years and then in the last days, the language of the Nazis inverted that of class revolution. (Goebbels, for instance, in the relative intimacy of his later journal, returned strongly to the rhetoric of revolutionary incitement.) Hitler would say to Rauschning, while searching for the typical justifications of avant-garde politics, "This is the great revolutionary significance of our long, dogged struggle for power, that in it will be born a new *Herren-class,* chosen to guide the fortunes not only of the German people, but of the world." The references to "a dying social order" are obsessive. "The worker today, from the political aspect, is as much a temporary symptom of a dying social order as the nobility and the bourgeoisie." What attracted him most in what he could learn from the Bolsheviks was apocalyptic prophecy. "The secret of National Socialist success is the recognition of the irrevocable passing of the bourgeoisie and their political ideas. . . . The era of democracy is over, inexorably finished. We have been drawn into a movement which will carry us along with it whether we like it or not. If we resist, we shall be annihilated. If we stand aside, we shall die off. It is a choice between taking action or being destroyed."[29] This is necessitarian politics, armed with prophecy and breeding violence. No political tone, no rhetoric, has been louder in our century. Inexorable is a key word, so is annihilation, and both were terms to be administered in the lives of many million victims.

4

Three Myths of Modernity:
The Metapolitics of Nature

During the interrogation before his trial, Adolf Eichmann discussed the minutes of the Wannsee Conference (which he wrote himself) within "the framework of the final solution": "The able-bodied Jews will be made to build roads as they are led into these territories [the deportation to the "East"]. A large percentage of them will undoubtedly be eliminated by natural diminution."[1]

Israeli interrogator Avner Less asked what was meant by the phrase "natural diminution," and the answer from Eichmann was "perfectly normal dying." He meant, of course, dying under the effects of near starvation, disease, and heavy labor. The language is instructive. The "normalcy" of death was a great support in Eichmann's mind and that of the other technocrats of the Holocaust. "Natural" and "normal" were words they utterly believed in, and that fact is what astonished their interrogators and judges, who came equipped to recognize moral monsters.

Interrogator Less read further from the Wannsee minutes: "Heydrich goes on: 'Since the ultimate survivors will undoubtedly constitute the most resistant group, they must be treated accordingly, since this natural elite, if released, must be viewed as the potential germ cell of a new Jewish order.'"

Less: "What does 'treated accordingly' mean?"
Eichmann: "That . . . that . . . comes from Himmler. Natural selection—that's . . . that was his hobby."
Less: "Yes, but what does it mean here?"
E: "Killed, killed. Undoubtedly."[2]

It would be useful to know what Eichmann's original German suggested, but the fact that a translator came upon "hobby" tells us something more about how the Holocaust language for "killing" distanced itself from reality. Was it Himmler's hobby to slaughter Jews? How does one cope with that aspect of the Holocaust? But perhaps to Eichmann major and minor descended to one level, without distinction. Thus his grisly occupation had created him.

But beyond that, the vocabulary of "natural selection," "natural elites," "resistant groups," and "germ cells" reveal a system of ideas that served not only as a shield but as a driving force, perhaps the chief force in the wholesale slaughter, and made it possible for people like Himmler, Eichmann, Rudolf Hoess, Ernst Kaltenbrunner, or Otto Ohlendorf to view themselves as deeply justified by natural law, the agents of nature's large and fated process.

They had faced a historic human problem, like a cure for cancer, for which they had found the "final solution." The Nazis liked to use metaphors of disease attached to man, the sick animal. The Jews and the Bolsheviks were bacilli, ulcers, toxic poisons, and Europe was a tubercular or cancerous patient. This was to be standard Nazi teaching, Goebbels announced to his underlings.[3]

Propaganda aside, in that world every killer hoped to practice his trade as a surgeon. By their prose you might know them. On the "final solution" Eichmann said soberly, ". . . that was a much-used expression. In the end, final solution meant extermination, but before that, it had other meanings, it meant exclusion of the Jews from the living space of the German people; that went under the name of final solution."[4] *Lebensraum*," the original and dominant Hitler concept, inevitably became the "death space" for others or their exclusion from "living space." One sees this as a calculating belief in evolutionary thought, and a call for self-preservation that no doubt supported an equally "natural" lust to kill. A brutal and primitive version of the Darwinian law brought verification to all the ancient codes of tribal aggression and war. And why not, why should peoples and races and nations passively submit to natural selection? Why not take it into their own hands? We can't understand the release from conscience effected by Hitler in his own people unless his vulgar but powerful naturalist creed is taken into account.

A pressing question for students of the Holocaust is how the German technocrats of death viewed their victims. It is futile to struggle with imagined monsters when something so commonplace, so "banal" in Hannah Arendt's distorted but real insight, is at hand.[5] When Eichmann referred to documents on plans to send some Budapest Jews to Palestine (the Kastner affair), he said, ". . . as far as I knew, the Reichsfuhrer-SS wouldn't consent to any emigration of Jews to Palestine under any circumstances. The Jews under consideration were without exception biologically valuable material, which made their emigration to Palestine most undesirable."[6]

The technocratic usage, "biologically valuable," is characteristic. The question becomes serious for those who wish to survive the use of this language. What is "valuable" and what transcends "biological" considerations? Where did such criteria originate, and how was the authority of science handed to the administration of bureaucrats? Eichmann, for instance, spoke consistently like an engineer following "guidelines"; he remained devoted to his guidelines, remembering the punishment for not following them better than his present trial and its stringency.

As historians have pointed out, the fact that the Holocaust was preceded by the Nazi euthanasia experiment has prime importance. It suggests that science was their firm and consistent authority for dealing with death. Death was circumstantial, a matter of nature's accounting, the life force in profit and loss. In this vein Himmler could speak of nature's heroes, his SS men, who had the courage to apply nature's law. We might prefer to see him as a more conventional murderer, but it is important to know the material of which he was composed.

It was a case of finding the inspiration for mass murder. Hitler told his generals in November 1939, "In struggle I see the fate of all beings," and repeating this theme often in more relaxed table conversation, he said, "The law of existence prescribes uninterrupted killing, so that the better may live."[7] There is no doubt that he held these ideas sincerely. Hitler could not have swept his world to his own pitch of cruelty without finding assent to his naturalist creed of force. George Steiner, for instance, with novelistic imagination, describes how the captured and aged Hitler still emanated a peculiar vitality, a psychobiological force in himself that reached and totally invaded his followers. In his novel, *The Portage to San Cristobal of A.H.*, Steiner has one character, a German war veteran, remember the Nazi era with gratitude. "We drank so deep of history that there can't be much left in the bottle," and "I wouldn't trade . . . God how we lived."[8] With licensed insight, the author gives exposure to a vitalist cult which sought the apocalypse as fulfillment. One can imagine what fed that zest. Was it the howling naked men, women, and children in line for the gas at Treblinka and Auschwitz?

"He [Hitler] was true to his word, a thousand year Reich inside each of us, a millenium of remembered life"—a millenium that cost twenty or thirty million deaths. What cheap Wagnerian heroics is this? the reader asks, and then must assume that it is Steiner's parody of what a court poet might have written in the last days of *Gotterdammerung*. Didn't Goebbels say similar things? Perhaps Steiner wished to capture the awe the world still feels for a murdering violence so extreme as to transcend judgment even today.

How in fact can we consider the poetry of death that surrounds Nazism? Rauschning, who listened more prophetically than most, heard Hitler say he dreamed a new man, a German youth who was "violent, intrepid, brutal," with the "pride and independence of the beast of prey."[9] Rauschning, and after him Leon Poliakov, were among the first to describe Nazism as a vitalist religion, requiring submission to "the racial soul, the blood and its mysterious appeal, . . . the higher power realized in the people (*Volk*)," and expressed in the "divine will" of their "high priest, Hitler."[10] The Jew, Poliakov points out, was the antirace, an antipeople, because that sort of devil was indispensable in a racist religion. And the führer admitted in his own words, Rauschning says, that if the Jew did not exist "we should have then to invent him."[11]

We begin to see the outline of a powerful naturalist religion drawing upon ancient reserves. Poliakov describes the readiness of ordinary anti-Semitism, with its deep roots in traditional Christianity and European culture, to provide the transcendent enemy whose shadow lay behind all other enemies—Bolshevism, capitalism, British imperialism, and the corrupt and degenerate democracy of America. But any discussion of anti-Semitism in its religious and cultural origin should not obscure the modern naturalist definition of a race or species enemy, one whose enmity is innate in his existence. There can be no concession to his existence, since he expresses a force that is removed from conscious will; the cause is not in a subject, and so must be treated as object, as cause and not as intrinsic effect. The contrast would define an ordinary true community, which constitutes a universe of subjects, committed in action toward and with subjects. The principle might be posed simply: the rule of causality makes objects, the endowment of choice makes subjects. In that sense a political naturalism extended to its totalitarian extreme equates with war; in war the dialogue of subjects ceases, and until war ends the enemy is a force, a material obstacle, to be destroyed or removed.

•

The belief in the law of life, ecstatically conceived as the élan *vital* engaged in successful struggle, has a price to pay, for the alternative in failure is extinction. Many of Hitler's minions who conducted his campaigns of annihilation held the sincere belief that a similar fate waited for them if they lost the war. They must have felt the particular truth of this in fighting the Russians, who after all retained a similar belief in the merciless route of historic conflict. Some of the accused at the major Nuremberg trial expressed surprise when the judges, in often admonishing the prosecution, affirmed the rules and ideals of justice. They had been trained to expect that victory took all the claim to justice. How often Himmler and his seconds told their troops to harden their hearts and follow nature's justice. We forget, in reading the record of cruelty and violence, how much the perpetrators were following a devout prescription.

What was meant by "total war"? The phrase haunted the minds of the Nazis and was used by Goebbels in a diary entry for February 1945 in proposing the ordered execution of Allied prisoners.[12] He meant war that did not obey restraints and simply equated itself with killing. Your enemy was defeated when he was dead, but only then. Eichmann in his interrogation also spoke of total war as the explanation for the slaughter of the children, the women, the old and the sick. First, because they used up available resources, and second, because they were biological enemies. The myth of the metaphysical enemy lies behind that dry bureaucratic reference. Its revival, with as much devotion as in old religious wars, explains the ferocity of conflict in our century. The historicist theme of class struggle and the naturalist theme of racial rivalry both raised human conflict to the apocalyptic plane where the being of the species was at stake. The fact must be faced that the Nazis conducted a campaign of murder for at least three years, that they did it methodically and with great efficiency, and that they did it with a clear conscience, even as they addressed themselves to killing women and children who were the biological reserve for future wars. It is that Nazi conscience, in its principles of belief, which compels obsessive study.

The first lesson is (and the "crime against humanity" teaches) that the Nazi Germans became the metaphysicians of war. Perhaps they defined its true nature for all the future. If the Holocaust was a war atrocity on the grandest scale, it cannot be reduced to analogy with any other. The difference is that the Nazis equated atrocity with war and war with life. It was no deviation, no lapse, no regression to primitive violence. In war men returned to their natural state, their norm of strength, their ideal of fulfillment. They governed accordingly. Reversing Clausewitz, they said that Fascism, the totalitarian order, is the extension of war by political means.

Accepting the modern eschatological view of race and class conflict on his own terms, Hitler was an idealist, a revolutionary, and a world redeemer. Cynicism is never so resourceful as a true ideological passion, but let evolutionary science add its weight and the result in general slaughter could reach the limits of the imagination. The biological struggle, the will to survive, the will to dominate, the competition for "living space," offered only the narrowness of death to the losers. The naturalistic outlook is very simple, like the violence which defines unmistakable results.

A group that lives primarily in terms of the competition for survival, whether race, nation, or class, forces the same principle on other groups. The more typically confessed war motive is almost always defense, rarely aggression. In any case, what developed in the nineteenth century was a fixation on the fear of group death. Darwin focused that fear on the rise and decline of species, extended by others to empires, nations, races. Theorizing the conflict and fall of classes, Marx completed a mental housing in which we still live, in part or in whole. Historic prophecies are taken correctly as threats. How did we manage to shift the blame for group violence to nature and history? Innocently, without malice, Kruschchev could say to the capitalist-imperialist nations, we will bury you. And would they then surrender to history and consent to being buried? It becomes important at that point to know whose hands hold the gun and the spade. It is important to understand whether our century of violence is the result of a great shift of moral responsibility from persons to historic and abstract forces. The personal direct will to commit violence is not easy to summon, is almost impossible for most people. The fact that army discipline and group loyalty had been captured by criminal leaders like Hitler and Stalin is not enough to explain the mass murders of our era. What dogmas of belief, what passivity of assent, gave them support?

•

The very last words from Hitler, written in the Bunker as his testament to the German people, explained the cause for which they and the world had suffered so much destruction. "Above all I charge the leaders of the nation and those under them to scrupulous observance of the laws of race and to merciless opposition to the universal poisoner of all peoples, international Jewry." This was the unfinished task of the six years of war, which will, he wrote, "in spite of all set-backs go down one day in history as the most glorious and valiant demonstration of a nation's life purpose." [13]

The "laws of race" were of course the "laws of nature," a talisman concept on which he relied from the beginning of his career. To know the laws of nature was to obey them. To his disciples, in private, he said, "One may be repelled by this law of nature which demands that all living things should mutually devour one another," but repelled or not, acceptance is required. "To act otherwise would be to rise in revolt against heaven."[14] But the command was from earth. "I dream of a state of affairs in which every man would know that he lives and dies for the preservation of the species." "The life of the individual must not be set at too high a price. If the individual were important in the eyes of nature, nature would take care to preserve him."[15] On these terms of fanatic logic and consistency, the incomprehensible Holocaust can at least begin to be understood—granted Hitler's hypnotic hold over his people, granted the disciplined obedience of his leadership cadres and the documented proof that they believed his gospel.

The argument was practical and tactical for Hitler, not merely the post-hoc rationalizations of a murderous hatred. He believed it could persuade everyone. For instance, in talking to Admiral Horthy, the ruler in Hungary, in April 1943, when Horthy asked what should be done with the Jews, he said,

The Jews are parasites. In Poland one took care of these matters in the most systematic way. If the Jews there did not want to work, they were shot. If they could not work, they had to perish. They had to be handled like tuberculosis bacilli, which could contaminate a healthy body. This was not cruel if one took into account that even innocent creatures like deer had to be killed, to avoid their causing damage. Why should one show greater leniency to these beasts which brought us Bolshevism?[16]

It is misleading to stress the irrational factor in Nazism, or its mystical romantic character, because they lead us away from the main point. The operation of Nazi minds was not only eminently "rational," that is, reasoned from their premises, but claimed the base of neo-Darwinian thought. If Nazism was "romantic" it was romanticized scientism, based on a glib and simplistic universalization of the message of science.

The destructive result was the emergence of a scientistic politics.[17] Zygmunt Bauman and others write with abundant documentation of the dominance of gardening and medicine metaphors in Nazi anti-Semitism and Holocaust language.[18] As Bauman and Lifton illustrate, the rhetoric led to drastic political tactics. Nations and civilizations were either healthy or sick, and the recommended therapy was not conversion, education, and reformation but purging and surgical elimination. The basis was Hitler's thought in *Mein Kampf*: "We, as Aryans, can only picture the state as the living organism of a nationality."[19] Citing the task of purgative healing,

Bauman quotes a Goebbels entry in his diary: "There is no hope of leading Jews back into the fold of civilized humanity by exceptional punishments. They will forever remain Jews, just as we are forever members of the Aryan race."[20] And so, as implicit in these words, extermination became not the covert crime, the uncontrolled atrocity, but the chief strategy for the Nazi "biomedical vision," as Robert Lifton called it.

The key of political relevance is offered by Lifton: "The Nazi project, then, was not so much Darwinian or social Darwinist as a vision of absolute control over the evolutionary process, over the biological human future."[21] But that, surely, is where normative Darwinism, its political "vision," leads. Lifton notes how the Darwinian term "selection" was the euphemism for making the periodic death sweeps through the ghettos and camps. Appropriately enough, the "selections" were conducted most often by doctors, a highly trained elite, and perhaps the most cultivated and ostensibly humane executioners that history can show. In essence, the Hippocratic dedication which Himmler extolled required only the shift of medical value from the individual to the group. Thus one killed for the sake of the health of the group in precise analogy with therapeutic surgery.[22]

As he reported to Lifton, one of the Nazi doctors promptly joined the party after he heard Rudolf Hess proclaim, at a mass meeting in 1934, "National Socialism is nothing but applied biology." This was an inspiration. In the most typical example of biological politics, Dr. Mengele was one who viewed himself as a "Nazi revolutionary" and a "biological revolutionary," "a man committed to the bold task of remaking his people and ultimately the people of the world."[23]

Did revolutionaries ever act with greater authority than this? Thus the Nazi vision of "applied biology" fostered the fatal crossing between will and necessity. To believe in your cause as a biological imperative—what would there be left to add to the intensity of a war struggle, or more to the point, to the coldness of surgical executions?[24]

"The Auschwitz self," in Lifton's expression referring to the camp functionaries and particularly the doctors, was a self frozen in abstraction. One gets the impression from Lifton's book, and others which deal with postwar responses of SS people and those like them, that they almost never conceive of what they did as in some possible sense deeply wrong and deeply forbidden. If we think that politics and medicine are particularly the crucial areas for human moral self-study, then this is the issue that eternally challenges explication. It is why Lifton's book has major importance though it necessarily remains unfinished. The Nazi doctors did not see the killing as a moral problem or burden but as a natural necessity dictated by race hygiene, as well as more particularly the social economy and hygiene of the camps. When they spoke to Lifton with any shade of remorse, they spoke in terms of a shock to the sensibility, rather like a student in medical school describing his first dissection. If they felt discomfort and revulsion, they only needed to drink and cloud their senses before and after the slaughter. In time, they said, one got used to it.

A doctor Lifton found more sympathetic in the interviews observed that their guide "was always pragmatic, on what worked—not moral or esthetic or any other such considerations . . . because that [area of feeling] was already blocked off. . . . No, 'Ethical' plays absolutely no [part]—the word does not exist." An older ethic may have had no part, but the Nazi doctors served a strangely inverted medical ethic brought to its pitch of absurdity by the popular writer, Ernst Mann, a critic of mass culture, who considered it the duty of doctors to cure disease by eliminating the sick, that is, by killing them. SS personnel, observing the mass of starved, sick, exhausted victims arriving at the death camps, could agree with Mann that "misery can only be removed from the world by painless extermination of the miserable."[25]

It is almost impossible to understand Nazism as a normative ideology, but it was that for many or most, its violence a sacrifice to the future with salvation for the "new man" at the peak of creative evolution. We forget that the cruelty of the camps expressed a command from the scheme of things, almost a religious service to divinized reality. The issue, in more moderate form, radiates in many directions, particularly with the increase of eugenic weapons. Referring to an article he wrote, claiming it was misunderstood, Stephen Jay Gould gave succinct summary to the problem of normative naturalism. He had written about the difference between "the evolutionary time scale, that is, the long run profit and loss in evolutionary terms of certain biological catastrophes like AIDS, and the personal fate or 'time scale' of actual suffering." In addressing the emphasis on the "long run," he said with great clarity that "we have here just one more case among so many (race, eugenics, intelligence testing) of the false search for ethical or human social guidance in the abstraction of biological evolution. The meaning, and the real tragedy, of AIDS lies in the fully appropriate scale of our short, personal lives—the only thing we truly know and have, and the untimely end of which marks the ultimate of human tragedies."[26]

What we must judge in review of the history now is that modern totalitarian ideologies succeeded in giving politics its absolutizing metaphysical

dimension. Peter Viereck chose well when he made *Metapolitics* the title
of his early account of Nazism.[27] "Metapolitics" has its source in German
Metapolitik, as used by one of Richard Wagner's followers in a letter to
him. "To be genuinely German, politics must soar to metapolitics. The
latter is to commonplace pedestrian politics as metaphysics is to physics."[28]
By this he seemed to mean, and as Viereck used the term, a politics that
combined natural and supernatural forces acting in the *Volk* collectively, a
pseudoscience, a supramundane aspiration close to religion, and a moral
collectivism as in socialism.

Metapolitics takes its most typical modern form in naturalist politics,
with the strict replacement of moral criteria, ideas of justice, etc., by cosmic
forces engaged in a fateful struggle that subsume and subordinate the
plans, hopes, motivations, and interests of direct political protagonists. The
chief categories of such suprahuman forces have been biological (race) and
economic and their specific effects are proclaimed in the politics of revolution and war.

To think of society (or the soul) "as a system of forces" sets the modern
trap. It becomes a characteristic to choose cosmic neutrality, standing
above the system, assessing causes and results, perhaps manipulating them
from the same detached standpoint. Manipulation is the mode in much of
democratic as well as totalitarian political behavior, since "forces" cannot
be addressed directly, or if "forces" think and choose they do so on a different level from those who would control them. The active alternative is to
sink into the system, be controlled, accept the rule of its "forces" by finding their immanence in instinct, blood, earth, race, power, and in the conflict itself for its revolutionary or redemptive apocalypse. The key, in my
sense, for naturalist politics is the dismissal of valid discourse and the respect for consensual agreement. The deeper key, and for this the thought
of Emmanuel Levinas has the utmost relevance, is the profound desertion
of "responsibility" to the Other in its personal as well as collective meaning. In its collective meaning Levinas observes that we engage with
justice.[29]

•

The politics of nature plausibly led to the Nazi cult of death, which, followed to its morbid extreme, came upon the Holocaust. Death invited and
repelled but had to be propitiated. The Hitlerian formula proposed racial
survival by trading on death to others. It is understood that primitive peoples ate the bodies of their enemies to capture their life, a form of literal or

symbolic immortality. What the Nazis proposed was different. It is a truism to say that those who kill have in one fashion conquered death. The ritual of the bullfight, the tradition of the gladiator, and the reality of war have their highest savor in imposing death on other living beings. What was heroism on the Wagnerian scale, for the Siegfried of spirit, if not the courage that demands testing against nature and nature's death? One wishes to master death but on its own terms—through its own force. One wishes to master mankind but only on the terms in which nature masters man.

By the time Himmler spoke to his SS leaders at Pozen in October 1943, the death program for Jews had become an ethic of violence that had cosmic goals, deep rationalizations of value. "This is a glorious page in the history of our people. . . . We had the moral right, we had the duty to our people, to destroy this people which wanted to destroy us."[30] The words teach us to imagine murder on that mass scale as a tribal ritual which offered Germans the sense of something larger than individual life. It was for a species of immortality in the life of nation and race, to which one makes sacrifice, and for which one lived in order to live life meaningfully. This was specific in Hitler's mind; he held the doctrine "of the nothingness . . . of the individual human being and of his continued existence in the visible immortality of the nation."[31] One gains somewhat better comprehension of the incomprehensible if we understand that in Nazi principle individuals did not exist. War was a gladiatorial battle in which whole nations, races, participated. Whether in thousands or millions they died as one; the abstract Jew was a single victim.

In the Nazi system death became nature's judgment and life's excuse. Mass killing was an effort to make the god appear, as in pagan days at some bloody sacrifice, but again and again, on a scale that stretched to the limit of the phenomenal world. Reality must declare itself, death answered a metaphysical hunger, it was a truth that could not be contested. The Holocaust suggests the old dangerous wisdom that the power to kill is a real temptation that urges its use and not for just a few. Psychologists of the Holocaust like Lifton and Bettelheim help us to understand this, and perhaps to save our social reason we must not consider it so great a horror. Accept it as a premise in naturalistic existence and one piece of wisdom emerges—that normative naturalist doctrine leads to the moral abyss. This had its early prophets. Peter Viereck described the nineteenth-century German "nature" cult and the atavistic return of "the demonic energies of old Germanic pantheism." He saw Heine reacting in 1834 to the nationalist romanticism of the school of Fichte, those "Nature philosophers" preaching a "fanaticism of the Will." And Heine was prescient. "These doctrines [of 'the primitive powers of Nature'] have developed revolutionary forces which only *await the day to break forth and fill the* world *with terror and astonishment.*" [32]

The *Lebenswertig:* Who deserves to live?

If one takes Nazi thought seriously (and how can we not), the focus must be on their thesis for the "final solution"—that it was indispensable that Jews be eliminated from their midst and finally from the earth, and that on this depended the "salvation," no less, of the rest of mankind. What was the argument they accepted before reaching that conclusion? As judges before such guilt or deformity, they should at least have been in awe of it. But the same thesis was argued routinely by Nazi doctors interviewed by Lifton, even the best of them, Dr. Ernst B., who won the gratitude of many victims and prisoners for his humane behavior. Long after the war, as Lifton interviewed him in his study, he proposed the same thoughts inhabiting the minds of acknowledged "monsters" like Mengele. "At times B. could refer to the overall issue of annihilating the Jews as though it were a serious question for men of good will to contemplate." [33] This is the puzzler. Was it a serious question for this intelligent, supposedly decent man? Then what was it in his experience or knowledge that gave him a basis? The frustrating thing in Lifton's book, with the advantage of interviews with living Nazi executioners, is that he fails to pursue the point. Interested as he is in their psychological responses and motivations, he does not come to terms with the authority they acknowledged for what they did, neither the moral authority nor, as scientists, the rationalizing empirical authority for declaring a "race" unworthy of sharing the earth.

For Jews certainly, for others as well, this remains the unsettling question, the one violating the mind: How could such judgments be warranted? What was it to be *lebenswertig* (worthy or deserving of life), that metaphysical concept of devastating effect? For the doctors it would be convenient to decide that sickness and health were sufficient bases for final judgment; they were after all the criteria of nature. Strangely enough, what defined sickness was not their affair; politics and medicine had become intertwined, with the politics dominant. Nazi anthropology and racial science were distant authorities that wrote their textbooks, and the doctors obeyed. In any case the unit of health was the indivisible national and racial organism. For that the proper medical authorities were Hitler and Himmler.

Those doctors who became executioners, how strange was their appearance in history, and their reversal of the moral premises of their existence. We cast about for support, and appropriately the best response might come from Judaism's Mishnah. "Man was created as a single individual to teach us that anyone who destroys a single life is as though he destroyed an entire world; and anyone who preserves a single life is as though he preserved an entire world." This teaching precept's felt antithesis is larger than a contrast between Nazi and Jew. All moral culture, particularly in modernity, must face the disparity between the mass and the individual, the long run and the short run, private and public, the ends and the means. All of moral culture must confront Nazi Germany's grossly enlarged triage principle on one side (where a human mass destroys another human mass for *lebensraum* or survival), and on the other the less murderous, more mundane practice of cost-benefit calculation where "interests" belong to groups, classes, majorities, and minorities. It may be that bureaucratic and scientistic reasoning has already destroyed the moral identity and function of the single individual. What is the "world" the *Mishnah* speaks of, that "entire world in a single life?" The abstract mechanism of the Nazi "world" turned individuals into component parts; their killing machine ate limbs and arms, organs and parts. For Judaism it was microcosm versus macrocosm, and the commentary, in a leap of faith, would make the two terms one. *Lebenswertig*, the hideous abstraction, can have no place of judgment here, in that true world which is the life of the single person.

If the term, *lebenswertig*, implies guilt, the metaphysical sweep of that judgment, its reference to an ultimate health and ultimate corruption, brings to thought the ancient accusation of deicide. If we examine modern anti-Semitism, which reached what might be called its intellectual peak in the late nineteenth century, we must ask why this should be so in the post-Darwinian age of naturalism. One answer might be that if "God was dead," as in Nietzsche's announcement, it would be plausible to call to mind the earlier crime. Perhaps he had been killed again and deicide still afflicted the world.

In Nazism the nature cult replaced Christianity rather effectively and still resorted to an anti-Semitic basis. Can we imagine something like "naturicide"? The nature god is endangered by the polluting race. If the Aryan race represents the god's chosen people, the saved, there must exist god's

enemies to oppose them. The evidence is clear that the Nazis sincerely
thought of the Jews as damned in nature. All their imagery and their acts
are proof in demonstration—the plague of Jews made literally equal to lice
and typhus. In that sense their death was a judgment for life against death,
a medical sentence beyond appeal. Against the Nazi god the Jews truly
sinned with the "original sin" of their biological nature. And, of course,
the punishments inscribed by the Nazis were in this sense consistent, since
first the Jews were forced to accept plague and starvation in the ghettos and
camps, and then they were executed for their sins of sickness and physical
degradation. When the Jews demonstrated they could not survive acute
physical deprivation, that is, when they were too young, too old, too weak,
could no longer work, or walk to the next labor station, they were destroyed, confirming the "law of existence," in the phrase favored by
Himmler.

In the original accusation of deicide, Christ demonstrates transcendence of nature in his birth and his death. Otherwise, why a virgin birth,
and why a conquering resurrection? Didn't the Jewish denial of the miracle
mean that they sided with lower nature and were its creatures? In traditional persecutions the Jew was the paramount symbol of naturalist reduction. Shylock wanted his pound of flesh and Judas his thirty shekels, and
the flesh and the money were interchangeable in symbolic definition of
Jewish guilt. If Nazism was pagan, the sin against transcendent nature was
reductive nature, and so deicide was confirmed again. For the Nazis the
devotion of the Jew to money and profit and parasitism was in unalterable
identification with the viruses and bacilli of plague. The rhetoric of pathology had swallowed and absorbed moral rhetoric and returned a thousand
times more fierce and unforgiving.

But there is a complication and, perhaps, a contradiction here. For the
true Nazi, alienated from spiritual Christianity, a perfect historic revenge
was available against the Jew on behalf of the basic pagan European culture, born with ancient Greeks and Vikings, carried by Germans, and, in
the words of Lifton's Nazi doctors, "undermined by Christian morality of
Jewish origin, culminating in a vast historic threat posed by Jewish influence to the Germanic race."[34] Conscience, Hitler said, was a Jewish invention, and he no doubt meant that sincerely. But if the Jew was the symbol
of moral transcendence, how could he also be the symbol of naturalistic
reduction? Thought is not at ease in dealing with such mysteries, except to
say that the ambivalence is historically typical. In one sense, the Nazis were
perfect nihilists; the aim of destruction was total, gathering physical reduc-

tion and spiritual transcendence into one great holocaust for life and spirit.

Even the nihilist, however, can be self-preserving, while the Jew could be the scapegoat for his nihilistic revenge. What was it the Nazis claimed to fear most insofar as the Jews were concerned? First, racial mixture or corruption, and second, racial competition for power and survival. In effect, they feared nature most and would discharge their fear by gaining mastery over it. But they also feared and hated moral restraint and judgment. In the Jew they could kill the threat on both sides. In every respect the punishment of the Jew celebrated the reversal of all forms of spiritual and moral transcendence, not simply the heroics of martyrdom but even the faintest trace contained in the human conventions of burial and mourning. The extermination of insects, the disposal of toxic wastes, these were the models for the Nazi way of death. The Jews were to carry the burden of organic flesh and suffer every insult of physical living. On this their persecutors were insistent, even to the point of translating hair and skin into commodities of use. That was the attack on spirit that most students perceive in the Holocaust. But it was also a revenge against nature, antinaturalism in the guise of accepting nature, applied against the Jews, reducing them not only to physical zero but to wholesale humiliation in the process.

There must be more significance than we can yet explain in the fact that in the other great cult of modern naturalist politics, Marxism, the Jew played a somewhat similar role of scapegoat sacrifice. Jacob Talmon observes that Marx himself, in the famous two essays on the "Jewish problem," equated liberal capitalism with Judaism and

with the abolition of all privileges—racial, family status, religious association— . . . [except] the privilege of wealth (which) had become the most decisive social datum. . . . In the turn of the wheels of history . . . the new society in which differences of class has been legally abolished had been seized by people of insatiable greed, which distorted all values and profaned all ideals. Nothing now had any value but everything had a price. The unacknowledged and illegitimate force which had become omnipotent was embodied in and symbolized by Judaism." [35]

That the liberation of mankind meant the liberation of mankind from Judaism was Marx's specific language, though he added that it meant the liberation of the Jews themselves. For the Nazis the Jew became the symbol and surrogate of reductive nature, or that within nature which "distorted all values and profaned all ideals"; for Marx the Jew was the equally reductive symbol and representative of the cash nexus, the new antisocial spirit of capitalism. That was why the world must be purged of them, or rather of "Judaism," which apparently meant a cultural identity and social role, not necessarily the Jews' physical existence. "The annihilation of Judaism will bring with it the liberation of the Jews." wrote Marx.[36] The radically drastic anti-Semitism of the Nazis refused to distinguish between annihilation and liberation, since their racial dialectic allowed for no conversion or redemption. But if Nazism has an intellectual tradition we must look for part of it here where the impulse toward extreme remedies was apparently endemic in nineteenth-century Germany. Talmon refers to a parallel remark from Wagner in his essay on Jews in music. "There is only one possible way of dealing with the Jews . . . annihilation."

The de-moralization of politics

In an interview published in the *New York Times* in recognition of his eighty-fifth birthday, Claude Lévi-Strauss was asked how he felt as a Jew who had lived (in U.S. exile) through the Holocaust. He admitted its serious effect, of course, but added that essentially it was a natural catastrophe, like those which had occurred to many peoples during history.[37] This was more than a personal reaction of a man perhaps too old to give a sharply focused judgment. It reflects a broad perspective in the science of human relations (anthropology), which he did so much to bring into popular styles of thought. Though he now disavowed structuralism and its followers, his phrase suggests an intellectual orientation by which we can measure the moral catastrophe which surrounds the Holocaust. Values and behavior are coded and decodable, as a language is coded. Values and judgments are descriptive and expressive and presumably deducible from social and environmental contingencies. But social violence on the scale of the Holocaust reduces judgment helplessly to the level of "natural catastrophe."

The really penetrating irony in this is that the Nazis themselves wished to think of the Holocaust as a natural catastrophe and themselves as natural agents in the event, the Jews no doubt as natural victims. For them (the theorizing Nazis, and perhaps the working killers as well), the dominant classification was perhaps that of plague, not fire, flood, and earthquake, but in the evolutionary process and the rivalry of races there was nothing unnatural about one race exterminating another, no more than the wiping out of one species in competition with another.

The theme points clearly to an opposite formulation. The Holocaust was a human catastrophe; the victims were human beings; the responsibility was in the hands of human beings; the relationship between victim and executioner was always human. To translate it into a natural catastrophe is, of course, to remove it from moral concern. The concurrent thesis is that the political terror of the twentieth century was supported and led by the substitution of objectifying historical and biological relationships for human relationships, race for the Nazis, class for the Communists, as the later Marx used the concept. Hitler himself surely read Marxist thought that way, great impersonal economic forces working to an ineluctable conclusion in the victory of one self-preserving biological interest over another. (In *petit-bourgeois* outrage, as Marxists might say, he stole the thesis of historically determinative struggle by substituting race and nation for the vital term, class).

The early Marx, in *Economic and Philosophic Manuscripts,* building from the basis of the class struggle, could formulate a hope for the future. After the final conflict, "[a]ssume man to be man, and his relationship to the world to be a human one. Then love can be exchanged for love, trust for trust, etc."[38] Such language was absolutely foreign to Hitler's mind. His view of how the triumphant master race would rule in the "thousand year Reich" can be imagined, but it would not be through "love and trust." In pure consistency of thought, Nazism and Fascism deemed "natural" relationships to be power relationships, and "human" or moral relationships were superstructural—useful myths or debased and weakening legends—to be built, demolished, transformed in the strategies of power.

Arthur Cohen brought the relevance of these terms into his discussion of a moral and religious understanding of the Holocaust. He wrote:

Until the end of the Eighteenth Century the political theory of Europe centered about philosophies of law, right, duty, and freedom. It was understood that the relation of citizen and state was somehow a moral relation, that the citizen was a person educated to freedoms and informed by responsibilities. In our time such language has virtually disappeared from public inquiry and debate. The language of politics is not that of moral interaction and representation, but the calibration and weighting of power, influence, need, control in such fashion as to guarantee for one's own constituency a larger and measurably greater security both for and against uncontested aggression. Questions of right and law, of justice and equity have virtually disappeared as moral criteria for social and political action. . . . What civilization once called murder or barbarism or cruelty or sadism has become a useless rhetoric in our day.[39]

Cohen calls this drastic historic change the "de-moralization of the political," a succinct phrase for a profound truth. Thereby the people who conducted the Holocaust found their greatest support. They had no language, needed no language, for telling themselves they were doing wrong. But the point is that we ourselves today have a kind of subtext of embarrassed language that finds itself hard put to debate Nazi premises. The resort in interpretation to crime or madness or "natural catastrophe" suggests that naturalist fatalism still creates a moral impasse.

To simplify greatly, every ethos of political behavior is founded either upon trust or upon threat, really, of course, a mixture of both, but we can distinguish among systems on this basis. If power is the confessed theme, the ethos and basis of action, then you will be dealing with terror. A power system, defining group relations based upon power, removes trust and substitutes threat. Power systems, therefore, insist on defining the enemy, stripping, isolating, annihilating him. To be sure the Germans were drunk with power, swept into the hallucinations of their leader, but they needed their own paranoid fears and the transcendence of that fear which violence against others provides. They needed the enemy, and they found him.

Intellectually, in all the strong systems of secular Manichean thought, we have lived in a world of threat for almost two centuries. If religion was an opium, it was good opium when it presented metaphysical threat as the work of God's judgment. Once human agency became separate and dominant, or naturalistic forces ruled through human agency, the field of threat from the metaphysical Other was all that remained. What choices did Hitler have to explain the defeat of the First World War, as he so badly needed to do? German failure and weakness? German sins and wrongdoing? A suprahistorical agency of fate and judgment? Only the racial enemy remained and became absolute, all resistance in nature to be directed toward him, as if death had no other source. We remember the explanation the German death squad leaders gave for killing children as well as adults.[40] They were the seed of future revenge. Can we believe then that a fierce, unrelenting naturalist jealousy on behalf of their own children led them to atrocity and the blindness needed to commit atrocity?

To summarize conclusions, it is the worst mistake to patronize Hitler's Nazism intellectually as the ideas of brute vulgarians or the criminally insane. Hitlerism had its roots in modern culture, and, therefore, we must regard it now, at the turn of the new century, as a matter of deep self-consideration. What then are the terms of evaluation? What are the ideas which have some basis in modern thought? And which of them can be critically revised, so to speak, in the light of their terrible consequences? For this, if for nothing else, the Holocaust justifies unceasing study, but to make our hypotheses we must dare to simplify.

First among these culpable ideas is the myth of inevitability which rewards or punishes forms of historic inadequacy, or a perceived failure to follow the prophesied direction of history. Second, then, is the belief that history, in this sense, is directed by forces uncontrolled by conscience or the moral will, the latter a term to distinguish from what Germans of Hitler's generations could call, after Heidegger, *Daseins-Willen,* the life will. The belief is that if the human conscience is worth attention at all, it operates as a mask to rationalize the deep interests and forces that actually work in human interaction. These forces are traced to biological and economic compulsion, the economic being simply the social expression of the biological force for survival, gratification, and power. For Hitler, race defined the instinct for species survival and dominance, where these equated with a biological vitality. This was not science, of course, but the hallucinatory myth which was its product and conditioned Nazi behavior. Murder on the Holocaust's large scale was not direct savagery; it was abstract; it superimposed upon the vital organism in the coldest, calculating way, exploiting both instinct and feeling where possible, repressing them where necessary. It could follow that the Nazi doctors interviewed by Lifton would be surprised by judgments that indicted them for serving what they thought were natural or biological imperatives. Rudolf Hess was enthusiastically sincere in naming his creed biological politics.

A straightforwardly simplistic Malthusianism defined a racial competition against environmental forces which restricted biological opportunity for Germans. Of course, in Hitlerism, biology and culture were inseparably linked, and if racial purity were the ideal it was because it led not only to victory over other species but to a cultural achievement which had to have a naturalistic base to be authentic. The Jews were substantively corrupt for Nazi Germans chiefly because of their racial difference; living in close proximity, whatever their qualities, they were a threat to racial purity. What is clear is that good and evil had been "naturalized," that moral threat and life threat had been equated, and all virtues had been subsumed in race and given the sanction of science. It is often presumed that Hitler's anti-Semitism began with cultural rejection in Vienna, in his "down and out" period, as when his paintings were found deficient for entrance into the art academy. This is flimsy as a wholesale explanation, but it is not farfetched to see Hitler helped on this basis (as well as by Germany's war defeat) to transfer cultural imperatives into racial biology and so defeat his presumed Jewish judges (and all Jewish traitors) on the level where "blood" and brute force would decide the issues between them.

In the end, we cannot discount the force of their naturalist ideology behind the Nazi drive to power, even if merely used to break down traditional moral barriers in war and politics. Hitler illustrates how dangerous it is to apply the "laws of existence" and the laws of history as sanctions for human events and acts. Those "laws," like all laws of human behavior, became masks for motives. To act with reductive justification from nature is an abdication from humanity, for humanity defines itself in adapting and transcending nature. So one would like to think, though the grand myth of our time, the naturalist and historicist myth, gains heeding from others and even gives license when a class, nation, or people act in its name. It seems that evil, like good, requires a metaphysical sanction. Edmund in *King Lear* felt so and declaimed, "Thou, Nature, art my goddess." But if acts can be judged as without higher sanction, as functions of the human will without nature's higher command, then the right of others enters equally on the field, becomes equally "justified," and the contest, if there is a contest, can be resolved only through direct conflict or through some form of truce or consensus. But truce is more than truce, and consensus is more than practical compromise when conflict becomes morally endowed. The important point is that conflict should be between moral agents and not as in a contest between human agents on one side and a historically and naturalistically imperative fate on the other.

5

Three Myths of Modernity:
The Cult of Power

"In the struggle against frozen forms of faith, the Enlighteners have left one religion intact, the most preposterous of all: the religion of power."
Elias Canetti

Those who too easily receive the epithet "evil" are at least half forgiven in advance. We distrust moral extremes in judgment. In the case of the Nazis it is not that their acts exceeded the possibility of moral description. It is rather that the capacity of moral response had been undermined before its occasion by decades of intellectual diffidence or actual cynicism. Who knew or understood a language to cope with the Holocaust? Could Nietzsche's lesson in the "geneaology of morals" help here? Those who first brought the news from the camps were accused of moral melodrama expressed in the incitement of conflict, or indulging in the paranoia that was the by-product of abuse.

And wasn't it true that Chaplin's images of the dictators dominated at least part of our minds? We were not always inclined to take Hitler's company with a gravity that matches the Holocaust in its scale of violence and measure of destruction. To be sure even now, in retrospect, there remains the trace of comedy in the view offered by that ghoulish quartet—Hitler, Goering, Goebbels, and Himmler. In one of his most ominous declarations, Hitler said that his enemies who once had laughed at him were now laughing on the other side of their faces. That was grievously true, but it takes nothing from a terrible seriousness to remember the ground of that laughter. There is contempt in comedy, and ill-licensed generally as it may be in the historic retrospect, it may deliver one part of the still receding, unimaginable truth. So we would see Goering, the sensualist and cynic; Goebbels, the Aryan black dwarf, the manipulator of hate in words and symbols; Himmler, the cold leader of the bureaucracy of death, the murderer who kept ledgers. And Hitler, What was he? His gift was hysteria, we thought. He was sincere to the point of madness; he was passionate for power and could move others with the same passion; and the result was to see him convulsed, jowls shaking, while his hearers, in indecent display, received the erotic thrust of his oratory, aroused to a collective lust to commit violence. At Nuremberg, in the splendor of monstrous political kitsch, he waddled slightly as he walked past those rigid ranks, glad to give up the burden of intelligence as well as conscience. Mock hero, more Sancho Panza than Don, driven desperately to revenge himself on those who, as he said, once laughed and would never laugh again.[1] Sancho, the embodiment of the spirit of war, ravaging through Europe? On this theme, at the carnival of Nuremberg, memory gives license to rage, and we laugh, as Hitler promised, "at the other side of the face." Was this the romantic idiot's revenge? And what did a Sancho-Hitler promise his people? An earthly paradise with every appetite satisfied, with every rival quelled? One rather envisions his German followers ruling over those mountains of gold teeth, eyeglasses, and body-stained clothing at Auschwitz, picking among them, scavengers and thieves in a wilderness of greed.

Did his people go to war in fear or in search for national glory? If there was fear, they could not rest until they imposed a greater fear on their enemies. The murderer who fears death has only murder for relief. The words "glory," "patriotism," "honor of battle," "honor of country" will forever remain insulted by the images left by the Nazi camps. But they did love power and that was for them sufficient glory. They strutted in their pride all over Europe. Was it vanity that was capable of releasing so much death?

The world moved from laughter to awe at so much power and then again back to contempt in the judgment of some historians who, unable to greet genuine evil with intellectual respect, were willing to patronize it. Of course, the record does that; it is still difficult to find a tragic seriousness on their side, the perpetrator's side, of the great devastation they caused. Hugh Trevor-Roper emphasized that omnipotent dictatorship only made possible a "political and intellectual fool's paradise in which such figures as Goering and Goebbels and Himmler, with their drugs and perfumes, their nihilism and mysticism, their flatterers and astrologers, could determine policy and such ninnies as Ribbentrop . . . could be regarded as experts in foreign affairs."[2] One sympathizes with his impulse to describe Nazism as "this vast system of bestial Nordic nonsense." Hannah Arendt did as much to dismiss awe from judgment in describing the Nazi evil as triumphant bureaucratic banality.

What does it do to our view of the Holocaust, the one modern evil that does most to challenge the moral imagination, if we agree with Trevor-

Roper and Field Marshal Lord Tedder (who wrote a brief Foreword for Trevor-Roper's book), that Hitler, a"hysteric," a "megalomaniac," despite his military and political genius, was "a man who by ordinary standards would be judged insane," or that Himmler himself, chief in command of the great slaughter, was, as everyone agreed, "an utterly insignificant man, common, pedantic, and mean." In addition, he was "stupid, devoted, ruthless, efficient, mystical."[3] Joachim Fest describes in Himmler an element of obsessional insanity "in the context of his world of ideas that was totally divorced from reality."[4]

Perhaps the spirit of nihilism is the force behind this sort of "comedy." It is a kind of sacrilege, whether against God or nature or mankind, to think of the power held naked in the hands of people thus portrayed as fools or insane. Something sinister and most deeply pathetic seems to grow out of human civilization itself with this report. Hermann Goering made his appetite for murder a part of his gross sensuality; he wore medals, they say, and gorgeous uniforms. And did the hysteric, Hitler, really rave and bite the carpet before sending his armies abroad and deciding the doom of millions? Can this be the answer to the question a witness saw in the eyes of the children of Auschwitz, Who is doing this to us, and why?

Everything in us rebels against attributing the moral and spiritual "*Tremendum*" of the Holocaust (in Arthur Cohen's usage) to the passion of fools, or even the alienated humanity of the insane. Historians speak of accident, improvisation, the contingencies of war, the blindness of bureaucrats, the cruelty of underofficers. The German "revisionists" make that point with more and more conviction. It seems we still don't know how to be serious enough before this most serious of human crimes. Surely the most dangerous and lasting effect of the Holocaust is the attack it makes on the self-respect of the species.

•

The serious truth is that in this historical instance an absolute power was wielded throughout Europe that had no relevant control or relationship with an ethical intelligence. Eichmann, under interrogation, said, "I never saw a written order, Herr Hauptmann. All I know is that Heydrich said to me: 'The Fuhrer has ordered the physical extermination of the Jews.'"[5] Modern totalitarianism has been an enterprise for extinguishing conscience. All those millions placed conscience in the hands of one man, and he in turn gave himself up to the historic "Will" inhabiting Germany, a fate in nature he embodied. But attention must be paid again to the creation of a man like Eichmann, who was happy to know nothing more than the führer's wish. That was the phrase most often used, the führer's wish, not even an order, something like a fantasy voiced, a daydream in air, an irresponsible mood. Indeed, no other man in our time has had such power, and how his Germans were hungry to be enslaved to it, reading orders from hearsay, hints, euphemisms, and rumors. Was it black whimsy, a kind of floating nightmare, or, as historians debate it, did that vagueness conceal fierce and long calculated design?[6]

"[Eichmann]: Who gave the orders for those actions? (The reference is to the mass killings of the *Einzatsgruppen*). The orders, the orders. Obviously, the orders were given by the head of the Security Police and the SD, namely, Heydrich. But he must also have had his instructions from the Reichsführer-SS, namely, Himmler . . . he could never have done such things on his own hook. And Himmler must have had his express orders from Hitler. . . ."[7] And Hitler had his orders from whom? Psychopathic murderers sometimes say they heard and were compelled by voices.

"I obeyed. Regardless of what I was ordered to do, I would have obeyed. . . . I can't shed my skin, Herr Hauptmann."[8] In that context, What was obedience, and what was an order? We may be certain, in that world of destruction, for such as Eichmann to obey power was his greatest fulfillment. The supranatural awe in power, its semidivine compulsion, was verified by the actual outrage in the orders given. He "obeyed," and a world took shape or a world was destroyed in his own hand, his master's hand.

While describing his command for the march of Budapest Jews to the border, toward Auschwitz (a gratuitous order close to the eve of German retreat), with many or most dying in the march before reaching the official site of death, Eichmann accepted a cigarette from his interrogator, saying "Gracias." Somehow, in context, the word appalls. The Hispanic grace, in that moment, defined other moments when he signed the death orders of millions. And the first leisurely puff, Was there reflection in it? Was he taking comfort in the memory of his power over death while now in close proximity to his own? This man in the glass cage with his furtive, flickering eyes and the uncontrollable tic of the mouth, How much was it his pleasure, or had he been forced to be the pimp of death? But there we confront the great void in Holocaust reports, the difficulty of giving these neuters, not monsters, a set of understandable reactions. The convicted murderer, the confessed murderer, never satisfies us with his account.

It is impossible to master these experiences with narrative when the event itself demonstrates the breakdown of any order of mind or language. There is a level of violence that is pure chaos and passes beyond language into groans, grunts, screams, and curses. Forget German bureaucracy and Prussian discipline, it was the goal of the Nazis to destroy consciousness and move willfully beyond the margin of intelligible experience. They would rule through chaos and above chaos, and chaos justified their power. It was power without qualities, power that was only power and, therefore, impossible to resist. Men want reasons and results from violence and would like to at least pretend to weigh ends and means. Even the victims want to know reasons and are frozen into shock when power is absolute and unpretending.

Hitler said to Himmler and Heydrich, in October 1941, "It is not a bad idea, by the way, that public rumour attributes to us a plan to exterminate the Jew. Terror is a salutary thing."[9] Terrorism was the essence of his political and military genius. It was based on communicating the certain conviction to victims and opponents that this force, these people, would truly stop at nothing to achieve their goals. The terror received was partly shock in confronting an unbending will—and at the same time a mystery of intention. This is why the word crime alone cannot be used, nor sadism, in reviewing the basic drive of the Holocaust. We are forced to add the mysterious ethic involved, the supposed "ideal" in his program. In October 1941 Hitler announced to the listeners of his monologue, "When we finally stamp out this plague we shall have accomplished for mankind a deed whose significance our men out there on the battlefield cannot even imagine yet."[10] But could he himself say what it was? Perhaps this is the ethos of power: an instrumentalism run amok, a violence whose momentum guarantees a metamorphosis of the human condition but also suspends all questions. A brute pragmatism, we should call it, that waits on no interpretation of significance. Its value is preordained, like a divine edict in history or nature, and in fact only the degree of its ruthlessness will measure it or its lasting results.

•

His deeds were "for mankind," Hitler said. He was speaking at one morbid degree for the spirit of apocalyptic politics which afflicted Europe and the world between the wars. Berthold Brecht would represent many when he said that communism was the only alternative to the "end of the world." Similarly, the lifelong message of Hitler was that his program made the only alternative to the end of Germany and the "Aryan race." With the widespread belief in cyclical decline for empire and nation, class and race, and with stress on moral and political corruption, Weimar was a particular target. The propaganda against the Jews was apocalyptic in this sense, therefore merciless. In modernist thought generally, images of decadence were deeply allied with redemptive themes of purging and purification and together led relentlessly to massive destruction.

Robert Jay Lifton and others have noted the relevance of apocalyptic expressionist writing in Germany in the 1920s, as background for the work of those university-educated Nazi doctors who met the trains at Auschwitz and Treblinka. The catchword was "*Rausch,*" meaning the intoxication and ecstasy of war as the Armageddon whose "end must mean a rebirth into a better world."[11] The Dionysian theme of renewal in destruction, made almost inciting in the impassioned language of Nietzsche, and Wagner's even more popular images of *Gotterdammerung,* stimulated the apocalyptic sensibility of several generations of Germans. Saul Friedlander, analyzing what he called the contemporary popular discourse on Nazism in Germany and elsewhere, found it filled with secret nostalgia and fascination. It revealed in itself "a deep structure based on the coexistence of the adoration of power with a dream of final explosion—the annulment of all power. . . ." The strong apocalyptic motif was "nourished by the simultaneous desires for absolute submission and total freedom," both of which, one might assume, being fed by "the dream of total power."[12] When toward the end Hitler received news of the destruction of his own personal SS division, *Leibstandarte Adolf Hitler,* he was heard to say, "Losses can never be too high! They sow the seeds of future greatness."[13]

The theme of redemptive violence inhabited the souls of the Nazis, and this was the basis of their murderous "idealism." They were obsessed by the exemplar values of nature and by the threat of species death in the conflict of species. They were obsessed by their own power, and in the peculiar logic of modern determinists they believed that they were mastering nature in submitting to its laws and directing history by following its current. This they could prove with the blood of their victims. They sought the modern apocalypse and wished to strip away custom, morality, civility, in the name of naked truth, a barest starting point on this planet. In this they were archetypal political modernists who borrowed from the cult of revolution.[14] The apocalyptic spirit knows only soiled values, lies, hypocrisies, a dishonesty that insults the true gods of life. The apocalypse installs death as the twin god, death as companion, as weapon, as agent of mercy and salvation. To invite the apocalypse is the ultimate respect one pays to power; it is power exercised in the day of judgment. Let it be the political day of judgment, and the result will be great revolutions and wars, and great human sacrifices, like that of the Holocaust. When was there greater intimacy with death than in Europe during the Holocaust? With the death's head their sign, the Nazis were the high priests of death, the first modern people who returned to human sacrifice.

•

Hitler erased any distinction that could survive between crime and war, crime and governing, crime and the assertion of power. For this we still fear his memory as if he truly forecast the end of civilization. But we might understand better if we see the cult of power as the product of twentieth-century reductionism which taught a brutal honesty against real or imagined evils (or established goods) and used violence as its certification. In Hitler's simplistic neo-Darwinism, violence expressed the "laws of existence." He took the simpler lessons from Nietzsche as well; he knew his justification in "the will to power." Even in the last days in the bunker he was appealing to the Germans to exercise that will, and when that failed he condemned all Germans to nature's destruction. It is always easy to find a will in destruction, and that too is power, even in the form of self-destruction.[15]

The will to power is first of all reductive. Laws, values, and ideals are its masks, shields, and weapons. At the same time, the ethos of power is reinforced by the myth of "necessity," a way of taking metaphysical authority for dealing victory and defeat, survival and death to the individual and species. Nature's law did service to the future through selective killing. In nature's law, murder became philanthropy, and the Nazis were quite serious in using the terms and logic of euthanasia. If we forget this, we forget what was historically unique in Nazi atrocities. Himmler meant what he said when he named their work "a deed accomplished for mankind" in his much-quoted speech to SS officers in late 1943, when the slaughter had passed its height. A profound megalomania reassures itself best by the degree of devastation it causes. To identify the will (defined as a will to power) with necessity can and did lead to the ultimate moral atrocity.

Hitler himself may be a case for the pathologists, but his program and success cannot rest with that explanation. In whatever form of madness he had, Hitler knew only two weapons in his political program and his war strategy, and these were to exploit fear and hatred and to use an absolute, unconceding violence. His own strategists pleaded with him during the

Russian campaign not to humiliate the Slavs and to win them over, since so many were ready to go to his side. The Ukrainians, for instance, met the first German conquerors with flowers and vodka. Immune to that gesture, neither he nor Himmler were able to respond to specific arguments that many Jews were valuable as a trained and skilled work force. He could have felt that any concession to practical needs in his war effort would dissolve the manic hatred so necessary to his form of war. Power to him based itself on war, war meant death, killing was its chief action. Rule meant threat and unswerving harshness. Death was what you administered with the weapons of war, and to stop short of death was to deny yourself victory. In his mind only one side could survive, or should survive, a war. He stretched power to its limit, there was no other means nor language by which to rule.

But meanwhile he associated himself with a modern apocalyptic cult which, worshipping power, linked death triumphantly with life and required blood sacrifice. The Holocaust has no status whatever as war strategy; but neither can it be allowed simply to represent ordinary and universal murder, even on a mass scale or as a collective sadism. It was an event in civilization produced by its own values, degenerate or obsessed, implicit or explicit. The determinism of power lies deep in modern technology, in the marketplace, in the strategy of nations, and power has become, even today, the first premise for understanding politics and psychology. That is why no contact with the Holocaust, by close or distant witnesses, fails to offer a blow to conscience, an impression of universal guilt.

What, more specifically, was the temptation of power in Hitler's mind, what did he contemplate when he imagined the Thousand Year Reich? What pleasures were there for Germany in its rule? Even at the end he was ready to sacrifice Germany with his own suicide. The authoritarian links the happiness of others to his will; the extreme authoritarian, the führer, demands the life and death of others to satisfy his will. We may suppose he was planning a new Rome. In fantasying the future, he did dream vaguely of esthetic pleasures, of building cities, of living as the artist-statesman, very much in the vein used in praise of Mussolini by Ezra Pound and the esthetics of order sanctioned by intellectual Fascists.[16] Who knows how much the dream and destruction of the Third Reich were incubated in a Viennese bohemian slum? The rage for order, even as expressed in the harmless megalomania of artists, cannot be separated from a lust for power and an equal craving for disorder. Those who believe that they are creating the future may also believe that the world is theirs to destroy.

The hypnotic influence Hitler had over the German mind remains a mystery, but surely he promised an absolute power over life, the power of the mass, immortal in its numbers. One can almost envy the Germans for their drunken ecstasy under his spell at the great mass meetings of Nuremberg. If sexual instinct has a role here it is to think of its climaxes compounded, many thousand times the force of single individuals. Sex claims two partners in a force to escape solipsist stalemate and dispersion. Mass sexuality, in its summoning of sheer energy without a near object for release, may command the spirit of war and mass destruction. The rituals, the flags and songs, the hoarse shouting voice that seemed to meet the extreme border where passion breaks free of language—they were all designed to verify a Dionysian ecstasy where power and order embrace.

•

Hitler's political policy, his whole war policy, was based on stunning the enemy with surprise. The march into the Saarland, the rearmament of Germany, Munich, the Austrian *"anschluss,"* his behavior with Chamberlain and Daladier, his secret dealing with Stalin, and then his final invasion of Russia—all were daring invasions of probability. So often did the improbable meet success that it might be understood why he felt nature, his god, would be always on his side, and that the caution of most men and nations did not apply to him and the Germans. The real secret is that Hitler equated victory with the limitless outrage of violence. By surpassing all limits he bound the German people behind him in crime. Surprise was a dimension of terror. He acted as if he thought his enemies would be astounded and paralyzed forever. In every respect Hitler gave impulse and method to the modern political art of terrorism. Instead of using hostages to bargain, however, as Himmler later offered to do, he used them as frightful sacrifices to throw panic, kill resistance, and empty the world of his enemies.

Leon Poliakov describes the compulsive search for Jews, in every corner of Europe that the Germans controlled or where they had influence over so-called allies. He uses the word "insane" to describe this. But can that be right? The killers reached out to those countries, their backroads and small towns, long after a threat in battle existed or could exist, and to people who in no time or condition of war could be a military threat. How could what seemed gratuitous slaughter be conducted with such method, plan, technological skill, and utter persistence? What lessons can be taken from an insane massacre? To use the term at all is to let down one's guard. It becomes useless as soon as we add the "method" in this madness. Method is what should concern us, and a system which drew in people who weren't insane but were compelled by the sheer "method" of power. The Nazis governed through terror; terror was their method, not madness; and fear was a rule of life, the natural accompaniment and weapon of power.[17] Any modern state which rules through external threat and internal terror keeps the Holocaust in its shadow.

The Nazis ruled and did violence with the help of lies, and any system which controls all information and uses the method of lies is dangerous too in that ultimate sense of threatened violence. Unfortunately for the Jews, the world accepted the rule of the lie in wartime, and most of the world interpreted the first news of the gas chambers and the Holocaust to have its source in war propaganda. Others who knew the truth heard themselves crying "wolf" and were forced into silence. What rival for truth was there except the self-demonstrating authenticity of power? Where power is worshipped there is only one truth, and the lie is its servant. "The men I want around me," said Hitler, in his conversations with Rauschning, "are those who, like myself, see in force the motive element of history, and who act accordingly."[18]

According to that theory, demanding victims for its proof, the strong have an existential need to search out the weak. Power theory could give the Jews neither help nor sympathy. They were totally powerless, and Hitler and the Nazis were totally powerful. Perhaps a power system was tempted to make the Jew the enemy, since naked in his weakness he could offer in defense only a moral injunction and reproach, expose in the Nietzschean sense "the geneaology of morals," and thus be de-moralized by the successful spirit of violence. Emil Fackenheim wrote an essay on the break in Jewish moral confidence during the Holocaust. That was a traditional faith in survival amidst the enemy, so long as it was believed that the enemy shared some of that confidence in ultimate justice, ultimate forbearance, ultimate guilt. What in power theory could defend them? What in power theory could even create remorse in their persecutors? It is certain that this was the secret of the universal betrayal, the silent witness, the passive and active collaboration the Nazis spread in their path. If the Jews could summon armies and weapons they could have some rights—without them they had none. They might be pitiful, but pity was a worthless sentiment and, in fact, a demonstration of the "moral" worthlessness of the objects of pity, according to the corrupted Nietzschean naturalist code. The leaders in the murder camps decreed that those who could most plausibly arouse pity—the old, the children, the sick, the women—deserved to die first. Pity in its aborted vocabulary for the Nazis became "euthanasia." They might call this nature's pity or biological mercy. And some of the accused murder camp operators actually saw it this way, years afterward, as in the witness of the Nazi "doctors" interviewed by Robert Lifton.

•

What was the source of the moral immunity felt by the Nazi killer forces? What enabled SS men to kill children, the old, and the sick with a sense of justification? Every basic question in ethical thought comes to focus here. What is conscience, how is it formed, and most particularly how is it transformed in collective behavior? Nazi racism boasted a form of conscience, a naturalist conscience; in Himmler's mind it was something like horticulture. Hitler was more straightforward in dismissing conscience as a Jewish invention. Perhaps after his deeds of destruction it has to be reinvented.

Certainly, whatever the earth tones of a vulgar Nietzschean vitalism, it was not a pagan freedom which rejected conscience. Rather the programmatic thought, scientistic, sociologically premised provided bureaucratic abstractions to motivate the bureaucratic machinery of death. The word "mass," or the "masses," for instance, so popular in usage during the early decades of the century, is a key to the politics of the Holocaust. The spirit of the crowds at Nuremberg was the true lasting spirit of Nazism in action. Hitler took this as the omen of his age. "The day of individual happiness has passed. Instead, we shall feel a collective happiness. Can there be any greater happiness than a National Socialist meeting in which speakers and audience feel as one?" [19]

But similarly for the Nazis, the day of individual pain had passed. Their victims had become a "mass" too, a set of statistics first, but then a giant organism that had to be destroyed. It is probable that in the camps the killers and guards could no longer imagine or react to individual suffering. They pushed and flogged and beat *crowds,* not persons, and the screaming and the weeping they heard was a sound much like that of their own weapons, or the fires they stoked, or a collective impersonal groan like that of a huge dying animal.

As Elias Canetti observed, the existence of crowds is morally insentient.

In *Mein Kampf,* Hitler said, "The psyche of the broad masses is accessible only to what is strong and uncompromising." But when did people begin to understand that they were "the masses"? Who invented the "psyche" that was to be permanently imposed upon them? And was any actual person ever inhabited by such a psychic force? Wasn't it always out in the street inhabiting someone else, someone to be feared and obeyed? Hitler would say that "they [the masses] feel very little shame at being terrorized intellectually and are scarcely conscious of the fact that their freedom as human beings is impudently abused."[20] This is the remarkable political cynicism that reflects his age but, unfortunately, also molded it.

The "mass" is an abstraction dealing only with abstractions. Progressively as crowds grow they give up eyes, ears, voice, and skin. The essence is that they are not reasoning entities; they do not participate in discourse, but they can be swept by surrogate emotions, most often and dangerously fear and hatred, and for dread results the former was more potent. The mass is a fictional monster though millions march under its slogans and are persuaded they belong to it.

Basically, the mass is the victim of its manipulators, of other masses, and of itself. Human beings are led or forced to shed their humanity, that is, their character in being, their autonomy. They cannot experience empathy for the mass of others nor can they feel it among themselves. An impersonal force inhabits the enemy, but the moral sense requires the transfer of self-identity to others. Power and conflict themes, like those of race and class, eliminate the self-identity of those faced in conflict.

If the German followers of Hitler and Himmler experienced a form of crowd hypnosis where, conscience disappearing, an external order is substituted, their leaders, too, were hypnotized by their own power. The mastery of millions was necessary to prove a transcendent strength, still part of nature but dominating it. It is after all natural death that limits the natural glory of the species. If one chooses to worship race, one must meet the ultimate challenge which reduces all races to equality. On that basis one can pursue understanding of the Nazi compulsion for the infliction of death repeatedly, without surfeit. For this, Elias Canetti has important insight:

> The moment of *survival* is the moment of power. Horror at the sight of death turns into satisfaction that it is someone else who is dead. . . . In survival, each man is the enemy of every other, and all grief is insignificant measured against this elemental triumph. Whether the survivor is confronted by one dead man or by many, the essence of the situation is that he feels *unique.* He sees himself standing

there alone and exults in it; and when we speak of the power which this moment gives him, we should never intellectually forget that it derives from his sense of uniqueness and from nothing else. (227)

. . . .

The dead lie helpless; he stands upright amongst them, and it as though the battle has been fought in order for him to survive it. Death has been deflected from him to those others. . . . Simply because he is still there, the survivor feels that he is *better* than they [the dead] are. He has proved himself, for he is alive. . . . The man who achieves this often is a *hero*, he is stronger, there is more life in him.[21]

Canetti speaks in the single person, as of the pathology of murder, but his meaning is transferable to his general subject—"crowds and power," and there in the context of the Holocaust his insight has great impact. He could be speaking for the mind of Hitler. How often, in public and private talk, Hitler and his chiefs spoke of a metaphysics of survival, and then, by logical sequence, power, and then further, of the immortality of their nation and race which seemed to equate with the assurance gained from the death of others. Accordingly, power proved itself by going to the limit, that is, it developed an insatiable appetite for death.

Canetti offers a new dimension in understanding violence, that one can be transfigured in the suffering and obliteration of others. Jean Améry, too, gave this much thought in considering the Holocaust as an effort to achieve sovereignty over life and death. He may have spoken directly from his own experience when he wrote, "In the world of torture. . . . A slight pressure by the tool-wielding hand is enough to turn the other—along with his head, in which are perhaps stored Kant and Hegel, and all nine symphonies, and the World as Will and Representation—into a shrilling squealing piglet at slaughter." The only path of transcendence was in the physical reduction of others. Améry saw "murderous self-realization" in the faces of his SS torturers. "With heart and soul they went about their business, and the name of it was power, dominion over spirit and flesh, an orgy of unchecked self-expansion."[22]

But that megalomania was collective, a power shared with others, multiplied beyond restraint and yet under discipline. The führer oath was this: "I vow inviolable fidelity to Adolf Hitler; I vow absolute obedience to him and to the leaders he designates for me."[23] Beyond morbid forms of crowd hypnosis, beyond Prussian discipline, the Nazis reached deeper than a military code to an ontological definition that could control all behavior. When Eichmann cried with passionate sincerity, "I obeyed, I obeyed," he meant that he obeyed truth, life, nature; he obeyed the only thing or everything that could be obeyed. If not the führer than what, than whom? And here the German violence, the catastrophe of the Holocaust, assumes its central role in a civilization's crisis of values.

•

Was Hitler capable of making the great and fatal choices which could appropriately lead to the destruction he accomplished? His early discourse with Rauschning indicates that he was minister and high priest to his own cult of power. "The will to power is for us literally the whole meaning of life." It could explain everything, achieve anything, it was the quintessence of life. Absolute as it was, power could breed all subordinate values. One could think of a new aristocracy, for instance. "The secret of our success lay in the fact that we had once more placed the vital law of genuine aristocracy at the heart of the political struggle. True aristocracy existed only where there was also true subjection." [24]

The basis was the brute führer principle, the source of the early triumphs as well as a determination to last to the end. Hitler and Himmler both sustained themselves on the ideal of breeding a race of leaders, and the racial policy was for them in one large aspect a grand style genetic experiment. It is also important to remember that for them the policy of the enemy was the same. The real interest of the Bolshevist rival, led by Jews, was to remove the strata of leadership in society everywhere and replace it with Jews. [25]

Thus the credibility given the power of leadership required more than displacement of the enemy; it required extinction. The extremism characterizes the naturalist politics which seeks to eliminate the opposing force at its root. As a form of political activism it demands extreme violence because its categories of defeat and victory are absolute. Fate does not negotiate with its victims.

In all this, Hitler could believe or pretend to believe in the Jewish empire described in the Protocol myth, which he would imitate as he would Bolshevism. In that context, opposing himself to his prime enemies, power and order were pure principles, ends in themselves. For instance, the Jews aimed for power by using the proletariat against the establishment. But then the Jews also gained and operated power through the rich, the financial oligarchy. Thus they won from both ends, opposing right and left against each other, but using each in turn as instruments for gaining power. Hitler would do the same, working the fears of the rich and the anger and rebellion of the poor. And for both he would identify the Jewish Bolshevik and the Jewish capitalist as the same enemy, whereby the Jews would be destroyed through their own double strategy. But the issue in the midst of seeming contradictions was always power, which put all ostensible values at its service. Power theories and the power phalanxes they create, even when connected to an ethical program such as the relief of oppression or the achievement of human equality, have that tendency to thrive with their own momentum, and leave behind their initial rationalizations of use.

There is no reason to isolate this form of political morbidity with the specific examples of the Nazis and Fascists. There is good basis for judging that doctrines of covert and pervasive power, more or less conspiratorial or, opposingly, oppressive, dominate the politics of our time. The theorizing of modern politics has been reductive in that sense for long, and finds no clear way out of its intellectual bind. Solutions are radical when, as in typical political argument, opponents disappear as political-moral agents and become the focus of abstract forces working in society and history, demonstrated as class, race, sex, or nation. And, of course, an entity defined as a force will inevitably be met by force.

Nazism lacked an important theoretical structure and could hardly match the Leninist-Stalinist creed of power for both explicitness and sophistication of thought. The latter doctrine was articulately totalitarian in offering all meanings, values, and judgments to control by the one seat of power, essentially the Communist party. Well before Stalin took complete rule, his major rival, Trotsky, stated in 1924, "None of us desires or is able to dispute the will of the Party. Clearly, the Party is always right. . . . We can only be right with and by the party, for history has provided no other way of being in the right. The English have a saying, 'My country, right or wrong.' . . . We have a much better historical justification in saying, whether it is right or wrong in certain individual cases, it is my party."[26] What does it mean to say that "the Party is always right," that it has to be right? Most simply it means that right has been equated with power; "history has provided no other way."

The climactic test of faith in these principles came later, at the Moscow Purge Trials, which for their peculiar morbidity of ethical judgment take rank with ideas traded by Himmler, Rosenberg, Goebbels, and Hitler himself. A year before his arrest in 1936, Bukharin expressed his "faith in the Party as the incarnation of history. . . . One is saved [from the difficulty of living, he said] by a faith that development is always going forward. It is like a stream that is running to the shore. If one leans out of the stream, one is ejected completely. . . . The stream goes through the most difficult places. But it still goes forward in the direction in which it must. And the people grow, become stronger in it, and they build a new society."[27]

This was the fatalism of power in history, leading a year later to his false confession and his willingness to serve the party even at the expense of truth and his own life. As Robert Conquest points out, "Their surrender [those accused making the false confessions] was not a single and exceptional act in their careers, but the culmination of a whole series of submissions to the Party made in terms they knew to be 'objectively' false." In the crises of the Revolution, they had experienced "an ever greater premium put on ruthlessness and will," and "at the same time the idea of the Party itself as an object of devotion."[28]

Another old Bolshevik, Pyatakov, tried and executed with Kamenev and Zinoviev in 1937, made the fullest statement of a creed that parallels the führer cult in Nazi Germany. Power, that is, the party, came first, he said in 1928, after being expelled as an "oppositionist" and repudiating his own principles in order to be taken back by the party. He was obviously referring to the quarrel between Trotsky and Stalin on the issue of socialism in a single country. Trotsky clung to the moral authority of history as witness for socialism's right to succeed. Stalin gave it the higher right of power, the right of the party he controlled, and, according to Pyatakov, was in this more consistent with Lenin. "The real Lenin," said Pyatakov, "was the man who had the courage to make a proletarian revolution first, and then set about creating the objective conditions theoretically necessary." The will to power, he said, created miracles that transcended historical contingencies such as the existence of large proletarian masses in a country already industrialized. And Pyatakov went on in a statement that sounds almost as if meant to parody and satirize the eventual judges who condemned him:

According to Lenin, the Communist party is based on the principle of coercion which doesn't recognize any limitations or inhibitions. And the central idea of this principle of boundless coercion is not coercion by itself but the absence of any limitation whatsoever—moral, political and even physical, as far as that goes. Such a party is capable of achieving miracles and doing things which no other collective of men could achieve. . . . A real Communist . . . that is, a man who was raised in the Party and had absorbed its spirit deeply enough becomes himself in a way a miracle man.

[And as] a true Bolshevik, . . . he would be ready to believe that black was white and white was black, if the Party required it. In order to become one with this great Party he would fuse himself with it, abandon his own personality, so that there was no particle left inside him which was not one with the Party, did not belong to it.[29]

In the end, Stalin and the party demanded that his victims commit moral and physical suicide—renounce their principles, renounce truth, and even order their own deaths—for the sake of the party and its power.[30] Can we say that this was not in the political air that Hitler and his colleagues breathed, granted Hitler's own confession of indebtedness to Stalinist Marxism? As Nazism entrenched itself, it was the führer that stood over his own party, totally fused with his will. He, of course, was considered a miracle worker above all others, and his victories of pure violence, the violence he equated with his will, almost succeeded in convincing Europe and the world.

•

The power concept, stretched to its extreme in Nazism, eliminates negotiation, consensus, dialogue, agreement. It substitutes purging violence. Hitler said most memorably, in a way that made him a prophet, "Dominion is never founded on humanity, but regarded from the narrow angle, on crime." In those words and the following, Hitler should be considered one of our best teachers of modern political amorality: "I also came to understand that physical intimidation has its significance for the mass as well as the individual. . . . For the successes which are thus obtained are taken by the adherents as a triumph symbol of the righteousness of their own cause; while the beaten opponent very often loses faith in the effectiveness of any further resistance."[31] Yes, no one understood violence better, no one was a better "revolutionary" in his sense of the word. But the psychology here reflected a metaphysical faith; the victory of power was self-justifying in the scheme of things, and even the victims of power would be persuaded of that truth.

Joachim Fest, speaking of Heydrich, took him as "the type of the modern technician of power who subordinates ideologies to tactics."[32] But with the Nazis power theory was their ideology, and they needed no other. Race, for instance, was simply the name for the power source, its gathered expression in the *Machstaat,* the Power State. Revolutionary doctrine became tactical doctrine almost immediately, since it gave total concentration to seizing and maintaining power. In this Hitler imagined that he outclassed his Marxist revolutionary models.

I have learned a great deal from Marxism, as I do not hesitate to admit. I don't mean their tiresome social doctrine. . . . But I have learned from their methods. The difference between them and myself is that I have really put into practice what these peddlers and pen-pushers have timidly begun. The whole of National Socialism is based on it . . . all these new methods of political struggle are essentially Marxist in origin.[33]

For Hitler, the Marxists were not so much his ideological enemies as his rivals in the race for power. Anti-Communism, on which he built so much of his early success, was less a strategy than a tactic, a superbly potent weapon.[34] He learned everything from the failure of the Weimar Republic to face the challenge from the left. The only way to meet the thrust of revolution was to construct another.

For himself and most of his generation history was always proof; it always taught a lesson. It seems certain that two events formed Hitler's political imagination: the defeat of the First World War (by the "traitors of November 1918"), and the Russian Revolution with its brief satellite episodes in Austria and Hungary. He, more than anyone, was the creature of war and revolution. But Hitler and those who contributed to his doctrine would not have accepted the description of themselves or their brand of Fascism as merely counterrevolutionary. The record of Hitler's discourse, not to mention the ideological and propagandistic efforts of Goebbels, showed that their ambitions reached further than that. "I need revolutions. I have made the doctrines of revolution the basis of my policy." he would say, according to the documentation of Rauschning. He was talking at one point of revolution within the ranks of his enemies which made them ripe for attack, as if the strategy which sent Lenin to Russia in 1917 was a classic maneuver for all future German conquest. "When he [the enemy] stands on the brink of revolution . . . that is the right moment." But he meant much more than an immediate and local victory. "Above all, we shall maintain our passionate desire to revolutionize the world to an extent unparalleled in history."[35] The borrowing from Marx was simple; he exchanged race for class. He said this explicitly in a conversation with Otto Strasser:

There is only one possible kind of revolution, and it is not economic, or political, or social, but racial, and it will always be the same; the struggle of inferior classes and inferior races against the superior races who are in the saddle. On the day the superior forgets this law, it is lost. All revolutions—and I have studied them carefully—have been racial.[36]

What did it mean for him, to revolutionize the world? The value was intrinsic and transcended specific goals. One supposes he meant to have an absolute freedom from moral commitments. "The revolution cannot be ended," he said. "It can never be ended. We are motion itself, we are eternal revolution."[37] It was order and motion in the pure quest for power; it was power as the politics of politics, or its master goal of fulfillment. And for historic absurdity, Hitler defined the Jew, his first enemy, in terms that applied to himself, as interested in power in all historic engagements, whatever mask the Jew carried. The Jews invented and used all ideologies, presumably Christianity at the start, and then Marxism for the century poised at the third millennium. Seeking total power, the Jew was every man's enemy. "The Jew was the enemy of the Roman Empire, even of Egypt and Babylon; but I have been the first to go all out against him."[38] Would he not then assume the Jew's role, in his universal, eternal, and single-minded ambition for power?[39] If he was mad, he was driven mad by his obsession with a monolithic principle which controlled and explained everything.

With power as the goal, he was able, he said, to obtain lessons not only from the works of Lenin and Trotsky but also to receive "illumination and ideas from the Catholic Church." Church, nation, empire were simply counters, the parts of speech in the grammar of power. "This revolution of ours is the exact counterpart of the great French Revolution," he said, but he would do with race what the French and Napoleon did with the idea of nation.[40] And if race could rule above class, nation, or empire it was because it sought ultimate sanction in the very first biological imperative of human struggle.

•

Understanding Nazism as originally preached and carried out by Hitler, we must judge that the psychology of war joined with race to form the single root of his thought. Much is made of the aftereffects of World War I in the rise of Nazism. But the clearest view of the matter is that for those most influenced by the Nazis the war did not end but was only interrupted. They were in the mental state of war and propounded the political culture of war from the beginning.

In a major way, Germany did share in the postwar disillusionment that followed the First World War and the modern radical criticism of the idealizing sanctions of war. But that only prepared the way to a cynical and reductive brutality which was to exceed all historic examples of war-making ruthlessness. In Europe generally, the revulsion from wartime moral propaganda did not support a trend toward pacifist idealism and internationalism, despite the League of Nations and the disarmament pacts. Quite the opposite. Even antiwar sentiment was a form of official moral hypocrisy and subject to the same disdain. The significant effect was to release, among artists and writers particularly, varieties of totalist or Dadaist satire, anarchist revolt, and that paradoxical cult of authenticity which esteemed the destructive apocalypse. This is the right historic context to study Hitler's rise and success. Without desiring war or needing revenge, the West still believed that Hitler's reductionist estimate of war's meaning and purpose was correct.

At the same time, Hitler's strategy was to assume all the moral privilege of the modern revolutionary spirit. He was not alone in this. In the age of ideological wars, cynicism and the use of brute force have always had a curious alliance with the sense of moral outrage. Hitler could define for Germans their own victimization; he could declare a covert international conspiracy, recite grievances again and again, and promise a Utopian purge of past, current, and future evil that finally justified the Holocaust. He succeeded in preparing a paranoid readiness in his German people which was always brought forth in his drastic offensives against the world.

That was the dangerous mixture, enough of the reductive spirit of war to release unrestrained violence and to justify it, enough sense of having been wronged. In the sum effect, of course, the first emphasis on natural and universal war was the strongest. It was consistent with the psychology of war, formed under his neo-Darwinist premises, that Hitler should have stressed repeatedly, and to the end of his life, the issue of a "life and death struggle." Himmler, his bloodiest disciple, spoke his master's language when he said, "True wars, wars between races, are merciless and fought to the last man, until one side or the other is eliminated without trace." [41] Annihilation, *vernichtung,* joined ordinary speech in the days of Nazi wrath. Even in his last testament, written in the Bunker while all of Germany lay waste around him, Hitler was able to say that the war had been "the most glorious and valiant demonstration of a nation's life purpose." [42] That was true even though the war and all its destruction was the whole responsibility of "international Jewry and its helpers." But then the Jews, too, advancing toward *vernichtung,* were presumably fulfilling their own life purpose.

Historians must ask how war and massacre could receive such cosmic justification and the assent of a virile intelligent people. Christopher Browning writes that most Germans were "acclimatized to mass murder as a widely practiced state policy" before the Final Solution became reality.[43] It was, in fact, quite long before, if we observe the role of modern

German thinkers who prepared the ground. Oswald Spengler was able to expect wide agreement when he pronounced the equivalence of war and life, and that the will to life in all living things could not be separated from combat.[44]

War had been given this metaphysical authority by crude naturalist thought, but the deadly aspect was the addition of an almost mystical fatalism, expressed in what nineteenth-century German thinkers called *Historismus*. Leopold von Ranke has been aptly quoted in this vein: "In power itself there appears a spiritual substance, an original genius, which has a life of its own, fulfills conditions more or less peculiar to itself, and creates for itself its own domain. The task of history is the observation of this life." And in the words of Heinrich von Sybel, "He who sides with the nature of things is always victorious."[45]

It was German logic to assume that the "state" could be the directly authorized agent of purposive nature and history, since the state was empowered, the *Machtstaat*. With the help of Hegel, totalist thought had found its way to the unity of metaphysics, history, and morality, the perfect compound for those who would exercise force with unhesitating conviction. And thus, as James Wilkinson suggests, German intellectuals who opposed Hitler found themselves contradicted by their own preliminary thinking about history, power, and the state. Fascist warriors, the *Einsatzgruppen*, those who tended the ovens and gas chambers, all the handmen of death who needed reassurance could find it, and "since the state alone gave shape to the nation's spiritual values, power and ethics could not be in conflict."[46]

In this context, adding to Hegel the texts of Sorel, Bakunin, and Lenin, and overall, the large and simple view of Darwinian teleology, one can better appreciate the command of Goebbels to his well-conditioned followers: "To cause outbreaks of furty . . . to organize hate and suspicion with ice-cold calculation."[47] Or the equally clear justification of mass murder from Himmler: "We had the moral right vis-à-vis our people to annihilate this people which wanted to annihilate us."[48] If cruelty needed philosophic warrant, nature dictated this advice to Hitler's generals: "Close your hearts to pity. Act brutally."[49] The words we hear in the Holocaust, below screams and prayers, are those of half-educated Germans expressing large metaphysical needs and hypnotized by totalist abstractions. Thus, lecturing to his officers with a mountain of corpses at his back, Himmler could say, "We know that these clashes with Asia and Jewry are necessary for evolution. . . . They are the necessary condition for our race and for our blood

to create for itself and put under cultivation in the years of peace . . . that
settlement area in which new blood can breed as in a botanical garden." [50]

•

In the Holocaust and in all such mass-scale crimes and tragedies, faith and
fatalism play a major role. In the case of the Nazis, the fatality of power
was itself almost their sole object of faith. Limitless ambition for one's
group, and all its claims and hopes, led simply and directly to the goal of
limitless power. And in exchange the will to power became perfectly arbi-
trary and opportunistic in its manipulation of ideals and ideas.

The question arises again in many contexts: How could a nation which
was the source of much of the moral culture that endows the world have
taken the Moloch of power as its god and created the moral devastation of
the Holocaust? There is no easy answer surely, though a partial answer
comes in what must be called the great reversal of the relation between
power and the values it serves. "The great reversal" is a high-sounding
phrase to match high implications, for its basis is in the tradition of reductive naturalist political thought which traces values, customs, ideals, and
beliefs in service to power relationships and power appetites. That judgment of the relation between cultural superstructure and the base, with
science offering the constantly multiplying instruments of reduction, has
had wholesale influence in modernity. And there the German intellectual
tradition played the major role, with the excavating work of Nietzsche,
Marx, and Freud.

The reversal of traditional moral logic, which inhabited the Nazi mind
and reached extremely violent expression, has had multiple application
while operating consistently in the political wars of this century. Recent
intellectual debate, particularly in France, has brought it into renewed
prominence, and one can view its summing up in the late published work
of Michel Foucault.

Foucault became the spokesman for contemporary updated versions of
European power theory, stressing the roles of Nietzsche and Marx in the
tradition, and in the process providing a remarkable précis of the Hitlerian
gospel. "It was Nietzsche," he said, "who specified the power relation as
the general focus, shall we say, of philosophical discourse—whereas for
Marx it was the production relation." But the production relation was in
effect a power relation in Foucault's sweeping schema, and to stress the
intellectual influence of Marx (as well as Nietzsche) on himself and others,
he commented, "It is impossible at the present time to write history with-

out using a whole range of concepts directly or indirectly linked to Marx's thought and situating oneself within a horizon of thought which has been defined and described by Marx. One might even wonder what difference there could ultimately be between being a historian and being a Marxist."[51]

The important relevance of Foucault in contemporary argument as well as that of the Nazi period comes in his specific selection of humanist liberal democracy, which he describes as philosophically idealist, as the target of contrast. "Modern humanism is therefore mistaken in drawing (a) line between knowledge and power. . . . and there is no point of dreaming of when knowledge will cease to depend on power; this is just a way of reviving humanism in a utopian guise." In published interviews striving to sum up his thought, he added, "I believe the great fantasy is the idea of a social body constituted by the universality of wills. Now the phenomenon of the social body is the effect not of a consensus but of the materiality of power operating on the very bodies of individuals."[52] The liberal doctrine of power as contracted, or ceded among contracting agents, was to Foucault a dead concept of eighteenth-century democracy.

Foucault carried the reduction of "bourgeois" ideality further than either Nietzsche or Marx, and in this he perhaps comes closest to implicit assent to the presumptions of Nazi thought and practice. "Nothing is more material, physical, corporal, than the exercise of power." And arguing with Marxists with whom he admits most correspondence of thought, he says that "power is not primarily the maintenance and reproduction of economic relations, but is above all a relation of force." The logic that follows is severe: "If power is properly speaking the way in which relations of forces are deployed and given concrete expression, . . . should we not analyze it primarily in terms of *struggle, conflict,* and *war*?"[53] (Italics in original.)

He assents to his own question: ". . . power is war, a war continued by other means," and points out in stress his truncation of the Clausewitz doctrine of war.

If it is true that political power puts an end to war, that it installs, or tries to install, the reign of peace in civil society, this by no means implies that it suspends the effects of war or neutralizes the disequilibrium revealed in the final battle. The role of political power, on this hypothesis, is perpetually to re-inscribe this relation through a form of unspoken warfare; to re-inscribe it in social institutions, in economic inequalities, in language, in the bodies themselves of each and everyone of us.[54]

The ultimate meaning to be assigned to the inversion of Clausewitz's aphorism "is that the end result can only be the outcome of war, that is, of a contest of strength, to be decided in the last analysis by recourse to arms. The political battle would cease with this final battle. Only a final battle of that kind would put an end, once and for all, to the exercise of power as a continual war." [55] This resembles the Marxist teleology, though Foucault himself doesn't describe the ultimate antagonists in the "final battle," nor how an anarchist utopia without the hierarchies and subsections of power institutions would function. That was perhaps not his responsibility, nor is it my interest here. The point is not to equate Foucault with Spengler or Alfred Rosenberg, or Mao Tse-tung with Hitler. The main point is to register the ubiquity of reductive power themes in politico-social thought of great sophistication, and to suggest the double face of such analyses, whether proposed in the interest of unrepressed, unoppressed existence (the Reichian and Marxist utopias), or in justification of "continual war," the use of force stretched to its ultimate outcome, as in the Nazi theory and practice of war and genocide. [56] In any case, whether modern power theory is treated descriptively or prescriptively, few weapons of analysis for the Nazi war and the Holocaust have better application than the power theorems of Foucault.

•

The language of power, even when raised to abstraction, is brutal and does not stay long for answer or rebuttal. Perhaps only the unanswered protests and appeals of power's victims can debate Foucault and sundry other reductivists on the subject of a humanism which Foucault finds mistaken and utopian, or on the possibility of drawing a line between knowledge (or values) and power. Chaim Kaplan may have been the most percipient of Holocaust witnesses when he wrote that "the worst part of this ugly kind of death is that you don't know the reason for it." That may be the question in the mind of every murderer's victim, but here it was repeated and compounded in the death of millions where murder had become a law of being. "If there is a system every murder might have a cause; if there is a cause nothing will happen to me since I am absolutely guiltless." Kaplan could only answer himself, "The system is a lack of system. The guiding principle is the annihilation of a specific number of Jews every night." [57]

Power systems of the Nazi extreme leave no reason, no cause that could satisfy Kaplan. They exist to generate power and prove power in killing. What Kaplan could not consider is that the Jews were the recipients of a hatred that would accept nothing less than murder for gratification.

Second, the Nazis, the Germans, had transformed themselves into a machine of death that generated its own power and had its own momentum, a system without reason or cause. Would they have argued for Foucault's thesis?

But Kaplan's irrepressible questions remain to be asked: How had they accomplished this? How had they willed themselves beyond cause? To say there is no cause is to bring blamelessness to everyone and to the event itself. The danger may be that in retrospect the Holocaust will be submerged in the oldest equivocation of war, that is, to say that the hand that holds the gun and pulls the trigger is a member of some "system," a part of some natural catastrophe, a blank function in the untraceable process of history.

Rightly then and with persistence, Jean Améry defined the issues of the Holocaust under the heading of violence done to "moral reality." Thus he writes about the imperative of resistance against the Nazis in the camps and elsewhere. Resistance was necessary in order for the victim to inhabit the world, but retaliation also brought the victimizer into the same moral world. "My resentments are there in order that the crime become a moral reality for the criminal, in order that he be swept into the truth of his atrocity."[58]

The criminal, unpunished, Améry calls the "antiman." "When they had led him to the place of execution [in punishment], the antiman had once again become a fellow man." "Antiman" is good usage of the word and cites the principle that must transcend the giant statistics of slaughter. The Nazis worked to become the "antiman," doing so most urgently in the effort to dehumanize their victims. The paradox for them is that now, for the great audience of history, they succeed in illustrating humanity in antithesis to themselves; their victims become surrogates, not heroes but representatives of humanity at the absolute margin where moral reality begins and has its a priori affirmation.

Like Jean Améry, Elias Canetti, himself a refugee from the Nazis, defined "moral reality" in direct contrast with the radical exercise of power. His text, *Crowds and Power*, might have been written based on actual Holocaust experiences, though he escaped the camps himself. The essay describes as accurately as one can the mental and physical processes by which the Nazis exercised power, and to which, unlike other rulers in history, in willed self-reduction, they consciously gave themselves up. Power, in its obsessive extreme, is a drive toward dehumanization.

Anyone who wants to rule men first tries to humiliate them, to trick them out of their rights and their capacity for resistance, until they are as powerless before him as animals. He uses them like animals. . . . His ultimate aim is to incorporate them into himself and to suck the substance out of them. . . . The worse he has treated them, the more he despises them. When they are no more use at all, he disposes of them as he does of his excrement, simply seeing to it that they will not poison the air of his house. . . . But, quite apart from the person who wields power and knows how to concentrate it in his two hands, the relation of each and every man to his own excrement belongs to the sphere of power.[59]

One should note here again the constant reference to the animal and animal excrement in Nazi invective and the purposeful torture of excremental functions. Canetti, in his own reductive insights, may be striving for an organic base, a kind of naturalistic absolute for the power drive:

One tends to see only the thousand tricks of power which are enacted above ground; but these are the least part of it. Underneath, day in, day out, is digestion and again digestion. Something alien is seized, cut up into small bits, incorporated into oneself, and assimilated. By this process alone man lives; if he ceases, he dies. So much he has always known. But it is clear that *all* the phases of this process, and not only the external and half-conscious ones, must have their correspondence in the psyche.[60]

Conceivably, Hitler and Himmler and most of their underlings could recognize themselves in Canetti's text. In the age of reduction, the barbarians and the primitivists simply raised to overt levels what analysts like Canetti describe on the internal psychic ground. But it is important to see "power" in this form to understand what we mean when we see it "naked" and separated from the countermeasures and restraints which civilization created or, rather, which created civilization. The Holocaust, and the Nazi regime in its entirety, was an extraordinary effort to reduce mankind to animalistic nature, and exercise power in its purest most elemental form, focused on survival, the taking of prey, and ingestion of other lives. That is why the Holocaust remains a case of civilization being tested in apocalyptic terms. And also why all forms of reductively naturalistic evaluations of social and political behavior must take pause and review their conclusions. The history of the Holocaust forms a permanently instructive appendix to the power philosophies of Nietzsche, Georges Sorel, Vilfredo Pareto and Oswald Spengler, of Gobineau and Wagner, and of Marx, Lenin, and Mao Tse-tung.

The brief comment by Hitler, that conscience was a Jewish invention, suggests that to him the Jews were not simply powerless victims, the right objects for a power exercise, but that they were also the chief ideological enemies of pure power. Conscience is our name for the consciousness which inhabits "moral reality." Tautological as it may be, within that reality mind does not exist without conscience.[61] In any case, it is instructive and showed insight on his part that Hitler should think himself the enemy of conscience. It is no paradox to say that the active leaders of the Holocaust were reactionaries on behalf of order, militantly applied, in ruthless attack on anarchic dissent, libertarian impulse, and all presumed enemies of state and race. The Jew represented that, but also the order of conscience and justice. The Nazi order was really power-mastery, *their* order, the aggrandizement of self-interest. With conscience dead, their order would fill the void. Chaos was whatever opposed their will.

After the modernist revolutions it becomes a truism to say that the authoritarian is the mirror image of the libertarian. The weaker the conscience recognized in oneself, the stricter the imposition of restraint on others. Without the rule of conscience one is filled with fear, not hope or limitless desire. Perhaps two opposing results are achieved: a release of will, desire, instinct (moving toward violence) in oneself; and a punishment of the same freedom in others. The god-force, the life-force, in oneself becomes the enemy projected in others. The repressive authoritarian sees "life" dissolve into rage against others and fear for himself.

Whatever the inheritance of German discipline might have been, the Nazis distilled it into a pure, apocalyptic violence. Perhaps it was conscience in its death throes, ready to destroy what it could not control. There is no question that Hitler fought hard to liberate his people from all moral inhibition against the use of violence. But he could only do so by making them swear total allegiance to himself. We may understand why modern revolutions turned so readily from liberation to tyranny, with "the revolution eating its children." Power has only power to devour when there is nothing to fill the void of conscience.

Nietzsche taught the death of conscience, not God. When did modern men assume that conscience was unreasoning, tyrannical, life-hating? Or else it was a commonplace conscience, without tragic heroism, most ambiguously endowed by Freud. The revolts against "puritanism," Victorianism, bourgeois philistinism, and, most vaguely, the "establishment" all helped to express the death of conscience, in different countries and on different terms, and banalities of the good became the only opponent to what developed finally into the worst historic "banality of evil."

But in the failure of the language of good and evil, one might speak more to the point of the modern death of discourse, that is, a failure of the dialogue of values and goals, motives and principles. If power theories tell us that reductive interests rule language, then discourse is a strategic manipulative game, fruitful only in stimulating calculated response. When language and discourse serve only bias, then finally all dialogue serves only power. Power is the judge of last resort among warring biases. And if language theories describe the divorce of language from reality, that in turn must be a divorce of values from power. The ultimate word for reality, stripped from the masks and evasions of language, is power. And any diminution of the authority of language increases the authority of power.

What is power, then, in the testimony made by the Holocaust? It is the proof of reality, the guide of behavior, left by the death of moral reason. Accepted in the sovereignty of nature, and confirmed in the betrayal of language and discourse, power beckons the suicide of a world that has willed to live outside the bounds of moral reality.

Alfred Rosenberg, Hitler's ideologue, once noted the image of "marching columns" for the Nazi form of power and its hold over the Germans. "The new German style . . . is the style of a marching column, no matter where, or to what end, this marching column may be directed."[62] There were other marching columns in that war—the Jews, for instance, on their way to the gas chambers—but their style was not the same. Franz Stangl, camp commander at Treblinka, said after the war that he saw the Jewish victims move to their fate like lemmings, but he was wrong too. That ghostly parade can be heard by us, below whisper or scream, in a language unformulated, without a vocabulary, the prelanguage of conscience.

6

Victims: The Metaphysical Jew

"The dead are nourished by judgements."
Elias Canetti

I

In reading the records of Ringelblum, Kaplan, and Czerniakow, it becomes apparent that the environment of terror never ceased. To the Nazis language was a tool and a mask. Reality was power. Now, in historic retrospect, words like atrocity, horror, and outrage fail before the surreality of their achievement. Power that was justified in its own name, unrelenting power, was the source of equally unrelenting terror in enemies and victims, for it grew from the realization that a force had been liberated in the world that could strike without conscience and, like a force of nature, beyond explanation or negotiation. Pure power, freed from the rationalization of its goals, has the greater ability to overwhelm resistance because resistance needs a ground of meaning, or else it is mere reflex and, therefore, helpless. Perhaps only the counterstrength of the Russians, based on their own system of totally mobilized power, could defeat the Germans. Both totalitarian dragons shared the strategy and the capacity to make all opposition impotent, and they lived by that principle.

One Nazi tactic became deeply embodied in the methods of political terrorists everywhere, namely, that of taking hostages. Under the Nazis, no man could resist without the knowledge that he was putting his family and his community in deadly risk. The consequence of one real or imagined offense could be the death of many. The practice was a daily routine in the Warsaw ghetto for smugglers, for escapees, for resistance to abuse, for failure to salute Germans or move out of their way on the street, for failure to wear the Jewish badge, for a glance or a word. And in every case the fear was not just for oneself but for family and friend, for neighbor and community, for infant and elderly. Hunger was the second great weapon the Nazis used to crush or prevent resistance, humiliation was third, but terror was the most deadly and persistent in the constant summoning of threat in every thought and word.[1]

Power that creates blank terror, without relief or qualification, is the power over life and death. At the camps the word to new arrivals was often this: separate yourself from your children and your old ones, for to be in their company means certain death. Nothing could more brutally tell these victims that they had arrived at a margin beyond life, a place where survival could be treasured only as an animal reflex. And even this, they were made to see, had no role, for the executioners treated the victims as one prepares corpses for burial. The effect was persuasive and so they achieved in many of their victims the passivity of corpses. To the SS this was easy, for in the administrative sense their victims were dead at point of shipment and dead on arrival.

The Nazis saw death in the gas chamber as only the last stage of a slow process of physical and moral destruction. They knew with the shrewd insight of professional killers that it was best to first loosen the moral hold on life. A major example of their terrible effectiveness comes from the records of the Lodz ghetto. During the days of September 4–6, 1942, the deportation of all children under ten and all old people over sixty-five was ordered by the Germans. The selection and the task was to be administered by the *Judenrat* and Jewish police under Chaim Rumkowski. The files of vital statistics in Lodz were sealed the night before, not by Germans but by the Jewish Resettlement Commission. No one was to be allowed to change the records and thus win escape for his children or meet a bribe in doing it for someone else. Meanwhile, the Office of Vital Statistics was surrounded by weeping, pleading people, hoping to change or eliminate the fatal records of birth.

Josef Zelkowicz was an eloquent witness in the journal he kept until his own trip to a death camp. The specific agony Zelkowicz reports will trouble historic memory for a long time, for it records the true nature of that "crime against humanity" that has challenged definition for almost fifty years. By this time the Jews of Lodz knew that resettlement meant death, the convincing proof now being the ordered delivery of young children and the very old. There was a community meeting that day in September to debate the task given the Jewish Council. One council member said:

They are asking for sacrifices and the sacrifices have to be offered. . . . There is no place to hide it and there is nothing to hide from you. All children up to the age of ten and all old people have to be handed over. The decree cannot be annulled. We can only soften it perhaps by carrying it out quietly and peacefully.[2]

This it seems was the voice of a Jewish leadership that found itself forced into the ancient necessity of bargaining with death in the name of the survival of a remnant. But it was starkly apparent that the Nazis meant to dishonor them by specifically offering the survival of some as a bribe against the death of many. Zelkowicz writes, "As a reward for their efficient and loyal performance they [the Jewish Commission and the Jewish police and fire departments] have been promised that their own families, i.e. their children and parents, will be exempt from the edict."[3] This was not a subtle demonism but obvious evil. The average killer is not interested primarily in the moral humiliation of his victims. But in the program of death and the principle that justified genocide the Nazis were intent on stripping their victims of human status, which included the essential moral sensibility of parenthood, of family and community. It might be considered that the victims were being reduced to the prehuman state of nature, but nature does not go that far. If a lioness will defend her cubs, the desperate triage case, as at Lodz, eludes her consciousness.

The nightmare reached its climax when the leader of the Lodz ghetto spoke at the meeting. Chaim Rumkowski was a man notorious for his dictatorial rule. Once known for his vanity, a petty Caesar, he is described now as shattered, weeping uncontrollably before he could begin.

In my old age I must stretch forth my arms and beg: . . . Fathers and mothers, yield me your children. . . . Yesterday afternoon, I was given an order to deport some 20,000 Jews from the ghetto. If not: "We [they] will do it" and the question arose: Should we have taken it over and do it ourselves or leave it for others to carry out?. . . I have to carry out this difficult and bloody operation. I have to cut off limbs in order to save the body! I have to take children, because otherwise—God forbid—others will be taken.[4]

There was nothing here to relieve suffering, and the words of witness met its impact:

People scream. And their screams are terrible and fearful and senseless, as terrible and fearful and senseless as the actions causing them. The ghetto is no longer rigid; it is now writhing in convulsions. The whole ghetto is one enormous spasm. The whole ghetto jumps out of its own skin and plunges back within its own barbed wires. Ah, if only a fire would come and consume everything! If only a bolt from heaven would strike and destroy us altogether![5]

The demonism of the Nazis lay in forcing a moral responsibility upon their victims for their own deaths. If, in triage effect, they were forced to share in the execution of their own children, it would be of a piece with the original cruelty to shift the dishonor for this to the victims. But every discussion of the Holocaust has to face this singularity of horror.

In that "enormous spasm" of terror and grief, what did those Jews think was the source of their suffering? Was this finally to convince them of their cosmic guilt? Those first Christian Jews, God's enforcers, believed and installed such words at the foot of the Cross, "upon ourselves and upon our children . . . " It may be argued that in historic Orthodox Judaism there is implanted the belief in salvation through persecution, the apocalyptic redemption of Jews registered in the magnitude of suffering and loss. Old questions arrive. Is there an affinity in the Jew for punishment, a curious element in anti-Semitism that takes the shape offered by the victim? Do the persecuted provoke persecution, and must the victim share the blame? Such speculation leads to an abyss of the mind, where one listens finally only to the screams from the Lodz ghetto.

One thinks, desperately perhaps, that the Jews of Europe were an opportunity for a collective pathological sadism aroused and redoubled by the passivity of the victim. Certainly it was stimulated by ordinary vulnerability. But how much more by the fatal Jewish acquaintance (through prophecy and memory) with suffering, survival, and redemption?[6] The belief that the victim will try to placate cruelty must be its strongest stimulus. It is remarkable, too, how much the prejudice in favor of the Jew's secret power was balanced by the visible weakness of the victim Jew. It may remain forever a mystery that he should be regarded as both helpless and a potent threat, but it was a combination calculated to arouse a fury. When the Germans met resistance in the final Warsaw ghetto uprising, they were at first stunned with disbelief, but it could only energize the slaughter.

Surely the Holocaust in its culmination would disprove any ground for hatred or fear, if the Nazis truly knew a tribal fear of the Jew. Murder cannot remain a criticism of its victim; the hatred that ends in murder transcends all grievance and can do little to explain the victim's nature, his psychic and social condition. And yet the question remains for Jews and non-Jews alike. How was so much hatred aroused, what was its cause in the victim, in the victimizer, in any conceivable character of the murderer or of those he killed? In a poignant moment during a conference on the Holocaust, Raul Hilberg admitted that after a lifetime of research there was one question for which he could not receive the trace of an answer. The question was, why? This is a question that cannot rest. It was at that same conference that Cyntha Ozick declared that such meetings should not be held by Jews, people who identify with the victims. Let the Germans, or their descendants, she said with some passion, devote themselves to answering the question, Why?[7] One agrees that in fact an important passage is missing in the history of the world's conscience, except for the rare phenomena of a recent speech made by the president of the West German Republic. Nevertheless, the question falls into all hands; the Holocaust demands moral closure, which is approximate understanding, the unsatisfied task of trying to meet the ghostly consciousness of the universal victim, the universal victimizer.

In the face of the Holocaust, both the well and ill-intentioned persist in thinking that if there is such hatred there must be a reason, not necessarily legitimate, but still reason that reflects in some sense upon the nature of its target. The German Jews had after all lived in their country for over a thousand years, the Polish and Lithuanians Jews as long. What could it have been that brought this on their heads? And what if it wasn't hatred at all but something worse in its insult to the victim, a god-like judgment of the *lebenswertig*? It is this as much as anything that brings up the mystery of the Holocaust. There is, unfortunately, a degree of evil that calls question not only upon those who commit it but those who receive it. And, in fact, the Nazi evil implicates the whole human race, and this in turn raises both the mystery and our helplessness before it.

Essays on classic anti-Semitism seem to have little assurance in explanation. It may be that the Nazi anti-Semite best resembles Shakespeare's Iago. To explain himself would remove the richest germ of his hatred, his "motiveless malignity," a passion that far exceeds any conceivable cause. In hindsight, how grossly implausible and irrelevant sound all the "reasons" given by Hitler himself. This is from his speech of January 30, 1939, the first instance where he threatened the Jews of Europe with destruction:

We are resolved to prevent the settlement in our country of a strange people which was capable of snatching for itself all the leading positions in the land, and to oust it. For it is our will to educate our own nation for these leading positions. We have hundreds of thousands of very intelligent children of peasants and of the working classes. We shall have them educated . . . and we wish that one day they, and not the representatives of an alien race, may hold the leading positions in the State together with our educated classes.[8]

This might be called the mundanely revolutionary class motive for attacking the Jews. But apart from its direct demagogic value it could hardly be sufficient to support the atrocity. Something much deeper, reaching life anxiety, a universal angst, must have been touched. In the Christian tradition, the Jew represents the metaphysical antagonist—man—both in covenant with God and betrayal of Him. The Old Testament, with its series of promises, covenants, quarrels, indictments, punishments, and rewards, is a closed story in the relationship of Christians with God. They are Saved Mankind. The Jew remains Fallen Man. As such he can receive all the self-hatred of the species. The Jew becomes the inevitable scapegoat within or outside religious belief. It was a plausible step into secular naturalism for Hitler, Himmler, and Rosenberg to think their way to representing the Jew as the subhuman. But what great irony that the Jew, who had attempted the most sophisticated dialogue with God, almost on equal footing with Him, should have become the subhuman. But this, too, is a clue. Perhaps the Nazi mind operated in a vengeance of the spiritual inferior. Transcendence seeking man, on traditional terms with deity, could be brought down to his naturalist image and so defiled by every form of biological humiliation.

If this was revenge, it must have had double force, with punishment coming from those who had felt the insult in modern naturalist thought. In this century, precisely at the German locus, the intellectual Jew, represented best by Marx, Einstein, and Freud, could be seen as the reductively naturalist thinker, at the extreme level most threatening to spirit and to all idealizations, whether religious or secular.[9] In that respect the modern Jew could be deemed to have repeated a deicide.

The thrust of typical explanation, doomed to inadequacy as it may be, traces the victim Jew to his role as exile, pariah, and scapegoat. In the Christian tradition, the Jew who killed Christ became the ultimate metaphysical exile, with no home in God's universe. The God one believed in was the guarantor of humanity in nature, space, and time. To kill Him was to kill the basis of one's being, the source of all meaning. That was much worse then to deny Him, since it was an attack on the foundation of being for all others. Therefore, though their leading thought was anti-Christian (volubly exposed in Hitler's "Secret Conversations"), the Nazis were following a traditional instinct in declaring the Jews subhuman and worthy of extinction.

The historic tragedy of Christian and Jew thus made the Nazi slaughter more of a "crime" in the cosmic sense which invokes heaven, hell, and the last judgment than the other great modern slaughters, like those of Stalin and Mao. To hate and kill the Jew was always on one side of ambivalence a matter of sacrilege, a violation of God's command and will. And yet in Hitler's petty post-Nietzschean thought the Jew carried the blame for

Christianity. It was in this respect that the Holocaust represented an apocalyptic revolution against both the classic religious inheritance and the Enlightenment.

The valid hypothesis suggests that the Jew was caught at the focus of that very deep modern ambivalence, the quarrel between traditional faiths and neoscientific naturalism. It may be that the ambivalence itself was the source of the most uncompromising hatred. Three dominant images or stereotypes which the Nazis exploited must have mingled explosively in the minds of their followers: the images of the Jew as philistine businessman, as rootless Bolshevik revolutionary, and as the prime figure of decadence in life, art, and literature. When mingled with the image of the "god-killer," it was possible to decide that "his character was unalterably negative," in the summary words of Karl Bracher's review of Nazis anti-Semitism:

Even in the preracist stereotype, the Jew was thought to be incapable of creativity and spirituality. He was the embodiment of everything negative which, under the heading "civilization," was counterposed to the higher value of true "culture." [10]

If Bracher and others are right on this point, then it is clear to see the Jew representing naturalistic man, on the one hand the subhuman worthy of every species of biological insult, and on the other "the soulless intellectual," "the rootless, shameless skeptic." It was a two-pronged revenge that could relieve an intolerable impasse of body and mind.

•

The crime of the Nazis that tasked the ingenuity of evil was the infliction of a moral death, a death to the world while in the world, upon many of their victims. In some respects, suicide was the most plausible of all reactions, and it was the choice made by many, in either direct or indirect form, as in the surrender of life made by the so-called Musulmen. But the other surrender, that of the active premise of a moral community, is the only way to understand the record left by Zelkowicz as he recounts the behavior of the Jewish leaders in Lodz, in that scene of moral anarchy, with all under suspicion of aiming to save their own at the expense of the others. At best, a desperate people accepted sacrifice in order to save the remnant of a community. But this was a hope that became more and more abstract. The tangible event made them collaborators in their people's destruction. [11]

Hindsight is always cruel, and perhaps the right to ask the pertinent question on the subject of the behavior of community leaders during the Holocaust belongs only to the dead victims. Etty Hillesum, for instance, was one who worked with the Jewish Council of Amsterdam and later died at Auschwitz. The journal she kept and her published letters, like the records of Chaim Kaplan and Emanuel Ringelblum, are invaluable historic testimony, though she wrote with greater privacy of feeling and often in spiritual exaltation. Much of her journal and the letters which survived her death were written as a privileged council worker, even while an inmate of Westerbork, the Dutch transient camp leading to Auschwitz. Here she records an effort to save a writer friend from transport:

Never before have I taken a hand in "fixing" it to keep someone off the transport. I lack all talent for diplomacy, but yesterday I did my bit for Mechanicus. What exactly it was that I did, I'm not sure. I went to all sorts of officials. Suddenly I found myself walking around with a mysterious gentleman I've never seen before who looked like a white slave trafficker in a French film. . . . one moment I had an interview with the Registrator and the next I was appearing before a senile little man who presumably holds a mysterious position of power and can get people off the transport when all seems lost. There is a sort of "underworld" here in Westerbork; yesterday I sensed something of it, I don't know how it all fits together, I don't think it's a savory story.[12]

But she senses something worse than moral chaos.

What the next transport will look like no one knows—the lists still have to be made up, and in the process all kinds of things are bound to go on behind the scenes. They are playing a game with us, but we allow them to do so, and that will be our shame for generations to come. . . . It is a complete madhouse here; we shall have to feel ashamed of it for three hundred years. The *Dienstleiters* themselves now have to draw up the transport lists [*Dienstleiters* were Jewish section leaders][13]

That same day the *Dienstleiters* were required to appear at the first night of a cabaret entertainment performed by the inmates and ordered by the camp commandant. They go home to dress in their best clothes and come back to laugh with the rest at a vaudeville comedy presented by Jewish entertainers. The parallel in perversity is the use of Jewish musicians at Auschwitz to accompany the march to the gas chambers. Mozart? Brahms? A Strauss waltz? The scene suggests *Walpurgisnacht*, a true record of the breakdown and defilement of a high culture.

Later, Hillesum was helping to ready the sick, the babies, and mothers for another transport.

Tonight I shall be helping to dress babies and to calm mothers—and that is all I can hope to do. I could almost curse myself for that. For we all know that we are yielding up our sick and defenseless brothers and sisters to hunger, heat, cold, exposure, and destruction, and yet we dress them and escort them to the bare cattle cars—and if they can't walk, we carry them on stretchers. What is going on, what mysteries are these, in what sort of fatal mechanism have we become enmeshed? The answer cannot simply be that we are all cowards. We're not that bad. We stand before a much deeper question.[14]

One faces it. What was that question, and in what fatality were they all enmeshed? Hillesum describes another scene in the barracks while a mother with a sick child is getting ready for the next transport and sobbing. "A woman comes up to her, a stout working-class woman with a kindly snub-nosed face, draws the desperate mother down with her on the edge of one of the iron bunks, and talks to her almost crooningly, 'There now, you're just an ordinary Jew, aren't you? So you'll just have to go, won't you.'"[15]

Those few words speak to the "deeper question." Surely, in all of Europe, victim and torturer were both under some spell, hypnotized by the overwhelming presence of elemental power, a power like death itself pretending to intelligent purpose, wearing a uniform, commanding obedience. Hillesum observes the paralyzing effect of sheer horror:

When I think of the faces of that squad of armed, green-uniformed guards—my God, those faces! I looked at them, each in turn, from behind the safety of a window, and I have never been so frightened of anything in my life. I sank to my knees with the words that preside over human life: And God made man after His likeness. That passage spent a difficult morning with me.[16]

The supposed passivity of those who filed into the death chambers can be attributed to many things—the inevitable thunderclap of terror, a stupor of disbelief and shock, exhaustion, hopelessness. But how much was implicit assent to death, a mass suicide?[17] Those victims may finally have felt something more repellent than cruelty, than hatred. They may have recognized an animal insensitivity that undercut all human worth. The world was not worth keeping in the company of the insane butchers who ruled it. To go on living was to live on their terms. In murder the degradation is mutual, and on this scale universal. On whose behalf should one resist? The will to live depends on some premises of value. How much does it depend on the assent to one's life in others?

Etty Hillesum writes in her journal at a time when she was being urged to go to work with the Jewish Council of Amsterdam in order to save herself from eventual deportation. (The following are all entries of July 1942.):

I simply cannot make active preparations to save myself, it seems so pointless to me and would make me nervous and unhappy. My letter of application to the Jewish council on Jaap's urgent advice has upset my cheerful yet deadly serious equilibrium. As if I had done something underhand. Like crowding on to a small piece of wood adrift on an endless ocean after a shipwreck and then saving oneself by pushing others into the water and watching them drown.[18]

In the end she chose the fate of the camp inmates and accompanied her parents and her younger brother, Jaap, a doctor and gifted pianist, on the final road to Auschwitz. But the earlier journal entry, made at the height of the season of massacre for European Jews, continues:

It is all so ugly. . . . I would much rather join those who prefer to float on their backs for a while, drifting on the ocean with their eyes turned toward heaven and who then go down with a prayer. I cannot help myself. My battles are fought out inside, with my own demons; it is not in my nature to tilt against the savage, cold-blooded fanatics who clamour for our destruction. I am not afraid of them either. . . . I know what is happening and yet my head is clear. But sometimes I feel as if a layer of ashes were being sprinkled over my heart, as if my face were withering and decaying before my very eyes, and as if everything were falling apart in front of me and my heart were letting everything go.[19]

The passage is keen witness to the ordeal of survival. The ones who did most to resist or escape were often adolescents, the very young, who chose the chance of survival while hunted through Europe by the SS and police. But for most, the choice seemed to be between one form of death over another, and they chose to die with their own people instead of alone or with a band in the Polish or Russian forests. They gathered themselves closer in their ghetto suffering. In the face of the horror they had nothing but each other as denial of an inhuman truth that had entered their lives. Even if not consciously, it may be that most wanted to die together, not alone, because the ultimate threat of the Nazis was the death of a world without humanity.

Hillesum makes a moving demonstration of these terminal impulses. It is striking, nevertheless, how much the sense of self-preservation was reduced to the community, then to the immediate family, and, finally—on the ramps before the gas chamber or in the camps with disease and starvation—to oneself. The Nazis were conducting a grand experiment in the breakdown of the human bond and of personal character. It would be cruelly naive to ask for heroism from these victims. But their report, as we have it, can teach what it is that maintains character and community, and the gigantic size of the evil that came for their destruction.

Hillesum herself was capable of a strange moral ecstasy in the midst of what should have been the stupor of despair:

> The misery here is quite terrible. . . . And then time and again, it soars straight from the heart—I can't help it, that's just the way it is, like some elementary force— the feeling that life is glorious and magnificent, and that one day we shall be building a whole new world. . . . We may suffer, but we must not succumb. And if we should survive unhurt in body and soul, but above all in soul, without bitterness and without hatred, then we shall have a right to a say after the war. Maybe I am an ambitious woman: I would like to have a tiny bit of a say.[20]

In the light of her fate (she writes in fullness of spirit but still far at that point from the ultimate ordeal of Auschwitz), it is difficult to do justice to the passage or even share in its emotion. She may have been strengthening herself against moral and spiritual surrender, perhaps even preparing her terms for martyrdom. How many like her there were we don't know, though one remembers and recognizes the tone and spirit of Chaim Kaplan and Emmanuel Ringelblum in the records they left behind. In them we see the response of a humane intelligence confronting an incomprehensible evil. We expect insanity or incoherence in the ordeal that preceded mass physical destruction. Instead, we have a clarity of spirit and a call to moral survival.

Etty Hillesum's life was cut off with her "say," though it ended with a transcendent effort to reach God. "My life has become an uninterrupted dialogue with You, oh God, one great dialogue."[21] One reads her words with the fullest respect, even with a strong desire to share her "dialogue," which does not absolutely require a supernatural partner. When she wrote the above entries in her journal in August of 1943 she had surely guessed with the others their almost certain fate. Her own words in a letter interrupted her thoughts like a sudden scream. "We are being hunted to death all through Europe."[22] Did it overcome her love for "God's riches" when that fate arrived?

What we ponder finally is a form of challenge. What did this victim, and other victims, want us to know and believe? What is their testament, resonant with an unspecific, undetailed moral resolve?

It could be argued that Hillesum was one of those made desperate for emotional and spiritual shelter. A deep personal love affair occupies much of the attention of her journal at a time when Dutch Jews were being brought closer and closer to extinction. She gives little notice to the actual war—politics of Allied resistance, the details of oppression—until she finally takes up permanent residence at Westerbork. In the journal, published as *An Interrupted Life*, it could be further noted that she retreats into a private religion with its resonances from Christianity, Buddhism, Indian quietism, a poetic vitalism, and nothing at all from Judaism, not even references to other religious Jews at the camp. But in that last emergency, sectarian differences become trivial. Was she not close, in any case, to the rabbis of the Polish and Lithuanian *shtetls* who persisted in prayer and Talmud study, and who, even facing the gas chambers, submitted themselves to their Torah? We hear her words against a background that makes prayer, of any kind, sound heroically determinative and self-defining.

So Hillesum, educated, enlightened, of pluralist and esoteric spiritual instruction, writes finally as follows, as I excerpt her words:

Very well then, this new certainty, that what they are after is our total destruction, I accept it. I know it now and I shall not burden others with my fears. I shall not be bitter if others fail to grasp what is happening to us Jews. I work and continue to live with the same conviction and I find life meaningful—yes, meaningful—although I hardly dare say so in company these days.

· ·

Living and dying, sorrow and joy, the blisters on my feet and the jasmine behind the house, the persecution, the unspeakable horrors—it is all as one in me and I accept it all as one mighty whole and begin to grasp it better if only for myself, without being able to explain to anyone else how it all hangs together.[23]

We may think this a characteristic fatalism and resignation that she elevates to divine comfort. But she goes on as if resistance were in her spirit and in her pen:

And I shall wield this slender fountain pen as if it were a hammer and my words will have to be so many hammer-strokes with which to beat out the story of our fate and of a piece of history as it is and never was before. Not in this totalitarian, massively organized form, spanning the whole of Europe. Still, a few people must survive if only to be the chroniclers of this age. I would very much like to become one of their number.[24]

Hillesum's own last communication was a postcard thrown from the train heading for Auschwitz. But her letters and her journal have the effect of that undeciphered message thrown from a train traveling toward death. One muses that what she in her last ordeal did was to charge us, the students of her fate, with the duty to complete the unfinished writing, her "bit of a say."

II

"We are a metaphysical people," Heidegger said of the Germans.

The much debated question of the passivity of Holocaust victims, their failure to resist except in dramatically isolated instances, focuses more on the nature of the crime and its true depravity than upon the psychosocial traits of the Jewish victims. The victims could not understand why this was happening to them, who was doing it, the nature of their guilt, why they were chosen rather than others.[25] As Chaim Kaplan's notes illustrate, in the first place they were stunned, not like "sheep before slaughter" but in the possession of human morally developed character. They were forced to confront death in its naked state, without reasons, beyond custom, rule, or expectation. In a certain sense the Nazi executioners had the right to claim what Robert Oppenheimer felt and spoke, from a Hindu text, when he saw the result of his work with the atom bomb: "I am become Death, the shatterer of worlds."

The "normal" basis for murder is a "motive"; even the victim is usually able to see that he is an enemy or obstacle to the aggressor's interest. The psychological difference between such a case and reasonless murder needs to be understood. To speculate on Nazi "reasons" is a morass. In any case, how could Jewish victims understand a motive that makes sense for a world that was to be *Judenrein*? That they were an obstacle to evolutionary progress? That their existence defiled the earth?[26]

As David Wyman and other historians observe, the credibility of the reports of extermination remained in doubt to the end, and even now are believed with a shock that destroys comprehension, a more important need for action than credibility. As usual, Hitler and the Nazis exploited the principle of the lie so big that it couldn't possibly be a lie, and facts so violent that they couldn't possibly be the truth. As for credibility, hindsight makes it easier, not more difficult, to understand the inability of many or most to believe the rumors of their impending destruction. It was the human universe that would become intolerable, not one's own existence. And there is a difference in the quality of despair between those judgments.

Hillesum's account in its salvationary aspects cannot be typical, of course, but we see from it how the victims were blocked when considering the possibility of escape or resistance. One factor was their wish and need to act collectively, without harming each other, as when in her case and that of her brother they decided on accompanying their mother and father to Westerbork and later Auschwitz when the rare real chance existed for both to avoid that fate. "Everyone who seeks to save himself must surely realize that if he does not go [on transport] another must take his place." She illustrates what the effort to escape as individuals could mean; she tells of a little boy who tried to escape a transport by running away, and how after he was captured fifty others, who had not been scheduled to go, were shipped as punishment. In tragic paradox, the Jews were helped to destruction by their readiness to act collectively; if it had been a true case of each for himself, the death count might have been much less, as in Hannah Arendt's view.

Close to the end, Hillesum wrote: "Ours is now a common destiny and that is something we must not forget." This was a great effort, she acknowledges. "Yes, I feel perfectly able to bear my lot, but not that of my parents," she writes to her friends.[27] She touches the paralyzing source of suffering, the witness they were forced to have of each other's agony, that of parents and children, husbands and wives. The tactic of the Nazis was to hold them all hostage against each other. It takes an effort to remember that the Nazis did not slaughter a numbered mass but families and whole communities who carried both the burden and the comfort of each other's presence.

It was in particular that experience of collective suffering in a "common destiny" which determines the features of the Holocaust and will no doubt endow it in universal memory. George Steiner writes, "To have been a European Jew in the first half of the twentieth century was to pass sentence on one's children, to force upon them a condition almost beyond rational understanding."[28] Who passes this sentence, and who is it that accepts it? Fortunately or unfortunately, the Holocaust, for many Jews, settled all questions about ambiguous identity. But how is it to exist defined that way, singled out as a victim to the mortal end? In the last extreme, what happens to the bond of communities and families? One image kept in witness is that of a pyramid of bodies in the gas chamber where people had clawed each other and climbed to reach air, light. What "identity" was that, and what does it mean to read now the words of Kafka which Steiner calls up: "Those who strike at the Jew kill Man?" Nevertheless, we cling to Kafka's words and cling to the paradox. The Nazis pushed and dragged the Jew to that margin of definable being, that void of identity, where the victim is both everything and nothing, and where a miracle of reversal must take place to fulfill Kafka's prophecy. "Those who strike at the Jew kill Man" because the crime is against all. It is this that communicates what Steiner calls "the peculiar dignity of his torment."[29]

Is it a flaw in suffering, a form of moral pride for Jews to adopt surrogatehood for humanity in the Holocaust? "Proprietorship, with all its exploitation advantages," some critics call it. It seems an inevitable metonymy to use the term "Jew" interchangeably with "victim" of the Holocaust, though one may hope—for the long run—in the Kafkean sense. No student of the Holocaust discounts the fact that thousands of Gypsies, homosexuals, and Slav leadership cadres joined the Jews in the classification of the *Lebensunwertig* (unworthy of life) who deserved a therapeutic death. We need a generic term for people of that destiny, and "Jew," lower case or not, will do quite well in view both of the exorbitant proportion of their numbers on the lists of death and the sweep and explicitness with which they were defined as worthy of extinction. This, however, is not to lower the importance of the Holocaust as a particular event in Jewish history, and the way in which that history, the character of the people and of their specific enemies, put a stamp on every feature of the Holocaust. Anti-Semitism itself, in all its nature, is almost enough to define the ideology of the Holocaust, if we can say it had one. But the subject is very, very large when it is broached as "to strike at the Jew is to kill Man." No one can deny Jews the right to give their detailed understanding to the first part of that phrase, and even to disdain the dubious honor of martyrdom, but it is a fact that general interest necessarily attends to the whole phrase, that is, toward the universalist features and implications of the Holocaust. This is for certain appropriate in an American museum of the Holocaust, in a country with a major commitment to interracial and transnational values.

The awe if not the dignity of Jewish torment has its background in their history, where they came to personify a cosmic fate affecting the world, afflicting themselves. Steiner put it tangibly: "Perhaps we Jews walk closer to our children than other men; try as we may, they cannot leap out of our shadow."[30] This was a people who were enclosed by a metaphysical identity that was unescapable, as the Holocaust illustrated in every detail. A man named Meck who tried to flee the Kovno Ghetto was caught, tortured, and hanged in public. It was Meck's mistake to send a last message to his mother and sister. The next day they were taken to the Ninth Fort, the place of execution outside Kovno, thus bound by death in his shadow.[31]

Avraham Tory wrote in the record, as the great slaughter began in 1941, "We feared for the fate of the men if they fell into the hands of the Germans, but we never imagined that they would murder women, children, and the elderly; and so far as the men were concerned, we never expected mass murder." [32] This was the shock of abstract identity, featureless but absolute, which crippled individual resistance. The mystery challenged the world, caught up in the Nazi superstition, and led it to give at least partial assent. For example, there is this: after reports of death camps reached Switzerland from Kurt Gerstein and the World Jewish Congress in August 1942, the Swiss government specifically ordered that all refugee Jews be turned back at the border, though non-Jewish refugees were accepted. The official explanation stated that since they fled on account of their race they were not to be considered political refugees. [33] The necessary presumption is that they were to be considered refugees without redemption, exiled from the planet and welcome nowhere. It could not have been the Nazis alone who felt that this had justice (or one degenerate modern form of justice—necessity) behind it, based on a metaphysical premise.

That existential premise (circumscribed and underlined by Jewish guilt) has to remain ambiguous, impossible to define because chiefly located in the blank principle of negativity. For Nazis like Heydrich, the Jews expressed their inherent nature in 100% opposition to everything Nazis stood for, as found in "liberalism," freemasonry, in Marxism, and, not least, in Christianity. To sum it up beyond these contradictions, Heydrich believed that the Jews had "declared war on us." Regardless of who had declared war, the features of the abstract Jew had to be found as the reversed mirror image of the abstract German Nazi.

Politically, the list of Nazi enemies was long, but it was necessary to find their common essence; totalitarian politics drives toward that simplicity. Hans Mommsen, an authoritative German historian, wrote that the "crucial function of anti-Semitism was to bridge the objective conflict between the anti-capitalist and anti-Socialist tendencies of the [Nazi] movement." [34] But even these issues of conflict seem mundane, inadequate for the scope of the Holocaust. The French philosopher and critic, Philippe Lacoue-Labarthe, makes a convincing summary when he points out that the Holocaust is different from the Gulag and other totalitarian massacres like that of Cambodia, where "a genuinely political, economic, or military issue [was] at stake." [35]

In the case of Auschwitz, things are quite different—despite appearances (powerful ideology, state of war, police terror, totalitarian organization of politics, extensive technological capacity, etc.) . . . the Jews as Jews were not in 1933 agents of social dissension (except of course in phantasy); they did not represent any kind of homogeneous political or religious force; they did not even appear to have any particular social cohesion.

And, he says, they could not even be viewed as a religious or historicocultural minority, in view of the assimilated nature of German Jews. "They were a threat as people *decreed to be Jews* . . . ," that is, a cosmic, unconfined threat to "a nation that was painfully lacking an identity or existence of its own." Thus Jews were described by others (the Germans) who really suffered or feared that void in themselves. It was an enmity and revulsion, Lacoue-Labarthe says, that "belongs to the realm of projection."

In effect, Lacoue-Labarthe is speaking of an ultimate form of dehumanization, again perhaps the projected fantasy of a people, like other modern peoples, profoundly shaken in their faith in the distinctive concept of the human.

The means employed in the Extermination were, in the last instance, neither industrial, military, nor those of a police force. . . . In its "final" aspect, the annihilation no longer had about it any of the features of the classical or modern figures of systematic oppression. None of the "machines" invented to extract confessions or remorse or to mount the edifying spectacle of terror, was of any use. The Jews were treated in the same way as industrial waste or the proliferation of parasites is "treated." . . . As Kafka had long since understood, the "final solution" consisted in taking literally the centuries-old metaphors of insult and contempt—*vermin, filth*—and providing oneself with the technological means for such an effective literalization.

It was reductionism on the cosmic scale, unprecedented in its consistency of meaning and purpose.

And if it is true that the age is that of the accomplishment of nihilism, then it is at Auschwitz that that accomplishment took place in the purest formless form. God in fact died at Auschwitz—the God of the Judaeo-Christian West at least. And it was not at all by chance that the victims of that annihilation attempt were the witness in that West of another origin of the God who was venerated and thought there.[36]

The sequence of Lacoue-Labarthe's thought is significant and marks the reaction of many who contemplate the mystery of the Holocaust on the level of metaphysical-religious questioning. In the end, the modern generic Jew victim inherits much from Christian anti-Semitism—to be outcast from the human is verified by the act of deicide. But didn't the Jew also inherit the Freudian crime, the murder of the primeval father? So Jean-Francois Lyotard suggests, and he adds, all forms of anti-Semitism agree that the Jew is nonassimilable, the utmost principle of negativity.

"The jews" are the irremissible in the West's movement of remission and pardon. They are what cannot be domesticated in the obsession to dominate, in the compulsion to control domain, in the passion for empire, recurrent ever since Hellenistic Greece and Christian Rome. "The jews," never at home wherever they are, cannot be integrated, converted, or expelled. . . . They can only assimilate, said Hannah Arendt, if they also assimilate anti-Semitism.[37]

This, then, is a totalism of resentment which can account for limitless punishment. On that level of the pursuit of an ultimate threat, it recalls the role of Melville's metaphysical whale, Moby Dick, in the mind of Ahab:

The White Whale swam before him as the monomaniac incarnation of all those malicious agencies which some deep men feel eating in them. . . . All that most maddens and torments; all that stirs up the lees of things; all truth with malice in it; all that cracks the sinews and cakes the brain; . . .

He piled upon the whale's white hump the sum of all the general hate and rage felt by his whole race from Adam down."

Certainly the style of monomania was Hitler's; he left evidence for it in his last words to the German people. The totality of rage, the ubiquity of the negative force, turning in self-hatred upon itself, fantastically supported the persistent myth that the greatest anti-Semites were Jewish or part Jewish. Richard Wagner, Heydrich, Hitler himself, were all rumored (and even investigated on that ground) to have Jewish ancestry. And indeed the larger history seems to illustrate examples of the profound inward-turning self-destructiveness of Jews, a negativism gone berserk, so to speak. There was Karl Marx in his explicit anti-Semitism for recent influence, as if to illustrate how necessary the Jew was in any salvationary doctrine. Julius Streicher, in a speech to German children, called Christ the greatest anti-Semite of all time. This has an obvious point when accompanied by the Gospel text and the preaching of the Jew Paul. The tendency to take the words of Jews as testimony against themselves (from the prophets to political and religious sectarians today) might suggest that historically anti-Semitism has been a collaboration between Jews and their enemies.[38] But the supreme example of negativity, of a force in the Jew that denies every sanctifying good and the source of good, remains the Crucifixion. Deicide is absolute, it cannot be conditioned or moderated, and those guilty of it are guilty in every form or mode of their existence.

Consequently perhaps, the Nazi persecutors never tired of the simple irony of referring to their victims as the "chosen people." They were touching an essence, for was it not their mission to usurp fate in confirming Jews as the "unchosen?" In the Nazi mind the Jewish drama of damnation was to be continuous, whether damned by nature, under the metaphysical law of race, or by the Christian God.

A fascinating instance of this way of thinking was provided by Robert Lifton in his study of Nazi doctors. One prisoner doctor cited in interview how when he first met Mengele he was impressed by the latter's professional friendliness and his cultivation in literary as well as medical subjects. When questioned by Mengele about his family, this doctor said his wife had come to Auschwitz with him, adding that she had been killed in the gas chambers. But when Dr. O. said his small children were still in France, "Mengele sprang to his feet [in anger] and asked, 'Why (did) they not come here as well?'"[39] The implication, of course, was that Jews had a duty to die and should know it. (Mengele expressed even greater anger on learning that the children had been hidden by French priests). If we can imagine this clearly we might understand the Holocaust better as well as the German Nazi mind. Power and order were to be ethical imperatives for victims as well as victimizers, and to be sure, in the context of Auschwitz, they became so. How could Dr. O. dare let his children escape their just fate? Surely this brand of anti-Semitism was insane. But the Jews were supposed to feel a profound self-directed guilt; how else could the Nazis keep their good conscience, as they seemed to have been able to with hardly any variation.

Reviewing Mengele's anger (the Jews had a duty to die), it seems that Hannah Arendt's criticism of the Jewish councils makes sense: all forms of cooperation were ways of legitimizing murder and helped Mengele's need to assume an ethical order in his work. The ghetto councils, the Judenrat, the kapos, *sonderkommandos,* and particularly the Nazi and prisoner doctors helped institutionalize and naturalize the Holocaust.

But the deeper philosophic dimension that challenged a Jewish "right to exist" gave terrible weight to the suffering of the victims. They were either dying in the hands of the insane or being killed in the impersonal justice of nature; and under the temper and order maintained by the Nazis, the latter was more convincing. The most significant response of the victims grew in their awareness that every step of the way was directed toward extinction. Every withdrawal of rights, every order and prohibition was a denial of their existential and affirmative being.

That was the message that came from a young man's diary written on the margins of a French novel entitled *Les vrais riches* and found at Auschwitz.

We're not human beings any more, nor have we become animals; we are just some strange psycho-physical product "made in Germany" . . . Hasn't modern humanity contradicted some original idea in the creation of the universe? What intelligence possessed of goodwill and foresight could create something so monstrous?

But he concedes the myth which had created him, to this extent:

If being Jewish is so strong, so "personal" and specific, if its difference from everyone else is so special, enough to provoke so much hate, hostility, sympathy, antipathy, then it must be a strong power *an und fur sich*.

What is to be done with that power if it can escape extinction? He answers for himself:

I long for a Jewish life in a Jewish state. I think that if the Jewish people had had no history but that of the last five years, it would be enough to justify a special entity, one which would not be mixed, since I doubt that even Jews will be able to understand all that has happened to us, let alone other nations.[40]

This is the mundane answer to a profound mystery, voiced at the edge of death. Jewish nationalism is an effort to escape from being the world's victim and martyr, the world's enemy and infliction. It would escape the fate of a metaphysical identity, defined and redefined as the miseries and fears of other men and nations dictate. The young man from the Lodz ghetto might be imagined to say this: if you ask who I am, I answer, "Here at the border of extinction I was defined, I derived my name from my persecutors and murderers, they named me in their violence and in their effort to annihilate me. But you can no longer write that script upon my body. I am no longer Man nor Anti-Man. If you would find me look for me in my own house, among my people. Perhaps as I defend myself from you, you will discover my real being and your own."

Call this an alternative resolution of the "Jewish problem," one preferred by Jews, no doubt, who would rather not retain the burden of carrying the problem of Man in Kafka's sense, the problem of the human essence and its valuation. The bleakest contrast, however, is the temptation to form Jewish identity exclusively or primarily on the fact of victimization. Elias Canetti supplies a stark portrait, writing in 1945 just as war ended:

The suffering of the Jews had turned into an institution, but it outlived itself. People don't want to hear about it any more. They were amazed to learn that one could exterminate the Jews; now, perhaps without realizing it, they have a new reason for despising them. Gas *was* used in this war, but only against the Jews, and they were helpless. The money giving them power earlier was useless. They were degraded to slaves, then cattle, then vermin. The degradation worked; the traces will be harder to wipe away from those who heard about it than from the Jews themselves. . . . The very ancient history of how others relate to Jews has changed fundamentally. People do not hate them any less; but they no longer *fear* them. For this reason, the Jews can make no greater mistake than to continue the laments at which they were masters and to which they now have greater inducement than ever before.[41]

This has a cold and bitter note, but a truth is behind it. The Jews who use the Holocaust as in old lament are wrong if they wish to keep it to themselves as their people's tragedy and suffering. On the other hand, the Jew who sees the Holocaust as paradigm in the drama of evil, who yearns to demonstrate a *Tikkun*, a moral turn for the world in it, who universalizes the terror and suffering, and who attempts to redeem an affinity of meanings for all mankind, is one who escapes victimization into martyrdom. To convert oneself into an abstract universal, on any level, is not a welcome fate, nor is it pleasant to play a role in the mythic metaphysics of other peoples.

If redemptive meaning is to be found in the Holocaust, let it be mundanely ethical (and political) and sternly secular. It is better to renounce sacrifice and the burden of salvation, though the victims have a statement to make and will have their "say." The first obligation for those who interpret their message is to point degradation and humiliation where it belongs—to the inflicter of it. The second is to restore dignity to the tormented, when that torment was the result of a true, unquestioned, and universal evil. That is why the spirit of the best texts on the Holocaust includes more than mourning, maintains the "peculiar dignity" reflected in the words of Chaim Kaplan, Emmanuel Ringelblum, Etty Hillesum, Primo Levi, and Jean Améry. Améry rose to the point when he wrote something for the civilized consciousness of the future:

I don't know if the person who is beaten by the police loses human dignity. Yet I am certain that with the very first blow . . . he loses something we will perhaps temporarily call "trust in the world . . . the certainty that by reason of written or unwritten social contracts the other person will spare me—more precisely stated, that he will respect my physical, and with it also, my metaphysical, being.[42]

What was lost might be regained, as "trust in the world" is redefined in the terrible clarity of the Holocaust.

III
The Survival of Judgment

These many years after the Holocaust the compulsion of interest still moves toward the testimony of survivors, many who are reaching their allotted span of life. Since I wrote the initial draft of this chapter and the two following, two books have appeared which have marked pertinence to the present discussion. *Holocaust Testimonies,* by Lawrence Langer, is a study of the reports of survivor victims; in dramatic apposition, *Ordinary Men* by Christopher Browning obtains testimony from a group of rank-and-file German soldiers assigned to the killing "actions" against Jews. The books give a rare opportunity to contrast the moral consciousness of killers and their victims, which is substance of strong relevance to the large questions of "meaning." The following review and commentary is then in the nature of an extended footnote which sharpens my theme and correlates with the final two chapters of my text.

•

Ordinary Men is a detailed report on the wartime activities of a unit of the German Order Police, the men of Reserve Police Battalion 101.[43] The record was based on interrogations and a very limited attempt at prosecution which took place in Germany in the years 1962–72, at least twenty years after the events. Most of the battalion personnel were average recruits from Hamburg, considered too old for the army and drafted into the Order Police. Such units were known as occupation security forces and eventually came into the chain of command controlled by Himmler, but they are to be distinguished sharply from the more professional killers especially trained as the *Einsatzgruppen,* units of the SS which operated closer to the front in Russia. As Browning stresses, only about a quarter of the men were Nazi party members, only two of the officers were SS, the average age was thirty-nine, and most of the rank and file were average in every other aspect for lower-middle and working-class citizens of Hamburg.

These "ordinary men" were assigned to the major transport activities which supported the death machines of the camps, but the focus of Browning's study is on their supplementary "actions" in rounding up and shooting Jews in the smaller towns and villages of Poland. In that direct role the men were each responsible for firing the bullets which killed people; they could see their victims die. That confrontation should have something to reveal. In their initial action the order was to shoot only the women, children, sick, and elderly, the men being rounded up for work camps. Browning observes that in twenty years of study, "never before had I seen the monstrous deeds of the Holocaust so starkly juxtaposed with the human faces of the killers" (xvi).

Yet, indispensable as the project was, Browning confesses frustration in his conclusions. The witness took place many years after; candid as many seemed to be, the men were facing the possibility of indictment, and whatever moral complexity of revulsion and guilt they felt at that time or later they were not likely to pursue it. They were opportune witnesses, however, because their commanding officer made the unusual move of allowing those who wished to do so to "step out" of the first action. A few did, and perhaps 20% claimed to have tried to evade full participation one way or another. Eventually the men were no longer given "the burden of choice," which made their conformity with orders much easier, and almost uniform.

The point carefully made is that evading the actions was not difficult and did not receive direct or indirect punishment. The interest then lies in their subjective responses as these can be gathered from the interrogations of the men of Battalion 101. Major Trapp himself was heard by his men to say "Man . . . such jobs don't suit me. But orders are orders."[44] Other comments were equally fragmentary and unenlightening in describing either evasion or performance, as in these examples:

"Presumably his nerves were not strong enough . . ."
"They did not feel up to it."
"[He] could not take it any longer."
"My nerves were totally finished."
"I suddenly felt nauseous."

Although Browning refers to the "shame and horror that pervaded the barracks" after the action, he also says, "By silent consensus . . . the Jozefow massacre was simply not discussed"; "The entire matter was a taboo" (69). One might have to choose between this statement and another, such as: "Truthfully I must say that at the time we didn't reflect about it at all" (72).

The chief source of pressure for the 80% or 90% who did not avoid the duty was that it meant admitting weakness and cowardice. One who evaded the action said, "They showered me with remarks such as 'shithead' and 'weakling' to express their disgust. But I suffered no consequences for my actions" (66). It was apparently more the fear of nonconformist behavior than the fear of authority which moved them. In any case, most of these, Browning later writes, denied they had any choice, despite Major Trapp's offer, which they claimed they did not hear or could not remember.

To define a conscience in such men in such circumstances apparently leads only to a stalemate. As Browning briefly notes, of those who did not shoot, none appealed then or later in interrogation to superior moral sanction. "They pleaded not that they were 'too good' but rather that they were 'too weak' to kill" (185). Those who did not shoot "only reaffirmed the 'macho' values of the majority—according to which it was a positive quality to be 'tough' enough to kill unarmed, noncombatant men, women, and children" (185).[45]

What finally challenges Browning's effort to find "a human face in the killers" is his own description of the "Jew hunt," a project conducted after the major part of the Jewish population had been killed, and designed to hunt down escaped Jews hiding in the countryside. There were always more than enough volunteers to join this project, and it caused no agonizing among the men. As Browning accurately points out, "The 'Jew hunt' is a psychologically important key to the mentality of the perpetrators." It was not a brief episode.

It was a tenacious, remorseless, ongoing campaign in which the "hunters" tracked down and killed their "prey" in direct and personal confrontation. It was not a passing phase but an existential condition of constant readiness and intention to kill every last Jew who could be found. (132)

That is where all analogies in the history of wartime atrocities begin to disappear, and where an effort to bring perpetrators and victims together on some level of moral intercourse seems impossible. Certainly the traumatic attack on moral consciousness reported by the victims seems to have no correspondence with anything on the other side. Perhaps that is a source for the deep spiritual disturbance voiced by most of the interviewed survivors in Langer's book.

•

Holocaust Testimonies enters as much as possible into the conscious witness of actual victims and survivors, who like Browning's subjects give their testimony long after the war experience.[46] Browning's treatment is soberly factual to a fault, much preoccupied with details of the several "actions" involving the Police Battalion, probing the actual testimony by the soldiers and officers, and offering a minimum of interpretation himself. Langer's book is richer in interpretation, again to a fault in the sense that he finds himself overly focused on the painful inner debate of survivors on the subject of their own "guilt," problematic as that could be at the extreme margin of survival. In the context of Auschwitz, to survive was to feel guilty, for survival was or seemed to be on the terms of deadly naturalist struggle.

In that respect, the two books move in contrary directions. In Browning's book, the soldiers do not face moral engagement and seem only to emphasize physical revulsion from the task as something horribly unpleasant before it settled into normal routine. The victims, on the other hand, describe such wounding shock in their moral natures, both in terms of what was done to them and in terms of their own passive, unheroic, and sometimes degrading responses, that their feelings of guilt encompass history, the world, the species—an actual moral apocalypse. The contrast with the testimony of Etty Hillesum and others who were not survivors— Ringelblum and Chaim Kaplan, for example—is striking.

The gist of much of the testimony is to recite how they had been brought down from human status and how the "human" itself had become equivocal and hypothetical, an illusion superimposed on unredeemed incoherent reality. What is sharply evident in both Browning's and Langer's reports is the loss of the sense of agency—as if both killers and victims had been caught in an overwhelming stream of natural force where the idea of responsibility had little relevance. In accepting what finally became a routine duty, the men, with the exception of a few sadists, had become the instruments of an order absolute in power but unintelligible in meaning. If some monster genius had the power to assign respective duties in a monstrous contest, it would be, "You, the Germans, your duty is to kill Jews," and you Jews, "Your duty is to survive." The victims in Langer's report, in a system otherwise without reason or value, clung to the instinct of survival as their own narrow principle of order. The phrase "choiceless choice" or valueless choice, which Langer assigns to the victims' sense of their condition, might with some important modification be also given to Browning's "killers" insofar as we credit their report.

The major difference, however, is that in retrospect Langer's subjects were able to judge the state to which they had descended, whereas Browning's "ordinary" men seemed still confined in the psychological discipline of their task. In that respect, Browning's study, while valuable for the factual record, is frustrated before the important questions in this discussion. Langer's subjects, however, exist and report from the very center of those questions.

•

The major theme of Langer's book is to pose a dualism which is simply illustrated by the distinction the victims feel between the "Auschwitz self" and their socialized identities preceding and following Auschwitz. They are deeply conscious of their "normal" selves, featuring marriages, children, jobs, careers, status with friends and family, everything composing the acceptable human order, and conscious simultaneously of the Auschwitz person who appears like a mocking ghost to stress the unreality of the "normal." "It is clear," Langer writes,

from the struggle of many witnesses . . . that they inhabit two worlds simultaneously: the one of "choiceless choice" *then;* the other of moral evaluation *now.* Harmony and integration are not only impossible—they are not even desirable. (82)

The duality so described is derived from the attempt to judge or evaluate the behavior of victims who had been torn from what Jean Améry called "moral reality," *our* world of later witness.

Langer writes, "It is virtually useless, as we soon discover, to approach the [Holocaust] experience from the reservoir of normal values, armed with questions like 'Why didn't they resist?' And 'why didn't they help one another?' (20) Langer acknowledges that many of course did. But that is not the point, and, as he says, the questions are misdirected. The victims had been brought to the level where such basic questions had no meaning, could not be answered in a space narrowed to include only the next piece of bread, the next doomed illness, the next roll call of death at a selection. The Holocaust proved, if it could prove anything, that it is possible to bring people into what Alvin H. Rosenfeld called "a double dying"—two deaths, the first more miserable than the last.[47] The fair observer must assume that the "Auschwitz self" was only one step away from the walking dead called "Musulmen."

They saw themselves as people translated out of their moral space, as in old tale the evil magician or a vengeful god could translate men into beasts. The interviewed survivors found themselves in fact waiting impatiently for the old and the sick to die in order to gain life for themselves, engaging in some instances in cannibalism which became a metaphor for their condition—and in the end feeling, whether in slight or significant truth, that their survival was somehow contingent on the deaths of many others. This is what Etty Hillesum sensed coming into the transition camp at

Westerbork, where she could still write in the plenitude of her moral sensibility. We have no report, of course, for her final ordeal at Auschwitz.

However, if there was a "crime against humanity," where does judgment arise and where does it apply? Langer, as I've said, writes freely in interpretation, as he should, but some of his judgments and perhaps his chief thesis are subject to misunderstanding. He speaks of "the requirement to suspend judgment, to revise our notion of the 'good.'" (26). We may suspend judgment of the victims surely, but must ask how an event that reached the climax of evil can be allowed to affect, that is, change, a definition of "the good." Whom do we judge? We judge the Nazis, not their victims, and judging them we use the standards the victims in Langer's book felt had deserted and betrayed them, we use a "reservoir of values," such as they may be or have become. One must pause therefore before the statement that "most of their [the survivors'] stories nurture not ethical insight but confusion, doubt, and moral uncertainty." Thus the Holocaust acted in its dreadful excavation of the grounds of judgment. In his interpretation of their report, Langer's witnesses corroborate those who welcome silence against the mediation of an ineffable horror: "One effect of common memory, with its talk of normalcy amid chaos, is to mediate atrocity, to reassure us that in spite of the ordeal some human bonds were inviolable" (9). But again one wishes to protest, atrocity is what it is *through* judgment, an inevitable and desirable mediation, and to cite human bonds is not to say that they are or were inviolable. To imply that only transcendent heroism in the extreme case could give validity to human bonds is to do humanity an injustice.

In distinguishing between the oral testimony he treats and written narratives, Langer observes that the oral offers a less self-consciously *represented* reality. He may be expressing here poststructuralist thinking, where, supposedly, mediations of form and closure construct meanings which instead of illuminating actual experience block access to it. This reflects a sharp paradox produced by Jean-Francois Lyotard: "It [the Holocaust] cannot be represented without being missed, being forgotten anew, since it defies images and words."[48] Langer writes that in a consecutive chronicle, "survivors who record their accounts unavoidably introduce some kind of teleology, investing the incidents with a meaning, be it nothing more than the value of regaining one's freedom" (40). Respecting the immensity of the event and one's incapacity confronting it, surely one must resist the stalemate of judgment. Langer's interpretation of survivor testimony brings to sharp focus the problematics of meaning I discuss at length in the chapter following. Meanwhile, one might pose the question: If Auschwitz destroyed the possibility of "meaning" and contradicted all moral history and theory, what are we to do with its memory?

Langer gains assent in speaking against salvationary treatments of the Holocaust, some going so far as to offer false martyrdom to the victims. He writes,

Unlike the Passover ritual, which gives Jews an opportunity to celebrate and com-memorate their liberation from bondage . . . the ordeal of former victims is an-chored firmly, via anguished memory, in its own historical reality, and nothing more. They cannot link their near destruction to a transcendent or redemptive fu-ture. (48)

"What future can such knowledge possibly serve?" Langer refers slight-ingly to "outmoded opinions of culture" (81).

The revelations of humiliated memory [in victims of the Holocaust] exhibit a "lower disunity" that has nothing to do with culture; we gain access to it only by suspending temporarily all values associated with that increasingly dim ideal. (82)

In the tragic sense, this is as true as death is certain. Primo Levi, with the best of witness credentials, wrote, "In the face of death, in the habit of death, the frontier between culture and lack of culture disappeared."[49] But should we now, in public witness, take on the "habit of death?" In any case, one may surely correct Langer's formulation; the Holocaust, that "lower disunity," has everything to do with culture, for unless all explanations are pointless, it arose from within culture and aimed for its self-destruction.

The "deep memory" of the survivors emphasized in Langer's report re-call, as I've said, the condition of the Musulmen. It is possible that ethical insight could never reach the terminal Musulman or clarify his own state to himself. But for those we call secondary survivors—those lucky to know the Holocaust only by report but necessarily committed to the future— the image of the Musulmen brings almost more light than we can bear, and "culture" is not a "dim ideal," it becomes a blazing passion. In fact, everything at last in Langer's text of witness moves away from the defeat of sensibility *toward* a hidden imperative, the unsatisfied conscience in search of ethical insight.

To this point I quoted some words from another survivor, Pelagia Lew-inska, who found herself fighting against destruction:[50]

But from the instant I grasped the motivating principle [to reduce her humanity] . . . it was as if I had been awakened from a dream. I felt under orders to live. . . . And if I did die in Auschwitz it would be as a human being . . . I was not going to become the contemptible, disgusting brute my enemy wished me to be. . . . And a terrible struggle began which went on day and night.[51]

What we witness in the testimony of survivors is a continuation of that terrible struggle. Langer writes of "the contradiction we still wrestle with nearly half a century after the event" (121). He concludes that "the Holocaust does little to confirm theories of moral reality but much to question the reality of moral theories" (198). This is in truth what he calls the "unreconciled understanding" of the Holocaust. If the road to a moral nihilism is left open in Langer's text, it is induced, I believe, from an honorable scruple against judging victim behavior on the heroicizing standard that seeks general redemption from the Holocaust disaster. Against behavior, moral theories are always questionable, but moral reality, the presence of moral issues in real experience, is not. Langer makes clear in his focus on victims how they were forced *outside* "moral reality." The only revision needed is the understanding that people *can* be forced outside it, but it was a "reality" from which they were excluded and not a "dim ideal."

Jean Améry had his own valuable understanding of "moral reality," and it should be brought into view if the issue is its disappearance within the violent reality of the camps and the Nazi regime. The eventual suicides of both Améry and Primo Levi may have been surrenders to what Langer calls "deep memory" and the "Auschwitz self." That is unprovable speculation (Levi himself set a precedent for it in discussing Améry's death), but both lived as if the contest for moral survival continued.

Améry in his testimony wrote that "the revolt against reality . . . is rational only as long as it is moral." He was speaking of resistance to Auschwitz in all its aspects, the action of the perpetrators, the effects on victims. He spoke for the dead and for survivors—". . . in the midst of the world's silence, our resentment holds its finger raised"—in order that "history become moral."[52]

This is an apt text to compare with the moral uncertainty and doubt nurtured by the witness narratives, at least as Langer interprets them. Améry's answer could not speak for everyone in the camps, that is certain, but memory in his case could add one response, a determination that "history become moral." What then was the object of his "resentment" and his resistance? He cites with perfect clarity the alternative to "moral reality" offered by Auschwitz, which some among his camp mates had been educated to accept.[53]

The power structure of the SS state towered up before the prisoner monstrously and indomitably, a reality that could not be escaped and therefore finally seemed *reasonable*. No matter what his thinking may have been on the outside, in this sense here he became a Hegelian.[54]

Primo Levi considered that Améry had returned to Auschwitz reality at some fateful point before his death. In what may have been bad omen for his own future suicide, Levi remembered and found himself quoting the still "unreconciled understanding" in Améry's own words:

Anyone who has been tortured remains tortured. . . . Anyone who has suffered torture never again will be able to be at ease in the world, the abomination of the annihilation is never extinguished. Faith in humanity, already cracked by the first slap in the face, then demolished by torture, is never acquired again.[55]

These men leave us with the question, and it goes to the heart of the ethical discourse that is our legacy from the Holocaust. When Levi asked himself why he wrote in memory's witness, he said he spoke for those who didn't survive. "We speak in their stead, by proxy." And of his own need to write, he said he saw in it

an atavistic anguish whose echo one hears in the second verse of Genesis: the anguish inscribed in everyone of the "tohu-bohu" of a deserted and empty universe crushed under the spirit of God but from which the spirit of man is absent: not yet born or already extinguished.[56]

This does not have the sound of Améry's resentment that would make "history become moral," but it makes the same appeal from the grave against an "empty universe" and for a "reality" of a different "reasonableness."

7

Redemption and the Life of Meaning

"Who will immortalize our troubles?"
Chaim Kaplan

I

Even today and more than yesterday, all who write about the Holocaust (and those who read) face, as in the title of a recent collection of essays on the subject, "unanswered questions." They may be unanswerable. Alternatively, the efforts at description can become morbidly obsessed and efforts at judgment morally trite or esoteric. Hannah Arendt accomplished more than she wanted when she cursed the subject for its banality. But that is the root of one obsession, that evil should have become banal or, on the obverse side, so mysteriously inexplicable that to discuss it is a kind of sacrilege. And then there are those who would treat it as a seizure of mass insanity, limited to a people, a place and time, even something like a natural catastrophe that wiped out a fraction of the population. For these the impressive facts are statistical. But it can be as much an evasion to call it a part of universal human evil as to limit it to a pathological scene and time. An evil latent in all people? And ready to break out in the right circumstances? Either way we dismiss its particular relevance, its focus on our civilization and its values.

Perhaps the difficult way critics, philosophers, and fiction writers have taken with meanings in language, or the languages of meaning, has come from the sense of its failure or betrayal in events like the Holocaust. If reality is inaccessible, at least one can prove mastery of language, and it follows that we might let language replace "reality" and be content to live in a world of words. But the Holocaust is a truth—a presence of truth—that will not be replaced, even if it exists beyond the power of words. One might add, in full irony, that if "reality" is not accessible in language it will be made more fully accessible through blows. The Nazis themselves, prompted by the skeptical linguisticism of their own time, made the effort to reach beyond words with their ferocious strength. If nothing else, the Holocaust illustrated what it means to know the assault of power, with no

141

words to limit it or make it familiar, no categories to soften shock, and no principles by which to judge or understand it. It was a conscious strategy of Hitler's—he speaks of it—to stun his victims in advance, paralyzing all capacity to resist. It would be one of his "posthumous victories," as Emil Fackenheim says, if he continued to stun the mind.

Echoing Theodor Adorno's admonition, George Steiner writes,

> If totalitarian rule is so effective as to break all chances of denunciation, of satire, then let the poet cease—and let the scholar cease from editing the classics a few miles down the road from the death camp. Precisely because it is the signature of his humanity, . . . the word should have no natural life, no neutral sanctuary, in the places and season of bestiality. Silence is an alternative. . . . To speak of the unspeakable is to risk the survivance of language as creator and bearer of humane, rational truth.[1]

Jean-Francois Lyotard has a similar thought, though delving deeper into that which "lies outside reason." He writes in *Heidegger and the "jews"* that the effort to express the inexpressible Holocaust only results in what he calls "secondary repression," a way of forgetting the "forgotten" by pretending to remember it. Rather obscurely, with strong Freudian implications, he writes of efforts "to make us forget the crime by representing it":

> It cannot be represented without being missed, being forgotten anew, since it defies images and words. Representing "Auschwitz" in images and words is a way of making us forget this. I am not thinking here only of bad movies and widely distributed TV series. . . .
>
> It is to be feared that word representations (books, interviews) and thing representations (films, photographs) of the extermination of the Jews, and of "the jews," by the Nazis bring back the very thing against which they work unceasingly in the orbit of secondary repression instead of letting it remain forgotten, outside of any status, on the "inside." It is to be feared that, through representation, it turns into an "ordinary" repression. One will say, It was a great massacre, how horrible! Of course, there have been others, "even" in contemporary Europe (the crimes of Stalin). Finally, one will appeal to human rights, one cries out "never again" and that's it! It is taken care of.
>
> Humanism takes care of this adjustment because it is of the order of secondary repression. (of the "unconscious anxiety" in and of the Other) One cannot form an idea of a human being as value unless one projects one's misery to the outside as caused by causes that one only needs to get down to transforming.[2]

Lyotard speaks of the repressed "inside" as an unconditionable force [of nature perhaps], which, to use his paradoxical style, is best remembered as the "forgotten" rather than forgotten as remembered. In any case, he wants the dignity of the "primary repressed," whether a great evil or something else, rather than the trivializing reform of "human rights." I take up that challenge in the last chapter of this text. There is indeed a "signature of humanity" in language and thought that cannot be surrendered. The instinct for protecting the "Unspeakable" with silence may have something in common with the silence of the Jewish *Sonderkommandos* on the train platforms of Auschwitz, and also the silence of media and diplomats and politicians in the face of the early news of the Holocaust. There were so many reasons for silence, but aren't they all shameful before, during, and after the fact? Silence suits only death itself, and even the clumsiest, most inept efforts to speak, tainted with "*kitsch*," have more worth. As for "human rights," however we express them, the Holocaust draws them to their absolute value.

•

Some have said we have had enough of mourning and reproach. Grief becomes piety, tragedy becomes sentiment. But it is not that sentimentality, or "*kitsch*" rhetoric, "*kitsch*" memorials, have exaggerated response. Rather they understate on all levels—factual, emotional, intellectual. Thus we welcome the factual sobriety of Raul Hilberg or Isaiah Trunk, and the dignified simplicity of Primo Levi. Mourning and complaint, the endlessly invoked guilt, the reproach never ceasing can seem to take the form of moral blackmail. To accuse guilt in the oppressor has proven its effectiveness on many fronts as a modern political weapon. But that is beside the point here. A valid study of the Holocaust pulls one to a disinterested level of judgment, or rather to where the interest has to be universal and beyond partisanship. On that level no one is immune from judgment, nor can distant relatives or descendants of victims claim meaningful compensation. The reproach in great crimes comes to all witnesses as well as agents and victims, and if there is a moral form of redemption, it is not discriminatory among groups or individuals.

The victims themselves were not martyrs and they were not heroes. There were a few desperate and hopeless struggles, as at the Warsaw Ghetto uprising, but in its traditional sense heroism has no relevance, not in dying and even less in surviving. Death was real, ugly, and incredibly wholesale in number; the suffering was real and exhausts the ability of the imagination to have a share in it. And yet though the event surpasses myth and defeats narrative, every premise of civilized existence remains on trial before it.

The Nazi German Holocaust enacted the apocalypse for victims, perpetrators, and witnesses, for those who knew what was happening, for those who did not want to know, for those who kept silent, for the churches, the media, the statesmen,the armies, for the *realpolitik* pragmatists, the ideologues and party loyalists, the scientists and philosophers in their distant abstractions, for artists and writers in their solipsist circle, and for the neutral readers of newspapers and the listeners to gossip who receive every experience but that of immediate and personal moral response. For all these it was the moral apocalypse, which takes place in a world were judgment is dead, where life has only the narrowness of pulse and breath, and where each person defends his bread and his shelter with teeth and with claws. It ends in the camps with those gray withered people who stopped feeling hunger, fear, pain, and slipped imperceptibly from their coma of life into the coma of death. But they are only the visible images of that absence of witness which afflicted the world of the Holocaust. It was a pause in civilization, a blank moment of animal fear, animal violence, and then a void of meaning that can only be grasped by one who still lives at the border of a human memory.

•

During the Holocaust, at the pit of its cruelty, Chaim Kaplan wrote this: "A simple old woman asks me each day, Why is the world silent? Does Israel have no God?"[3] That first question remains to be answered. And because the second expects no answer, the weight of the first becomes greater on the world's conscience. There is no lack of words in their absurd deficiency, and yet the question remains and propels language. The most sensitive observers still envy silence even as they write. Arthur Cohen placed the dilemma.

I cannot make the *tremendum* of the Jews so distinctive that nothing can be said of it. Language requires some measure of similitude, some *analogia*. . . .
    If we stand on the contention that thought is essentially incapable of compassing the "*tremendum*," that it must fall silent and dumb before its monstrousness, there are additional consequences. . . . The first and most pressing is that the past that pressed against us before the *tremendum* is annihilated . . . and if, as is signaled by our language, *tremendum* means historical immensity for which there is neither a satisfactory analogue nor historical model, the history of the past becomes irrelevant.[4]

This is characteristic; a weight rests against language almost impossible to support, yet charging it with unlimited seriousness. The apology for speech contrasts with those who kept a record and thought their witness a sacred obligation. Chaim Kaplan had this to say for his diary's message to a later world, our world. "Anyone who keeps such a record endangers his life, but this does not frighten me. I sense within me the magnitude of this hour, and my responsibility toward it, and I have an inner awareness that I am fulfilling a national obligation, an historic obligation that I am not free to relinquish."[5]

That urging of testimony is universal in the documents left by the victims. The legacy has given us a massive, still growing literature. The act of witness has been brought so far as to become an act of redemption. On a plaque before the entrance to Yad Vashem in Jerusalem, the words of Baal Shem Tov are inscribed: "Redemption lies in Remembering." Elie Wiesel, the most widely appreciated of all memorialists, forecast his life work in this way: "That boy [himself—at the margin of death] was convinced later that were he to survive, he would tell the tale; he was convinced that if he would tell the tale history would be redeemed."[6]

There is a trace of this spirit of the apocalyptic Messiah in all who write about the Holocaust, though frequently accompanied by the sense of facing the same wall of silence the victims faced. Those of us who are not survivors but claim spiritual membership in survival are compelled to write. Under compulsion we "write" as though to replace the verb in Paul Celan's verse from "*Die Niemandsrose*": "O you dig and I dig, and I dig towards you." The whole poem, well known as it is, should rise into consciousness at all those moments when the urge to silence intersects with the command to speak.

> THERE WAS EARTH INSIDE THEM, and
> they dug.
>
> They dug and they dug, so their day
> went by for them, their night. And they did not praise God,
> who, so they heard, wanted all this,
> who, so they heard, knew all this.
>
> They dug and heard nothing more,
> they did not grow wise, invented no song,
> thought up for themselves no language.
> They dug.
>
> There came a stillness, and there came a storm,
> and all the oceans came.
> I dig, you dig, and the worm digs too,
> and that singing out there says: They dig.

O one, o none, o no one, o you:
Where did the way lead when it led nowhere?
O you dig and I dig, and I dig towards you,
and on our finger the ring awakes.[7]

What is most defeated is the urge to explain. The first and last question, "Why?" Why were they killed? remains perhaps forever out of reach. Raul Hilberg asked the question in surrender:

Why, why? I sometimes, though never answering the question myself, ask it, especially of Germans—. I never get an answer at all. It seems as though here is an entire nation that is utterly incapable, despite the fact that there are still eighty million Germans on this earth, of explaining its own action. . . . This is a problem beyond rationality and irrationality; it is useless to ask what they got out of it. It's useless even to ask what impelled them. I heard the word this past month from one very articulate German, "*Ein Rausch,* something that just took hold. It's almost untranslatable." He says he believes the two attacks on the Soviet Union and the Jews "sprang from the same source beyond rationality, for its [sic] own sake, for the experience of it, for the making of this history.[8]

We have here the human case, the subjective case of violence. You cannot supply historical circumstance very convincingly to explanations of the Holocaust. The long history of anti-Semitism does not really lead to it, or all the way to it. You cannot cite threat to the Germans or group rivalry with Jews. There was no doubt a tremendous superstition; hatred created its own myths, attributing to the Jews all misfortunes and frustrations, all evils, ranging from capitalist exploitation to revolutionary subversion, from moral license and degeneracy to ancient moral prohibition, begun presumably at Sinai. Hitler could put himself into or out of this madness as if by will. Once he said that race hatred and conflict was his choice to rival the class hatred of the Bolsheviks. And he once said that if the Jews did not exist he would have to invent them.

Joachim Fest and Alan Bullock describe Hitler, particularly in the war years, as occupied only by the dynamism of battle, driven forward without any intelligible goal or anticipated achievement except the survival of his power. In the end it was not clear whether he wanted his German soldiers to kill Russians, or the Russians to kill Germans, or the Germans to kill themselves, so long as all was laid waste. Thus the victim Jews could not see the point when they searched for the *reasons* for the Holocaust slaughter. How could such hatred exist and what could have aroused it? They could not see that they were the convenient objects of destruction; in their powerlessness they invited the action of pure power and could provoke the apocalypse.

The dead cannot judge; they do not state or decide. Their silence contains eternal possibilities that we must imagine and understand. Certainly the dead are an audience to any accounting of their deaths. But though the dead do not give lessons, it is still a duty of the living to reclaim meaning; the value in survival or further life is in meaning. The issue is this, How shall the dead be remembered and by whom? For the Nazi killers who survived punishment they were a living corruption who poisoned the world, were Bolsheviks, spies, capitalist swindlers, and were a life threat even to the youngest and oldest among Germans. To repeat such a list is grotesque, and it is for this the dead are silent, in the face of political "reasons" that were like the babble of thieves and murderers over their bodies.

•

Tikkun, a mending of the world, is Emil Fackenheim's own theme of religious meditation on the Holocaust. He talks about a new Good Friday, though one without its Easter. "Only through self-exposure to the horror can Christian faith and thought preserve their integrity—and hope to be astonished anew by its old Good News. In our time, this old-new News is not that all is well, that nothing has happened, that now as before, it is Good Friday after Easter. It is rather that . . . a terrible new Good Friday was every day overwhelming the old Easter." He goes on to say, as if to cover his ground against degrading pieties, that "there could be no thought of using (or, which in this case is the same thing, abusing) the Holocaust for any kind of Jewish-Christian debate, one about redemption included." In fact, he speaks for many when he writes, "The attempt to justify the Holocaust as an evil means to any good, however glorious, would be blasphemous—and is impossible."⁹

Fackenheim's thought is complex and ambivalent if not inconsistent on the subject of *Tikkun.* He implies that the story of Job is a better pattern than St. Matthew. If there is to be a "mending of the world," there must first be a rejection of Job's comforters, a denial beforehand of all spurious talk of redemption which erases the horror and forgives the guilt. Justification is not what the dead in memory want, no closure with an Easter rebirth, no religious fantasies under the gas. If redemption is for humanity, what could possibly include those killers in their particular incarnation as Nazis? And what is, was, and will be the world in which they thrived.

The theologians are sorely troubled. Fackenheim refers to a German Christian theologian whose inconsistencies are typical and perfectly genuine. "Johann Baptist Metz has written that Auschwitz was 'the apotheosis of evil'; that anyone wanting to 'comprehend' it has 'comprehended nothing'; that a Christian theodicy in this sphere is 'blasphemy'; . . . [and yet] 'to listen to Jews as Jews not as victims' is a theological as well as a human necessity, since 'by Auschwitz everything is to be measured.' "[10]

There could be assent to "by Auschwitz everything is to be measured," but what does that mean in the face of the silence hanging over the camps? So Fackenheim positions himself in writing of the necessity for *Tikkun,* a mending for Christians and Jews and seculars.

It is [as] unthinkable [that ages of good will and faith should be broken apart as] that the age-old fidelity of the religious Jews, having persisted through countless persecutions and against impossible odds . . . should be destroyed forever. It is unthinkable that the far less ancient, no less noble fidelity of the secular Jew—he holds fast not to God, but to the "divine spark in man"—should be smashed beyond repair. . . . It is this unthinkability that caused in my own mind, on first confronting it, the perception of a "614th commandment," or a "commanding Voice of Auschwitz," forbidding the post-Holocaust Jew to give Hitler post-humous victories.[11]

One such victory would be to place its comprehensibility beyond reach, which would be the same as to nullify it according to a Hitlerian nihilism.

Fackenheim presses his question to the limit. The Holocaust must offer the spiritual search of a *Tikkun* to philosophy and Christianity as well as to Jews and Judaism.

Were it not for the Jewish *Tikkun* then and there—and that of quasi- and honorary Jews [of those non-Jews suffering in the camps] . . . all authentic future philosophers and Christians would be sick with a permanent fear—in this case, the fear that, were they then and there rather than here and now, they, their prayers, their philosophical thoughts, would all be indiscriminately prey to the Nazi logic of destruction. This is what was meant . . . by the above assertion that the Jewish *Tikkun* in the Holocaust world is not only enormous in significance but world-historical.[12]

He is saying, as I understand, that the mending of the Jews (which might be particularistic with the rebirth of Israel, and the survival of specifically Jewish life), entails the mending of both philosophy and Christianity on their own terms. What quintessential value or sense of value could it be that bridges all faiths and communities and threatened all in the Holocaust?

"Yet philosophers and Christians today and tomorrow . . . are reached by a blessing across the abyss, coming to them from the darkest Jewish night. It is a blessing the like of which the world has never seen." [13] One can understand how the Holocaust can arouse the passionate desire for a miracle of salvation. But what is this blessing for the whole world? How can the Holocaust be revelation and miracle in any world other than that of the Jews? Typically, the majority of Jews might want to keep what salvation there is in it for themselves. They are not jealous for martyrdom. But as a redemptive event the Holocaust might mean the end or drastic weakening of anti-Semitism, or at least give it a bad conscience. That would be something if it remained true, even if the revelation was only that of remorse. To suffer guilt would be a natural and just punishment. And meanwhile the world might benefit by the legacy of conscience.

One welcomes the forms of partial redemption, the founding of Israel for instance, if that were the only good consequence of the Holocaust. After all, the victims had only one collective thought during the height of the slaughter, that a remnant should survive, and a refuge be found. One welcomes the effort of Christian churchmen, the Catholics particularly, to revise their doctrine to modulate its implicit or explicit anti-Semitism. And yet the ultimate level we seek is an understanding of the Holocaust in the interest confronting all people, all societies, on the terms of every relationship between governments and individuals, between nations, races, classes, and ideologies. Only this would be a blessing from the "dark Jewish night."

•

It seems vainglorious and a spiritual mockery to think of the Holocaust as the founding event of a new religion based on guilt and sacrifice. Fackenheim and other Jews of faith may ask for *Tikkun*, a mending of the world; they may pray for it, but for now and for long the imaginable God of any religion must remain shocked into silence. He must obey the silence of the churches during the Holocaust, and even the passive and active participation of those of the religious congregations of Europe who performed the Nazi will. If there is a God, He must say, do not ask redemption from Me, ask that you become human first, that you speak languages, build cities, found families and a true civilization on its true basis. But since politics has provided the strongest mass religious experiences of the twentieth century, perhaps there is a political salvation available that purges those political cults that fathered the Holocaust. It may have to speak in the negative, in proscription of a very violent and obvious evil, just as basic Judaic-Christian doctrine began with proscription. The Holocaust may function in memory as if it were the original sin of politics as well as the culminating catastrophe. Hitler brought the apocalypse, he preached the earth's destruction and the death of man. He promised hell and brought it to the world, and all were saved from him, the anti-Christ, and not just the Jewish remnant. But then, Is there inspiration in the death of millions under the utmost of sordid conditions? Is there a martyrdom that teaches through shame? And do our political allegiances, strategies, conflicts, and theories of conflict show any true signs of being "saved"? There is an embarrassment in the Holocaust, an embarrassment on behalf of man so great that an endless future might be spent in redeeming human self-respect. But that may be a basis for vows and atonement in the political sphere at least.

Christianity founded itself upon the image of a brutal death. At its inception it was a religion based as much upon dread as upon God's love. But such is the moral dialectic; we imagine brotherhood in the presence of overbearing images of violence. We want the Holocaust to bear within its overpowering shade of horror the catharsis of tragedy. We want the Holocaust to transform shame, precisely the shame the Nazi executioners meant to impose, the shame of animal death under the gaze of indifference.

•

The literature of the Holocaust has been dominated by demands for meaning as if the world faces an eternal day of judgment focusing on a new, more drastic version of "original sin," a second fall of man. Necessarily much of this writing is portentous and obscure in its rhetoric. Some of it is cryptically to the point and unforgettable, the work of Levi and Améry as example. When Theodor Adorno administered the death of poetry after Auschwitz, presumably he meant that writing poetry required minimally positive assumptions on behalf of its audience and its subjects in this world.[14] For instance, one might imagine Anne Frank writing her *Diary* with the expectation that victorious Germans and their collaborators would supply her chief audience after the war, or that her text would rest in that museum of Judaica planned by Nazi cultural authorities. Her stunned fear and blocked pen, Adorno might be suggesting, would now afflict all poetry.

Emil Fackenheim was explicit on that doomsday where "all authentic future philosophers and Christians would be sick with a permanent fear." It is natural for religious thinkers like Fackenheim and Cohen to view the

Holocaust in the pattern of the world's fall in the age of Noah and that of Sodom, and to seek redemption. But the same awe of a climactic event, of a turning point in the world's moral history, is exhibited by historians and general commentators. One German writer's view is succinct in proposing that the Holocaust can be seen as "nothing less than a moral equivalent of the Copernican revolution." [15]

The Copernican image is apt for an event that saw the moral dimensions of judgment destroyed. "The most frightening aspect of our present world is not the horrors in themselves, the atrocities, the technological exterminations, but the fact at the very root of it all; the fading away of any human criteria." [16] This is the impression that lasts far past the shock of the first news of the camps. But why should so many thinkers and memorialists have this thought so long after the event? And doesn't that supply an added urgency to still more consideration? One of the most prominent and active of German historians in the recent debate over Holocaust guilt, responsibility, and reparation, Ernst Nolte, wrote that, unlike other epochs and their disasters, the Nazi past does not fade. It "seems to become more alive and powerful, not as model but as specter, as a past that is establishing itself as a present, as a sword of judgment hung over the present." [17] Nolte, like many Germans, may be making a restrained protest, but the condition is exact, and, as a sword, judgment still harshly demands interpretation of past and present meanings of the Holocaust. [18]

Judgment, however, seems either obvious or impossible. This appears to have been the case at a recent conference entitled "Writing and the Holocaust," held at the State University of New York at Albany, April 5–7, 1987. The speakers were almost all American Jewish writers and historians, some with distinguished careers spent in attempting what they now declared beyond reach. The audience heard in closing sessions some strong words of disillusionment, expressed, one can say, in the context of large claims for a "Copernican revolution" in the morality of states and nations. And as if arguing with anguished theologians, some of the participants explicitly rejected the role of martyrdom given to the victims.

Cynthia Ozick made a blunt case which remains challenging: "For me, the Holocaust means one thing and one thing only: the destruction of one-third of the world's Jewish population. I do not see a 'redeeming meaning' in a catastrophe of such unholy magnitude." The search for it is obfuscating, indulges in "opacity and mystification," and she doesn't want mystification, but the facts, the events which are brutally hard and clear. "In thinking about the Holocaust we have to take into ourselves a different possibility, an alien thesis, one that we have never been taught . . . that goes against the moral grain." It was the expression of a radical nihilism and can breed only nihilism in its effects, she says. ". . . it leaves us, like Lear, unaccommodated . . . like Lear, it leaves us howling on the heath." She concludes: "What we have been trying to do in this conference, I think, is to bring a moral umbra to that which cannot sustain or maintain or contain a moral umbra." [19]

In particular, what is being rejected is the language of redemption which implies a kind of safeguarding transcendence, a surmounting of utter horror and evil, and an effort to include the criminals themselves in the redemptive benefit, all mankind sharing the crime and the salvation from it.

Apocalyptic events lead toward hope or its opposite, and it is most difficult, knowing fully its action and style embedded in nihilism, to make the Holocaust promise a "mending of mankind" on any level, practical or spiritual. A most respected literary and cultural critic and consistent political moralist, Irving Howe, expressed himself as follows. Somehow in all the talk of the "incomprehensible," he said, there remains a disappointment, a sense of major failure, that "even the most dreadful event in history has brought little change in the thought of mankind." [20] "Exactly what it might mean to say that after the Holocaust consciousness has been transformed is very hard to say. . . . For good and bad, we remain the commonplace human stock, and whatever it is that we may do about the Holocaust we shall have to do with the worn historical consciousness received from mankind's past."

Howe quotes Primo Levi: "It is foolish to think that human justice can eradicate" the crimes of Auschwitz, and adds "Or that the human imagination can encompass and transfigure them." This is impressive witness, but it should be evident that Levi went further than most in encompassing the crime within a sensitive and imaginative conscience. Surely it is a mistake to set ourselves an impossible task and then call it a defeat of the moral imagination. To say that Nazi crimes have their source in the "commonplace human stock" cannot be allowed to subtract seriousness from "the most dreadful event in history."

There are really two problems here, in profound paradoxical linkage. One is that any talk of justice and redemption brings a form of adjustment to a crime that transcended all limits. It even implies a sort of forgiveness. The other, even more depressing, concludes mundanely that the Nazi crime was an expression of universal human nature. And between the banal and the unspeakable or incomprehensible, the moral imagination is caught stranded and helpless.

Howe ends his essay with some lines quoted from the work of the Israeli poet, Don Pagis, "Written in Pencil in the Sealed Freight Car":

> Here in this transport
> I Eve
> And Abel my son
> if you should see my older son
> Cain son of man
> tell him that I

Thus the poem ends, and Howe addresses it by saying "that sentence will never be completed." It is a virtue in poetry not to end a sentence with something grossly inadequate or inarticulate. But it is not a virtue in life, in our best prose. That message was written to us by someone interrupted in his speech and driven into silence. It was meant for us to complete as well as we can, or as a mystery nursed and carried away; we acknowledge, as Howe did, its violent and mortal interruption, but we do not give assent to it.

The record of the Albany Holocaust Conference, almost as if designed to end such conferences, leads to more acute disillusionment when authoritative historians like Raul Hilberg or Saul Friedlander agree with the conclusion that the search for meaning in the Holocaust is hopeless. Friedlander writes that "we return constantly to this issue, all the time looking for coherence, for closure, and even for a redemptive sense on the side of the victims. . . . There is no redemptive message in this at all. . . . But, even beyond that, to look for a meaning or a message on a more general level has failed whenever it has been attempted. I think we should try to face the fact that we have to live with this without following our natural tendency to find meaning."[21]

But can that search be repressed? Friedlander goes on to say that "strangely enough, over the last two or three years, this past [of the Holocaust] has come back into Israeli consciousness in the most vivid way, as it has almost everywhere else. There are today more books in Israel about the Shoah than about probably any event in Israel's history, certainly more than have been written about the creation of the State. Novels, theater pieces, discussions, . . . the whole issue is coming back."

If it is coming back, it must be because there is something irrepressible in the search for conscious understanding. Friedlander says, however, that the standpoint is different, and doing so he clarifies what the resistance to interpreted "meaning" may be. "There is no attempt to place it [the Shoah] within a framework of heroism in order to give it a meaning; there is no attempt, so far as I know, to identify it as part of a great historical interpretation." This he proposes should be a general resolution where "we can forgo the attempt to enclose the Shoah in our various worldviews." It is difficult to disagree with this, and we know the abuse. But the thought needs only one reminder; the Holocaust took place under the auspices of a "worldview," a *Weltanschauung* of grandly inspiring proportions to its believers. This is a "meaning" that still has us by the throat and must be exorcised.

"Reconsider," Friedlander urges, "the hope of finding some redeeming aspect in it; . . . simply face it as it was, a catastrophe of absolutely untold magnitude." But that does not take away "meaning" but simply reduces it and puts it from moral consideration, on the level of planetary catastrophe, a great drought or flooding of a continent. And he says, as if to frustrate deepest feeling, that "the most difficult task we face" is "precisely not to look for redemption in these events." Of course, redemption can seem an anachronistic term, worse than fatuous and insensitive in the context of the Holocaust. But perhaps it needs translation, perhaps it means survival, a reemergence into a "moral reality" that we, as if we were in fact survivors, need and wish to inhabit.

One thinks of a hypothetical trial of Heydrich or Himmler for mass murder, on trial forever in the world's memory. Would they not be eager to include themselves as victims of this "meaningless" catastrophe? And the victims, could they be content with this judgment of their suffering? The cry for justice is always in some proportion redemptive, though it cannot reach the dead. It is *our* need, *our* passion, that will not be satisfied by talk of incoherence, the lack of closure, the lack of intelligible meaning that threatens the basis of conscience itself.

The despair of meaning is a true despair from which we need redemption. Irving Howe quotes Camus: "To talk of despair is to conquer it," and replies in brief irony, "Is it now?" He may miss Camus' point, I think. To recognize despair, or the annihilating act which causes despair, is in a basic sense to go beyond it. This is not a judgment that refers adequately to the debasement and subhumanity of those who accomplished the Holocaust, but it may meet our sense of what they almost achieved. It was nothing less than the death of meaning, as characterized in the words of Saul Fried-

lander, "the sense of total chaos and senselessness" which close study of
the Holocaust conveys. The catastrophe of absolute magnitude is the catastrophe of the world's moral destruction.

Cynthia Ozick, after arguing so strongly against the effort to find "redemptive meaning" in the Holocaust, admitted that she felt partly converted to another view (expressed in an essay by Norma Rosen) which she
calls "the universalizing sanctification of memory." And indeed Ozick
must recognize that to dispute "meaning" is to help destroy memory. She
goes further toward the possible meaning of "redemption" in this case.
"There *is* an appropriate universal 'use,' in her special sense, of the language of the Holocaust: as a way of sensitizing and enlarging us toward
mercifulness." [22]

"Mercifulness" comes too close to forgiveness, and forgiveness is not
the issue. The problem in Holocaust writing is to find a different mode,
not of reconciliation but of moral resolution and revival. It wasn't the lack
of mercy that horrifies us in the Nazis. Enlarging us, yes, sensitizing us,
yes, but toward what result? I would argue for a moral readiness that may
touch the basis for all human connectedness. Ozick suggests this herself
most meaningfully: "In theory, I'm with Theodor Adorno's famous dic-
tum: after Auschwitz, no more poetry. And yet, my writing has touched
on the Holocaust again and again. I cannot not write about it. . . . I am not
in favor of making fiction of the data, or of mythologizing or poeticising it
. . . [but] . . . I constantly violate this tenet: my brother's blood cries out
from the ground, and I am drawn and driven." The door remains open to
gross sentiment, gross simplification, "*kitsch*" of every kind, and personal
and political exploitation, but those of us who write, and will write, are
"drawn and driven."

II

It is obvious that Nazi anti-Semitism distinguishes itself sharply and shock-
ingly from the ancient trials and sufferings of Israel. Traditional religious
anti-Semitism wished to displace the separate revelation of the Jews, and
in the process make them members of the salvationary religious community. The Nazi prejudice was *against* assimilation rather than against the
self-chosen exceptionalism of the Jew. Christianity was ostensibly interested in saving *souls*. Political religions are more terrible in that they tend
to minimize the possibilities of conversion as opposed to elimination. With

no souls to save, and only racial biology and imperial power to believe in, the Holocaust could take place on its own terms of conclusive and merciless violence.

Religionists who attempt to find a traditional form of redemptive martyrdom in the Holocaust will not succeed, despite the recent engagement of Cardinal O'Connell of New York and the pope himself. If anything, it was a grand effort to *prove* the death of God, almost successful in the only way such efforts could be successful. In and for the Holocaust God *was* dead, but the closer and equivalent truth is that *Man* was moribund. The apocalypse came through the political religions or ideological myths of our time, and redemption, if there is one, must find its way through and beyond those same secular faiths or, rather, that quintessential faith put into question, a humanism of the species in full and rightful possession of the planet. The Holocaust renews moral insight because it achieves an absolute where we thought no absolute in judgment was possible. It defines the premise by which humans exist, a margin of self-identification beyond which they dare not pass.

No one can question a prohibition against genocide. The command is obvious, but the understanding behind it and the consequences that flow from it are not. The premise is positive, not negative, and defines a relationship which makes genocide the self-extinction of the species. The Nazis proclaimed a limited human community consisting of themselves, the Germans, and a few Nordic, so-called Aryan, groups. Their principle of exclusion has its denial in the solid, the deeply founded sense of a totally inclusive human identity. Tested in the massacres and wars of the twentieth century, this may have a personal resonance, a personal base of security as strong and stronger than traditional nationalism and group chauvinism of any sort. In other words, redemption, the *Tikkun* of our years, has a deeper meaning than the charity of grief or the salvation of judgment, and longer consequences than memorial archives and buildings can hold.

•

If one wishes to be militant in favor of a new secular form of charity, one should renounce in traditional Judaism and Christianity those elements of vengeance which associate with their central myths of martyrdom. The very idea of martyrdom entails revenge, even when it takes the form of a judging and punishing forgiveness. While recognizing firmly the distinction between a naturalistic political myth and essential Christianity, the mystery remains. How could Nazism so easily take over anti-Semitism, with its religious roots, and exploit it? Could a philosophic naturalism explain the willingness to kill young children?

There is absolute absurdity here in the word "sacrifice," in the invitation to martyrdom, well-meaning as it may be. There can be no bells, no rituals, no communion meals for the sad starved ghosts of Auschwitz. But there was a sacrifice, nonetheless, testamental, most meaningful, though without grace or glory. The task is to specify it, and, if we commune in that sacrifice, to what communion do we belong?

The issue cannot limit itself to that between Jews and their oppressors, or to the special nature of the so-called Jewish question. What in any view could have been that question, or problem, for which a "final solution" was needed?[23] What is it now? Nevertheless, the Nazis themselves specified the problem when they spoke of the Jews as subhumanity. In the first place, they did so in order to make their crimes possible for a vestigial human conscience. But second, and in major part, they confess they recognized that their crimes were indeed against humanity.

Their victims died mostly without resistance and were not aware of a sacrificial struggle. How link their fates to a moral cause? They were the purest of victims. And yet just because they represent images of life destroyed at the very margin of existential claims which construct a moral humanity, because they represent defeat in the world of unfreedom and inequality, they have become for us sacred images. We raise them in memory and in forecast of our own reduced condition—the biological subexistence that borders what we call the "human estate," our self-affirmation in the world. A man who has lost that claim on being cannot be an object of indifference, nor an object of shame, for he demands from us, in an otherwise empty world, our affirmation of that which he has lost. So we think of those reduced to impotent, mindless, and abject misery, because we recognize integral being in this context, not in heroism but in its opposite. Character, or the human identity, has a dual dimension; it is always known against the background of animal existence and the void.

•

Can the Holocaust be rightly named as Tragedy? The religious parallel exists before all in the revelation of moral commandment. The event, whether we use the word sacrifice or not, brings universal witness against evil. What are the tragic parallels? There is a suffering at the center which challenges all normal measure and judgment. But what was the flaw and the pride and who shared the roles of protagonists? The victims were so completely victims and the perpetrators (foreign as those words are to tragic meaning) so purely agents of destruction that the conclusion must be that here, at the Holocaust, humanity failed tragedy, failed it to a degree that perfectly defines the antitragic.

Nevertheless, those capable of witness have been brought to the level of tragic judgment. There was a culture that flung itself headlong into the embrace of history, believing in science and the instruction of new technology, accepting the gods of necessity and power, taking single passionate faith in nation and race, mastering the future in utopias of conquest. There was an egomaniac ruler whose only belief was in his will, personifying and inhabiting his claimed race. There was a naturalist creed which freely taught murder, because the serious sanction against murder was dead in God's own death. (Ancient tragedy always implicated the gods.) Beliefs in evolution and progress, and in the creative will of man who will forge a new world according to his liking, the rebellion against old restraints and taboos, and the amoralism of politics had taken monstrous form in the hubris of the cult of revolution. And power had become naked with the failure of elites to keep authority and rule with codes of honor and scruple. Above all, the attack was upon human honor, and so the tragic sensibility must answer. The Nazis killed without a code, without scruple, so that at the end, facing defeat, they kept only the will to destroy the world with their defeat. Therefore, tragic judgment, which transcends the void, must respond.

The Holocaust is the tragedy of modern civilization for whose catharsis of recognition we still strive. Basically, it is a tragedy which teaches from the edge of the abyss, but it is wrong to say that the Nazis were primitives, bringing the world down to their level. Rather they were leaders of a most highly civilized people at the peak of twentieth-century consciousness. Technology and a cult of science, nationalism, and a religion of race, the strongest belief in order and community as well as in physical and moral self-development, emancipation from superstition and repressive moral systems, the spirit of competition and victory, of gain and profit, an obsession with history and the evolutionary decline of species, a belief in the primacy of struggle and conflict as well as a typically reductive modern analysis of motives, a passion for racial honor and virtue founded purely on naturalistic premises—all these were the substance of German civilization in the fatal year of 1933.

There are theories of the Holocaust which deny tragedy, such as, for instance, that it was the product of madness, that it was moral sickness, the achievement of moral retardation, that it was a crime like other crimes but on a tremendous scale, that it was the product of contingent historic circumstance such as the suffering of Germans from depression, inflation, the Versailles treaty, Prussian militarism, Teutonic authoritarian discipline, and finally that it was the product of war spirit and necessities, a war atrocity among others, unplanned, unmotivated, a random desperate violence in the general field of apocalyptic violence.

To invoke tragedy is to see these "reasons" as out of scale for viewing the Holocaust; to speak of tragedy is to search for an instrument for weighing its seriousness. But it is not necessary to apportion tragic dignity to mass murderers on the measure of destruction that they reached. Nor is it necessary to awake the Musulmen victims from their stupor to another more heroic role. We think that the murderers were an outcropping of ourselves, we think that we who feel guilt are the protagonists who must be worthy of being protagonists in that history. And we are the victims. Unless we give back their dignity to the actual mortal victims, it is we of the human species who have lost it. We invoke tragedy in order to clarify the emotions we experience in the face of the Holocaust and purify the shame we feel and transform it.

•

Tragedy is never pure, and those who treat it as such create havoc. Hitler in his bunker was that kind of tragedian. Tragedy belongs to its contingent elements of character and conflict in real human lives. The stage for the Holocaust was politics, and it is there, in the ultimacies of conflict in war and racism, that the tragic inquisition of motives takes place.

There is war to condemn, total war, in its ruthless engagement with the whole world as the object of destruction. All sides participated in total war in that epoch of conflict and share its guilt; it is hardly needed to invoke Dresden and Hiroshima for that. But the specifics of war, that is, violence, demand a response deeper than a renunciation of war itself, defensive or offensive, or of imperial nationalism and chauvinism. The weight of moral resolution may fall upon racism, in all its range from petty snobbery to xenophobia to murderous fear and hatred on the scale of the Holocaust.

Racism is not the issue between the victim people and their persecutors and executioners. That issue and their confrontation belongs in some supernatural sphere where souls are judged in eternities of punishment. We, the survivors, are left with the mundane issues of survival, and racism is one of them.

If we look toward the future, racism has profoundly universalistic meaning. The antithesis of racism is not tolerance (that cheapened word), and it is not a prohibition against prejudice or hatred only. If we condemn racism with a full redemptive turn, it must be for something that racism specifically denies, something whose positive presence makes racism a great wrong. Do we need to ask for more than what seems rational or possible in relationships between strangers? One issue, of course, is the definition of the stranger. When does the man outside our immediate world cease to be the stranger? It seems that two major events, Hiroshima and the Holocaust, have determined that on this planet it must be that either all are strangers or none.

The need to take gratification from a group identity may be irrepressible. Racism (which I take as the inclusive word for the varieties of group chauvinism) is more intense and more dangerous than ordinary nationalism because it has no rational structure, no practical binding, and belongs with superstition and esoteric religion. But its emotional force is what is considered representative of group competition and conflict. Its latency is universal. But the issue is not that of refraining from racism. It is a question of making it impossible in the same emotional and characterological complex in which we exist. What imperative, what loyalty is it that confronts racism in the human conscience?

It is a question of redefining the enemy. We create enemies in our words and acts, and it is not easy to define where they begin to exist. In that respect, the word "racism" is only a paradigm for that which we wish to prohibit or censor in ourselves. Nationalism in war can become as great a danger, class militancy still another (though it is doubtful if it exists very often except where mixed with other sources of hostility). Enmity begins before declared conflict; it begins in memory, ideology, in the tradition of prejudice before we create an actual enemy in words and acts. Enmity is a metaphysical category before it becomes concrete, it is opposition, estrangement, the hostile Other in a beleaguered existence. That fear is always ready to be called up. It may be an atavistic recall of tribal dangers, it may even be biologically innate, the fear of the stranger. In the Nazi extreme, it was painted as a competition for survival in elementary living space. It seemed that they could not express *Volkgemeinschaft,* their own clustering unity, without defining an enemy.

•

We come to Holocaust history to be taught a metamorphosis of value. One might say that it is moral simple-mindedness to think that anything good could be the result of that relapse from civilization. And yet we use judgment still, and when we judge that evil in its extreme dimension the result must fall into the dialectic of the Good. If we say that the horror goes beyond the judgment of good and evil, then we must answer that no humanly created horror could. The nihilist and the misanthrope have their points, but if they were consistent would not know what to make of themselves, much less the Holocaust. For they would have no name, no image, no judgment for the horror they feel. The dialectic of the Good means that we know evil by the premise of good, and good by the existential fact of evil. Intent on living, we find the way and means which oppose themselves most clearly to the Holocaust. It is not enough to refrain from murder. It would be absurd to say that was the lesson. But as people who live in constant moral re-creation, people of humanity, we renew ourselves and remember the Holocaust as a great touchstone of moral history.

In the last account, we may amend our revulsion from the word "sacrifice." Those victims were denied martyrdom, but what is a martyr? A martyr is basically one whose death renders testimony; the martyr exists for those who can read martyrdom in his death and take a resurrection of value from it. The Jews who died in the Holocaust did not seek martyrdom and felt none of its accompanying grace or transcendence. But death never belongs only to the dead, nor is redemption theirs. The question persists, In what sense a martyrdom, and on whose behalf? Surely for all mankind, since the victims died as an exiled and rejected part of it. This martyrdom must be demonstrated in the most intimate nonabstract sense. The strongest action of moral lives is to raise memory above death in its utter depth of reduction. The crime was death inflicted in such a way as to have no meaning, at the extreme opposite of martyrdom. But that is the point. To find what was redemptive in the Holocaust requires that we look first at what was intended for destruction. Is it possible that Nazism invented a new death, a more complete, dehumanizing death than men had ever known? They destroyed the transcendentalizing moral dimension of living and dying. Even the victim of a murderous rage occupies the moral sphere, is even a sort of martyr to a principle. His existence is attested to by the murderer's self-interest, or hatred, or revenge. He is part of a purpose, whatever minimum comfort there may be in that.

Lear, naked on the heath, addresses himself to "unaccommodated man." He meant the tragic fall of humanity, not from high purpose but from all purpose, from any structure of value. This is what was meant by the writers who speak of the "meaninglessness" of the Holocaust. In profoundest empathy they face what the victims faced and are reliving the death of meaning itself. But doesn't that give the Holocaust a greatest of meanings, "the first idea" of the moral life? Unaccommodated man whose accommodation was human can be reaccommodated. Stephen Crane's brave assertion, "Sir, I exist!" gets no response from the universe but should, in fact must, from man.

It is intolerable that death should remain mere death, to prove nature's indifference. And so we would make those many victims martyrs in defiance and give them back to meaning. Death is always something else— utterly beyond us—but the dead arise immediately in our affection, our guilt, our longing for them to be one with us. Martyrdom is for memory. Life is sacrificed to a thought, an emotion, to our spiritual substance. The issue is not their dying but the manner of it. The manner of their dying, yes, because it did so much to violate the true essence of living and to deny their place in memory. Therefore, we resurrect those victims into memory, in the name of all meaning.

III

To be witness to the Holocaust is an exercise in conscience. We dwell on conscience; it becomes our obsession, and we equate it with memory. Terrence Des Pres writes, "In the literature of survival we find an image of things so grim, so heartbreaking, so starkly unbearable, that inevitably the survivor's scream begins to be our own."[24] This is where conscience starts, not in law or proscription, not in abstract right, but in painful empathy where Kant's rule or that of Rabbi Hillel begin enforcement.

To a large extent, the Holocaust was a terrible, almost final victory over conscience. The Nazi ideology, the German army system, the war psychology, the führer complex—all collaborated in evacuating conscience for individual Germans. The archetype was Goering who is reported to have remarked, "*I have no conscience. My conscience is Adolf Hitler.*"[25]

Des Pres, in his evocative and most pertinent book, *The Survivor,* speaks of response to the Holocaust and calls it the horror that "arises from the visible wreckage of moral and physical being." The shock, "as Nadeshda Mandelstam suggested, is life's own cry of dread and care, of recognition and refusal and appeal to resistance . . . This response, this *response-ability,* is what I wish to call 'conscience'—conscience in its social form; not the internalized voice of authority." But Des Pres's thinking meets a typical quandary here. Understandably, he wishes to find conscience in interactive, immediate relationships and not in mere obedience to command or rule. But he cannot escape the weight of historicist sociology, and so he writes in what seems to me contradiction to the valuable concept of "response-ability":

Conscience, in other words, is a social achievement. At least on its historical level, it is the collective effort to come to terms with evil, to distill a moral knowledge equal to the problems at hand. Only after the ethical content of an experience has been made available to all members of the community does conscience become the individual "voice" we usually take it for.[26]

That point is subject to acute misunderstanding. Whatever the anthropological and psychological explanations of the origin of moral culture, when conscience acts authentically it is an individual conscience. Des Pres's words imply that we attend to "all members of the community" before we can voice conscience. But in our time the abuse of conscience comes as a "social achievement" and "collective effort." The collectivity as such, and in action, has the distinct effect of blurring or eliminating conscience, much as SS troopers were able to follow orders of the community in committing atrocities. In effect, Des Pres contradicts himself after speaking of the "survivor's scream as our own," or, as Nadeshda Mandelstam expresses it, "life's own cry of dread and care." This is a cry that no community, as community, and no abstract entity can hear.

It may be the mistake of modern moral thought. We displace conscience in the attention we pay to historic genesis and social enforcement. It is true that character as we know it is inconceivable outside social existence. But as living agents, not parts of an organism, we cannot refer the function of conscience outside ourselves. It is *within* social existence that the conflicts of conscience take place, and it is *against* social acts and experiences that conscience is most often uniquely what it is, a claim on individual judgment, a call to individual will and choice. That does not mean that conscience acts alone, for conscience always speaks to another conscience and in the end becomes, we always hope, the active judgment of a community. But we cannot mistake its point of reference. There is no conscience outside an agent; it does not exist in a church, a party, a leader, it does not express itself in history or in a social cause, or even in a set of laws and commandments. These are classically the instruments of conscience for good, or the masks of conscience for bad, that is, its imposture deadened, displaced, or corrupted by formal practice, abstraction, dogma, and inspired fanaticism. Laws and institutions instruct conscience but only as they offer choices and are exercised in judgment. In sum, conscience as such cannot be displaced by abstract dogma or authority. In assent or dissent, in its response-ability, it acts. If there is something that can be called a collective conscience, it is in itself subject to a higher conscience, seated in individuals who can hear "life's own cry of dread and care."

•

Terror, the intimidation of power, was not just a political strategy, it was in a sense metaphysical, the effort of supermen to outreach themselves and achieve the control of being as well as the mastery of millions. We think the Nazis made themselves death's legislators. They were familiar with it, they would be its constant companions, its privileged *sonderkommandos,* and so gain a special form of immunity. It is after all natural death that limits the natural glory of the species. But perhaps memory of the Holocaust can be redemptive in this sense. It can also borrow metaphysical sanction; power faced death in its universality, power sought to dominate it by wielding it as a weapon. But death, in the community which all men join and none escape, can instruct us in the commonality of our being, so that if the bell tolls for death, it also tolls for life and brings us into it together.

For extension of this thought, it would be helpful to go to the work of a philosopher comparatively unknown in this country, Emmanuel Levinas. The relevant statement is in an extended interview on his work published in English under the title *Ethics and Infinity.*

Q. Nowadays you extend your meditation on responsibility for the Other by a meditation on responsibility for the Other's death. What should we understand by that?"
E.L. "I think that in responsibility for the Other one is, in the final analysis, responsible for the death of the other. Is not the rectitude of the other's look an exposure par excellence, an exposure unto death? The face in its uprightness is what is aimed at "pointblank" by death. What is expressed as demand in it certainly signifies a call to *giving* and *serving*—or the commandment to giving and serving—but above this, and while including it, the order is not to let the Other alone, be it in the face of the inexorable. This is probably the foundation of sociality and of love without

eros. The fear for the death of the other is certainly at the basis of the responsibility for him.[27]

This is a strong voice from contemporary philosophic humanism. Levinas, in defining "the humanity of man as responsibility for the Other" lays the simple premise for salvaging and clarifying judgment for the Holocaust. "Positively, we will say that since the Other looks at me, I am responsible for him, without even having taken on responsibilities in his regard; his responsibility *is incumbent on me*. It is responsibility that goes beyond what I do."[28]

Levinas goes so far as to say that this is an existential attribute upon which personal identity or immanent sensibility is based.

Responsibility in fact is not a simple attribute of subjectivity, as if the latter already existed in itself, before the ethical relationship. Subjectivity is not for itself; it is, once again, initially for another. In the book [Otherwise *than Being*], the proximity of the Other is presented as the fact that the Other is not simply close to me in space, or close like a parent, but he approaches me essentially insofar as I feel myself—insofar as I am responsible for him.[29]

Responsibility is an absolute insofar as primary being in the sphere of the human is an absolute condition upon everything else. Levinas no doubt would not deny that one can depart from the sphere of the human. But in that result he suggests the void, a blank of consciousness, and this is why he stresses "the face of the Other," upright and alive, "the look" of the Other, and finally his death, which is a contingency directly posed against one's own, more than a warning but a dependency. How then understand the responsibility for death in the millions?

The barest life in this world requires an allegiance to humanity. The true misanthrope survives on spite, that is, he simulates the awareness through attacking it. But the question nevertheless remains; we know that SS men could go home to play with their children after a day's butchery. Perverted men, or a perverted awareness of themselves as human? Levinas would have us leave that aside when another scene is summoned. One sees the old, the children, the women, the men, families, no less, the nucleus of universal memory, being marched naked to their deaths. The SS officer, listening to music, having his dinner, abruptly fades from vision. He is an impossibility, that is to say, simply not one of us, not human. And as for the others on their march, one somehow sees them all, equally naked, equal to each other and equal to our own vulnerability. But we overcome shame in gazing at them and transcend the pity that is actually for ourselves. Before being killed they were meant to be stripped of their identifiable, that is, shared, existence. But that was a mistake. The greatest humiliation and torture that could be devised succeeds only in exposing their common humanity at the place where all begin their being.

8

Existential Democracy
and Human Rights

One asks the purpose of a museum of the Holocaust that presumably holds the quintessence of a special knowledge. Is it to confirm our prejudices? What crosses over and adjudicates between the prejudice of the Nazis for death and the prejudice of the Jew for survival? Nothing but strength? Is there a reality to confront prejudice? Is there an umpire to determine Reality and Value and Truth? What distinguishes such terms from ignorance and prejudice? At some Olympian level of consciousness, do all such terms fade into one another? Or is everything that people call knowledge and truth to be regarded as a weapon to be used on opposing sides of the barricades of power?

That vein of thought threatens democracy itself. A free democracy of debate has to assume the possibility of transcending "points of view." Democracy demands a process by which to reach consensus. It assumes that people can be instructed, that there can be a sharing of knowledge to open the blockages of fixed belief and warring interests and prejudices. If that does not exist, the only mediation that is left is the contest of force. Not necessarily physical force. One can yield to a majority point of view, to pragmatic interest. One can negotiate or compromise. But unless the avenue of agreement is left open there is only a truce in all this, and the truce itself is held only by the fear of open conflict. For some this is democracy enough, and for many this is the moral failure of democracy, that the negotiation of interests is all that it offers, a trading place where values are submerged. What is the difference between a value and an interest? Who can define it? What is the consequence of failing that distinction?

To accept the compromise of interests may seem a worthy submission on behalf of peace, but in the last analysis it is a submission to the power of the majority. The latter is meaningful only if it holds the prospect of the reconcilement of values and interests. And this means one must have faith in a higher knowledge term, a place beyond warring interest and point of view—not a neutral place but one which the mind can approach. In the minds of members of a democracy there must be faith in the ultimate refer-

ence of truth, or else the voter dialogue is corrupted and has simply trans-
ferred the power of weapons to the power of manipulative words. And if
we say all words are manipulative, and all discourse a rhetoric masking
power and interest, then we again lower sanctions beneath words to physical force. The catastrophic danger of the twentieth-century political discourse has been this: to reduce all facts to the viewpoint of a passive skepticism, all argument to the relativism of point of view, and the forms of
resolution to the assertion of power. It is at this focus that the study of the
Holocaust forms themes of crucial importance.

To regard power as the ultimate arbiter is to sacrifice both moral agency
and moral goal. To cultivate power is to invite the force in events, one's
self, or one's opponents, which may be thought to achieve results of any
moral or amoral description. Power exists where agency or goals are irrelevant. Power is in the precivilized state, an animal condition. One of the
marks of the ethical superiority of Marxism over Nazism is found in the
way in which it originally viewed the neo-Darwinian struggle for existence.
For Marx and Engels the goal was not to confirm the laws of nature but
to transcend them. In the resolution of the final conflict, Engels wrote,

The struggle for individual existence disappears. Then for the first time man, in a
certain sense, is finally marked off from the rest of the animal kingdom and emerges
from mere animal conditions of existence into really human ones. The whole
sphere of the conditions . . . which have hitherto ruled man, now comes under the
dominion and control of man, who for the first time becomes the real, conscious
lord of nature.[1]

The theme has sharp focus. Engels was conceding that only "the final conflict" and proletarian victory would bring man out of the "animal kingdom." At least that was a moral objective. It is conceivable that Hitler
imagined "the final solution" as an exit from the naturalist world of power.
Of course, there is no evidence of that, and it is incompatible with everything to which Nazism, as a true primitivism, was committed.

If the Nazis succeeded in surpassing the imagination of evil, it is because
evil requires a point of view that can judge it. But the Nazis seem to leave
no place of view or point of judgment. Still today, fifty years later, one
resists assimilating the event of their atrocity, one resents and resists all
analogies, refuses to bring *that* behavior into conformity with ourselves
and what we accept as human. The reason for this is that we in fact *have* a
standard; it was the basic standard by which we measure human existence
that the Nazis violated. In actually experiencing a total evil one can lose
comprehension since the floor of judgment itself has been destroyed. It is

for this reason that so many of the victims could not believe what was happening to them, even before that last moment when all meaning was extinguished. They had been forced into the moral void.

Paradoxically, the language of the "void" was dry, euphemistical, bureaucratic. Himmler is quoted as saying that "even from there [the labor camps] the Jews are some day to disappear, in accordance with the Führer's wishes."[2] This was the authentic voice of that schoolmaster of genocide. We notice the not surprising resurgence of "disappear" in the language of the "death squads" in Latin America. For the Nazis the death language included the phrase "the Führer's wish." It was the führer's wish that the Jews be destroyed. His wishes had no control, no limit, no measure. They were fate and not subject to judgment. The führer principle was obviously a device to erase conscience. Conscience, (that "Jewish invention"), Hitler said in his casual talk, "is a blemish, like circumcision."[3] Brute power recognizes its primary enemy.

In that respect and in the view of many in the early twentieth century Hitler could be seen as a liberator. If we trust Rauschning this was how he thought of himself. "Providence has ordained that I should be the greatest liberator of humanity," Hitler said to his confidants. "I am freeing men from the restraints of an intelligence that has taken charge; from the dirty and degrading self-mortification of a chimera called conscience and morality, and from the demands of a freedom and personal independence which only a very few can bear."[4]

It can be a relief to discover that Hitler was the creature of ideas, no longer simply a monster controlling strange forces from the depths, no longer abstractly evil, but a historic human being whose creative source we can reach and attack. For instance, he could say something so banal, so "modern," for his time as "Our uprising has nothing to do with *bourgeois* morals."[5] Rauschning and others give evidence that he borrowed from avant-gardist attitudes and the campaign against moral philistinism which had become commonplace in France and Germany between the wars. It is customary to give stress to Hitler's war against Bolshevism, which became of course Judeo-Bolshevism to him and his followers. In the process we forget how much he shared in the spirit of *epater le bourgeois* with revolutionaries and avant-garde modernists generally.

In this context, Lacoue-Labarthe writes significantly of how a generation of thinkers was attracted to the varieties of totalitarian politics and ideology. In partial defense of Heidegger's temptation by Nazism in 1933, when he actively supported the regime as rector of his university, Lacoue-

Labarthe asks, "Who in this century . . . whether of 'right' or 'left' of the various revolutionary projects, has not been duped? And in the name of what? 'In the name of democracy perhaps?' Such things can be left to Raymond Aron, to the official philosophy of Capital (of the achieved nihilism for which anything *goes*)." [6] And he lists the great so duped in this century (as opposed no doubt to the unheroic protagonists of liberal democracy, such as Aron), Hamsun, Pound, Blanchot, Drieu, Brasillach, Céline, and "in the other camp, Benjamin, Brecht, Bataille, Malraux" and Sartre. "What did the old world have to offer them with which they could have resisted the irruption of the so-called 'new world.'" It should be easier to answer that question now, despite Lacoue-Labarthe's gesture of contempt for "bourgeois" democracy. The imposing list of the figures of art and intellect that he presents only increases the shock and dismay which any reading of Holocaust history offers. Call it "Heidegger's mistake," as a paradigm for the sins of the intellectual vanguard since Nietzsche, how they formed the great reactionary thrust against the democratic tradition, and the overwhelming prestige they brought to totalitarian ideas. [7]

●

In America and the West we should remember Hitler, the ideologue, best (and know ourselves better) in his hatred for all aspects of liberal humanist democracy. If we have any devotion to those principles, for us the Holocaust will remain a permanent touchstone. Theodor Adorno, in reference to Nazism and the Holocaust, spoke of a needed reactive "democratic pedagogy." [8] Nothing deserves deeper assent, for here there is argument still, a conflict of ideologies which focuses on the lessons of the totalitarian era.

Jürgen Habermas made the same point in recommending the continued reindoctrination of the German people even forty years after the war. "A loyalty to the universalist principle of constitutionalism, one anchored in conviction, could be inculcated in the cultured German nation only after—and by virtue of—Auschwitz. . . . Whoever wants to suppress the blush of shame, destroys the only reliable basis of our Western *loyalty*." [9] This would seem a solid position when made during the debate of the *Historikerstreit,* where Habermas lodged himself against German revisionist historians. But the same debate made him think twice about lining up too closely with the West. [10] He could see how Holocaust literature, which concentrates on antitotalitarianism and gives the Nazi regime its representative identity, could become a weapon of the postwar anti-Communist campaign. The Cold War, of course, had to recall the Nazi propaganda effort to persuade the Western allies to make a separate peace and unite against the real common enemy, Communist Russia. At the time, the controversial visit of President Reagan to Bitburg where SS personnel were buried seemed to be the occasion for forgiving and forgetting the Holocaust in the name of the old-new alliance against communism.

It was a dilemma and remains a trap. There is always somewhere the effort to explain the Nazis and justify one's particular political or national cause by putting their actions into a class with those of Stalin (the Kulaks and the Gulag), with capitalist imperialism, with South Africa, Vietnam, and Israel. After the war it became a battle between the superpowers to see who had better claim on the Nazis as their chief enemy. I have cited the recent study by Arno Mayer (*Why Did the Heavens Not Darken*), which makes the stronger case for Soviet communism. However, that is arguable; the record shows that Hitler regarded bourgeois democracy as his natural enemy (or victim) to be destroyed, and that Bolshevism, though surely to be destroyed, was less a moral antithesis than a dangerous rival which shared the same ultimate goals of power. It is certain that an honest indictment of the Nazis by a Communist of Stalinist conviction has to take a different color and direction from that of a liberal democrat. There is much that the Holocaust does not clarify in metaphysically religious and moral meditation but obscures to the point of despair. In one area, however, it does have clarity, transforming clarity, in my view, and that is in ordinary secular politics.

It is in fact the Holocaust which most sharply discriminates between totalitarians and democrats. The case against the Nazis requires multiple comparisons so that we understand what is at stake. It is Orwellian doublespeak to accuse liberal democracy of nurturing Nazism, though true in the sense that the natural victim nurtures its natural predator. On the other hand, Hitler acknowledged his methodological debt to the Marxists and Stalinists. Whatever we make of the Cold War, the truth remains that the West did not, early or late, unite with Hitler against Bolshevism but explicitly did the opposite. Whatever the tentative maneuvers of 1939, it was Stalin, not Chamberlain, who forged an alliance with Hitler. The West clearly if belatedly saw Fascism as the immediate and greater evil, and, if any side can claim that an ideological component in the war equaled or transcended the interest of self-preservation, surely the British and Americans have a better claim than the Soviets. The bewildered German propagandists of 1944 and 1945 might testify to that as they discovered that the Allies, near victory, were not ready to turn their guns on the Bolsheviks and save them from destruction.

Nevertheless, it was Hitler's game, and it was the Communist game to see the battle between communism and Fascism as the only battle that counted. The ideological climate thus generated has had greatly destructive effect, from which we just now may be beginning to recover. In the moral and political ambivalence which has been its infliction for more than a century, Western democracy still has not truly accepted that in the battle with Fascism the chief historic target of destruction was itself. Some of the victims knew this well. At the climax of Jewish suffering (and a few months after America entered the war), Chaim Kaplan wrote, "Is it in the power of a human being to endure hardship in this degree? We had one consolation in our lives: our faith in the victory of democracy; our belief that its powers were greater than those of the other side, the enemy of the Jews and the enemy of humanity."[11] If the war had any moral reason, and if any lasting political result of the war makes sense of great sacrifice, it is in the survival of democracy and of the public conscience that governs human rights. For this truth the Holocaust remains a monument of terrible cost.

•

It is important to remember that the Jews were chosen as political enemies of Nazi Germany, and that the connection with religious anti-Semitism is exceedingly hard to make, except as one analyzes the cultural subconscious, so to speak, of the German people and the collaborating Europeans. In the long intellectual or theoretical tradition of German anti-Semitism, the Jews came to be considered exponents of the liberal Enlightenment, which tallied, of course, with their own emancipation. No doubt in contemporary conspiracy theory they were the allies of Napoleon. Treitschke, the nineteenth-century German historian of great influence, accused Jews of importing French rationalist thinking, ideas of rational justice, in addition, of course, to materialist interests and values, their native vice and corruption.

Alfred Rosenberg linked Jewish power with the French Revolution, which brought the Jews out of the medieval ghettos. Jewish emancipation and legal equality was made to represent "the decadent" ideas of liberty and equality overall. The great betrayal of November 1918, which Hitler never allowed the Germans to forget, was perhaps only symbolically linked with democratic and pacifist ideas. But the difference between symbolic danger and direct conspiracy was minimal in his mind. It was automatic for Hitler to equate internationalism with Jews and nationalism with anti-Semitism. The profound conversion of his life came when he saw these relationships. He writes in *Mein Kampf* that "for me this was the time of the greatest spiritual upheaval I have ever had to go through. I had ceased to be a weak-kneed cosmopolitan and become an anti-Semite."[12] It may be hard today to see that one can be converted to anti-Semitism, that it could mean a change of life, a finding of faith, and that it meant commitment to a totality of political values. But this became the dangerous "metaphysical" nature of anti-Semitism, signifying its transfer from cosmic religious eschatologies to a modern political struggle with equally fateful and totalist significance. Both Hitler's fanaticism and the messianic power of his "metapolitics" stem from that source.

It would have been grotesque at the time for Jews to see themselves as the chief ideological enemies of Nazism. But now, after the Holocaust, we must give more credit to Nazi belief, even if Jews were selected to spearhead democratic values in order to deface them. Of course, they were used to represent Bolshevik values almost in the same gesture, but in the Nazi perspective Bolshevism was confounded with internationalist egalitarianism, clearly a threat to nationalist and racialist hierarchies, on one side, and, on the other, it was in fact a rival totalitarian power, to be emulated and defeated. Even if the Jews were pathetically innocent of leading opposition to Hitler, should we not now accept that imputed representation of liberal humanist and democratic values? To understand what the massacre meant, and that it was not meaningless, one cannot view it without regard to what it was specifically that the Nazis wished to destroy. They honor their victims by imagining the polar antithesis with themselves.

A question is why Hitler pursued Jews everywhere, in countries he had no intention of absorbing, such as Finland, Denmark, and Norway, and in Poland, Hungary, Rumania, where they were an untrusted and despised minority, rarely even allowed to join the resistance where it existed. No objective danger existed from them. Perhaps he understood that ideas were dangerous and that every Jew left alive anywhere must perforce from tradition and makeup, from the circumstance of exile and pariahhood, generate ideas that would always threaten the New Order. The exile and wanderer may be a moral threat to a closed community, the source of alienation and fragmentation in a traditional culture. But the positive belongs with the negative. The moral promise of such a people may be an offering to the future, a cosmopolitanism which is benign, in fact, progressive, and gives the basis of harmony in a world of necessary differences. The Jews did not offer themselves as victims, but victimhood does not require consent. And the fact that the Holocaust is entailed both with the moral advancement and degeneration of the species should not surprise students of Jewish history. If anti-Semitism equates with antihumanism, and it does as all racism does, the only basis for surmounting it is humanism itself. That part of the dialectic of racial and group oppression must be understood.

•

Jean-Francois Lyotard, perhaps speaking typically from frustrated cosmic needs in philosophizing after and about Auschwitz, scoffed at the prospect of the world's redemptive turn concentrating on "human rights." "One will say, It was a great massacre, how horrible! Of course, there have been others. . . . Finally, one will appeal to human rights, one cries out 'never again' and that's it! It is taken care of." [13] For many, like Lyotard, there is an unerasable sense of philistine presumption in the notion that the world can achieve reforms that can atone for the Holocaust or prevent its recurrence. It is certain that in most people's minds politics cannot engage with or do justice to either the full-sized truth of Auschwitz or its moral and spiritual implications, particularly when both poetry and metaphysics are dismissed in that effort. Again, Theodor Adorno has caustic thoughts on this subject: "Our metaphysical capacity is paralyzed because actual events have shattered the basis on which speculative metaphysical thought could be reconciled with experience." And going further: "If thought is not measured by the extremity that eludes the concept, it is from the outset in the nature of the musical accompaniment with which the SS liked to drown out the screams of its victims." [14]

The thought arises that one should try to arrest this progress toward intellectual despair, just as one would have liked to arrest Jean Améry's or Primo Levi's advance toward suicide. But with the mundane comfort and redemptive solace from a commonplace political moralism? I argue here that the second premise of ontological ethics (following Levinas' injunction of "thou shalt not kill") is against suicide. Of these two injunctions, an adequately equipped ethical philosopher might make the basis of a creed of "human rights." The world today has been enormously attracted by the faith in human rights, ingenuous as it may be, and whatever its basis, a simple pragmatism or humanitarianism, or a more deeply philosophic humanism. To see the Holocaust as testimony for this need is neither an insult to intellectual pride nor moral sensibility.

•

There is a logic that leads from the first abuse of human rights to genocide. The ultimate "human right" and the premise for all the others is the right to exist. The Jews began to lose their right to existence when they were denied equal treatment before the law, the right to move across borders, the right of refuge and all forms of pacific defense against power. These terms are elementary. But an equal share in the power of governance is entailed in the primary right to exist, and the right to exist is entailed in freedom of movement and freedom of expression. In the human state, existence must be defined, it has a nature and qualities. The existence of someone free to attend a university or engage in a business or profession is not of the same order as someone who is not. The existence of someone free to speak, listen, or read, free to think and develop thoughts, free to obtain information, is of an entirely different order than one who is not.

Radical inequality on these terms under the Nazi regime, as, for example, between Germans and Poles or Germans and Jews, invites murder and all lesser forms of violence. For murder, in one's conscience, is most inhibited by the recognition of shared existence and equality in being. There is a scene in Tolstoy's *War and Peace* where Pierre Bezuhov is brought as a suspected spy to the French general, Davout, and they stare at each other from two perspectives of being—that of Pierre's imprisoned state and that of Davout's army rank and rule—and for a moment a glance between them crosses the barriers to existential equality. The fact that Pierre is not ultimately executed as a spy is barely noted and perhaps is only incidental. What interests Tolstoy is the radical contrast of conditions of being, and the momentary bridge which crosses below and above the suddenly shallow forms of general, judge, Frenchman, Russian, spy, and defeated enemy.

A gloss on this passage from Tolstoy is best derived from Levinas, pertinently instructive as his thought is in any discussion of the epiphanic moment of moral immediacy.

I think that across all literature the human face speaks—or stammers, or gives itself a countenance, or struggles with its caricature. Despite the end of Europocentrism, disqualified by so many horrors, I believe in the eminence of the human face expressed in Greek letters and in our own, which owe the Greeks everything. It is thanks to them that our history makes us ashamed. There is a participation in Holy Scripture in the national literatures, in Homer and Plato, in Racine and Victor Hugo, as in Pushkin, Dostoyevsky or Goethe, as of course in Tolstoy or in Agnon.

But I am sure of the incomparable prophetic excellence of the Book of Books, which all the Letters of the world awaited or upon which they comment. The Holy Scriptures do not signify through the dogmatic tale of their supernatural or sacred origin, but through the expression of the face of the other man that they illuminate, before he gives himself a countenance or a pose.[15]

Gives himself, or is given, by the murderous stereotypes.

•

The Nuremberg laws redefined existence for the Jews on a metaphysical standard transcending law. With the images of devastation and death in the Holocaust, all lost freedoms become sharply visible as ontological in their nature. Human rights denote efforts to protect existence and give it feature and fulfillment. In the Holocaust, death dominates the scene and presents itself as pure extinction, without reason or practical motive, without sensible purpose or design. In their attack upon freedoms and rights, the Nazis approached death as their ultimate recourse. Death remained the border of even those rights that remained in a totalitarian society, and the Nazis governed everywhere with the automatic reflexive threat of death over the people they ruled. Power was interpreted to mean that and gained its conviction from millions of actual and potential deaths. In a totalitarian regime, we say that power precedes and endows existence, and if you exist you do so by the one ruling sanction of power. Properly understood, a democracy gives existence priority over power, and in a deeper sense, over the hierarchies of rank and function. The subject says to the ruler, if you rule you rule under terms that qualify and preserve my existence. These we call human rights.

Writing on Christmas day, 1939, Chaim Kaplan saw the contrast the Nazis presented. A new force called Nazism, he said, has arisen that will establish a new world order on the wreckage of the old with principles and foundations completely different. "The right to live is given only to the strong. The tender and the weak have no place in the world. Strength is the source of law. All the laws of nature are laws of strength. Only the strong can take possession. Humanism is a stumbling block to the world, humanism weakens and rots it, and this is against the laws of nature established since the world was created."[16] It is poignant to hear someone near death appealing against the laws of nature. But that, for humanism, is exactly the ultimate place of defense and its trial of justification.

No scale of evil brings the Nazi leaders into kinship with humanity. It still shakes one's sanity to contemplate their work. But despite that, one has to say that the Holocaust is a lesson in positive democracy. If the sentence sounds like shocking trivialization, it is because we have trivialized the meaning of democracy in our minds. There can be no great negation that does not imply an equally great affirmation. That is why we respond to the story of the Holocaust not only with terror but with an expectancy that resists despair. Perhaps we may search for Kaplan's inspired sense when he wrote, "I sense within me the magnitude of this hour and my responsibility toward it." [17]

•

Emil Fackenheim and Elie Wiesel join in saying that at Auschwitz not only man died but the Idea of Man as well. Rather perhaps this was its threat, which becomes the obligation of a world of survivors (man in the twentieth century is that kind of survivor) to reverse. "That human personality is an end in itself," Fackenheim writes, was what was at stake in the land of Kant and Nietzsche. "As for the Third Reich, its heart and soul was the aim to destroy just this principle—by no means only in the case of Jews . . . but also, and perhaps above all, in the case of the 'master race' itself." [18]

"The individual is transitory, the *Volk* is permanent," Hitler proclaimed as a new "imperative" for his people, and he offered Germans "the sacred collective egoism which is the nation." [19] The Jews, Nazis thought, had no "volkdom," were no nation, were incapable of founding one and, therefore, were imitators and corruptors of other states. Thus in their alienation or exile, imposed or self-imposed, they were excluded from personality or autonomy, and any protection of fellow being. But that exactly is why their fate questions the "idea of Man."

Though we generally agree that something that we call dehumanization took place in unparalleled form and effect during the Holocaust, we are still not quite sure of its meaning. The Nazis themselves clearly had an obsession with the term "human," elaborating on the subhuman for the most part but implying always the *Ubermensch*. And that polarity may indicate how little ability or inclination they had to conceive the human in itself, without gradation. Resistance writers and intellectuals, reacting from Fascism during the war and after, found it necessary to resort to their own fixation on the human. Paul Nizan made his interest blunt: "How many times the word 'man' recurs in my writing. But there is no other. The real problem is to define what meaning it contains." [20] Sartre, his friend and

philosophical companion, wrote in the inaugural issue of *Les Temps Mo-
dernes:* "We openly affirm that man is an absolute." [21]

The strange fact is that the humanist ideal was actually used against itself
in Hitler's system. [22] German humanity, the racial type, was indeed set in a
hierarchy of valuations. The large design of the Nazis was to prove that
their victims did not belong to the same species, therefore the extraordinary effort to reduce them to the Musulman condition. Perhaps there
would have been less destruction if there had not been so high a valuation
of the human and superhuman. It may be that the secularization of the
"idea of man" in the nineteenth century led to a berserk and destructive
humanism. Each race or nation would impose the test on others—but using what as criteria? Blond hair, white skin, a cast of features? No, something more definite, more consistent was needed. Man would demonstrate
his humanity, or value, not through his morally developed being, or endowed soul, or conditioned Kantian relationships, but in his strength and
power of domination. Death would be the testing ground, survival in victory the proof of the right to live. This was explicitly in Hitler's mind at
the end, when he urged the self-destruction of the German people as a
form of natural just punishment for their defeat, according to Albert
Speer's report.

That desperate consequence of a "humanism" that based itself on the
will to power and led to the war apocalypse brings Richard Rubenstein to
reject "secular humanism," because, like Nazism, it has a conception of
"humanity in general." [23] He draws on Hannah Arendt to support this
thought where she says that "the process whereby Jews were turned into
men in general, lacking all concrete legal, political, and national status, was
the final preparatory step to turning them into superfluous men whose
extermination was of no consequence to any existing political group." [24]

That has a practical truth in its grievous consequences, but in its moral
implications it is misleading. Arendt mistakes, Jews were not "men in general" to the Nazis; they gave Jews a discriminatory definition, that of the
"subhuman," the antithetical species. It was to them a legal and political
term. It is precisely a concept of humanity in general that the Nazis did
not have. Or we should say of humanity in general *and particular,* for if
the term means anything it has to express a concrete universal.

The rejection of "humanism" was supplemented and confirmed by Rubenstein's further judgment that after Auschwitz "human rights are no
longer credible." He based himself again on agreement with the even more
influential scholar of totalitarianism and the Holocaust.

> As Hannah Arendt has pointed out in *The Origins of Totalitarianism,* there is today no longer any credible intellectual basis for affirming the existence of *human rights.* Such rights in the abstract are meaningless. . . . The only rights an individual has are those he possesses by virtue of his membership in a concrete community which has the power to guarantee him those rights. Without such a community, a man can rely on no residue of universally accepted human rights. Such isolated individuals are totally without rights, as were the death camp inmates.[25]

Rubenstein concludes, "Regrettably, the word *power* must be underscored." As an issue of stern political realism this is correct. As a tautology on which to base political and ethical values it is not. Does the statement mean to imply that the right of a million and a half children to exist vanished because they were defenseless? And is that how each side in a confrontation of weak and strong are to measure rights? It is in fact precisely because the Holocaust engaged victims in a void of institutional defense that Auschwitz focuses eternally on the ground and nature of human rights, and gives us "the intellectual basis for affirming their existence."

Rubenstein underscored the word "power" in speaking of human rights. But the Nazi religion of power, a primitive regressive religion, requiring blood sacrifice (the death of others being the testimony of one's power over life), necessarily calls up a reinvestigation of what we mean by human rights as *apart from* and opposed to power. The basic concept of "rights" is antithetical to force, an assumption *against* power that prepares the ground for justice. Concepts of freedom and justice are in one effect efforts to restrain the unlimited rule of power. They are not mere negative terms but imagined values that make demands, and are rivals to power in their essence, themselves the objects of cults of reverence. Democracy, as the institutional embodiment of those cults, is weakly considered when viewed only as the constitutional check on power centers, distributing their force, balancing and dispersing them. That defensive role has been its handicap in the rivalry of world systems. Is freedom only appreciated by those just liberated from oppression? Or is it an empty space to be filled with content by each oppressed and separated person or group? The doctrine of human rights appears as if to fill a void in democratic values.

The issue comes to a head here. It is a question of identities: How is the "human" formed? Of what does it consist? An empirical politics and ethics wishes to specify, to find the outline in exact sociological, geographical, racial, economic terms. Arendt and Rubenstein share their misgivings with Marx where the Communist Manifesto, in attacking romantic and utopian socialism, rejected the general category of the human. As the manifesto

declared, such thinking claimed to represent "not the interests of the proletariat, but the interests of human nature, of man in general, who belongs
to no class, has no reality, who exists only in the misty realm of philosophical fantasy."[26] But the issue is which "fantasy" or abstraction one chooses.
The question now is: Which has more ethical reality, the categories which
label a race, or class, or political friend or enemy, or the concrete and universal humanity found in direct experience? Almost any page in the writing
of Holocaust or Gulag survivors could provide the answer. An ethical humanism posits the universal in the intrinsic immediate existence of persons
before it generates any other values or definitions, and it is a value which
is prelegal and transcends the categorical.[27] All abstractions are categorical,
and the true universal is based on individual existences and the mutual
recognition that are inherent in them.

•

The study of what happened to the concept of the "human" and humanism in the nineteenth and twentieth centuries is indispensable for the understanding of modern political ideologies. The focus must be on the two
dominant systems which judges would agree have been, ostensibly or explicitly, most indifferent to the value of individual lives. In Nazism the human was reduced to biological abstraction and treated in racial terms. A
biological politics entails a biological ethos. In Marxism the human being
disappeared in the abstractions of class and economic forces. In war and
ideologies of war, in biological and economic politics, the individual is
obliterated and becomes an abstract category, a type, a class, a race; he
becomes a force, he becomes a problem. He is a function in an equation
or solution and will be treated on those terms. Murderous caricature
though it may be, Nazism, the system of Hitler, was a complete effort to
press bureaucratic thought and technological procedure to their inhuman
result. The recent work of Zygmunt Baumann, *Modernity and the Holocaust,* presses this question. If we need or want a definition of humanism,
it must be understood on the level of what contrasts with it, the major
forms of antihumanism in this century.[28]

    Who are the antihumanists? It is difficult to avoid a pejorative reference,
but the topic deserves intellectual sobriety. This is what it receives from the
most distinguished of liberal humanist scholars, Isaiah Berlin, most recently in a brilliant series of articles published in the *New York Review of
Books.*[29] Berlin traces his theme in the writing of Joseph de Maistre, whom
he describes as the very early teacher of modern Fascism. To Maistre's post-

revolutionary mind, in the early nineteenth century, the factor in human relations was power.

In Maistre's scale of values power comes almost highest, because power is the divine principle that governs the world, the source of all life and action, the paramount factor in the development of mankind; and whoever knows how to wield it, above all to make decisions, acquires the right to obedience, and is by that token the instrument chosen by providence or history, at that particular moment to work its mysterious purposes.

As a nineteenth-century conservative, Maistre, according to Berlin, locates power where it must securely lie, "in ancient, established, socially created institutions," and where it is "the working of the divine will."

All usurpation must fall in the end, because it flouts the divine laws of the universe; power resides only in him who is the instrument of such laws. To resist them is to put the fallible resources of a single intellect against the cosmic stream, and that is always childishness and folly, and more than that—criminal folly, directed against the human future.[30]

The invocation of divine will and purpose, of course, is anachronistic when considered in the context of modern power philosophies, which have been explicitly and devotedly naturalist. If higher powers are commanded, they are used in elaborate systems of deception that exploit primitive sanctities and demonologies. These belong to the techniques of persuasion, so widely developed in modern political practice, but behind them, we regularly assume, are the dominant, the exclusively important motivations of material and biological interest. The economic interests of groups, the interests of races and nations in the competition for power, the laws, so to speak, of class conflict, race conflict, and imperial rivalry, form the structures of explanation for politics which have received intellectual respect.

Value judgments then fall into the distinction between superstructure and base, but where the base is entrenched in history and nature it can be as imperatively determining as Maistre would expect. Moral argument becomes the instrument of power, rather than the reverse, where power would be considered the instrument of moral goals. And the line of assumed honesty is to patronize or disdain moral rhetoric, while tracing expressed values to the group interests or power interests that masquerade below language.

This is a position that still has great intellectual respect, particularly in the academy, but also in the implicit assumptions of most practical politics and journalism. Perhaps no one has been as forthright at the higher levels of discussion than Michel Foucault, who, in summing up his thought, describes with great exactness the reversal in the relations between value and power, between rationalized goals and the forceful means of achieving them:

> My general project of the past few years has been, in essence, to reverse the mode of analysis followed by the entire discourse of right from the time of the Middle Ages. My aim, therefore, was to invert it, to give due weight, that is, to the fact of domination, to expose both its latent nature and its brutality. I then wanted to show not only how right is, in a general way, the instrument of this domination—which scarcely needs saying—but also to show the extent to which, and the forms in which, right (not simply the laws but the whole complex of apparatuses, institutions and regulations responsible for their applications) transmits and puts in motion relations that are not relations of sovereignty, but of domination.[31]

Sovereignty in Foucault's usage embodies the legitimacy of right, and domination refers to the effective actualities of power. Accordingly, he would say sovereignty is an obfuscation.

> The system of right, the domain of the law, are permanent agents of these relations of domination, these polymorphous techniques of subjugation. Right should be viewed, I believe, not in terms of a legitimacy to be established, but in terms of the methods of subjugation that it instigates.[32]

The force of Foucault's argument is more an attribute of its bluntness than its originality. For generations, political activism of several degrees has proceeded on this basis, the inversion of values, the dismissal of legitimate sovereignties, that is, not only the sovereignty of ruling hierarchies but the sovereignty of *ideas* of justice and right, with the conviction that those ideas are the instruments of dominant power, or as it may happen, of a would-be revolutionary power.

The classic expression is the work of Marx in the project of inverting Hegelian principles. "It is not the consciousness of men that determines their existence, but, on the contrary, their social existence determines their consciousness."[33] Historically, there is subtle paradox in such emphatic determinist judgments which turn out to be incitements of the political will. When we view the extreme violence with which political aims have been pursued since the First World War, it is a warrantable hypothesis that the unleashing of violence and the elevation of conflict have direct relationship with the subordination of consciousness (the conscience of consciousness) to existential modes of action. The fact that this stems from theory or ideology is a logical contradiction perhaps, but it does not bar its effects.

In this context, three major historic events of the twentieth century take their special significance. They are, respectively, the Gulag, the Holocaust, and the Nuclear Bomb, the last being the paradigm of the ultimate arbiter of power in war.[34] All three illustrate the subordination of rights, values, and mediating discourse to power as the ultimate authority in human events. In effect, they practice Foucault's inversion. That being so, each can be used as a touchstone for judgment at all levels of politics and statecraft. Under the threat of these immense catastrophes, self-preservation requires that they come to memory at every bend and turn of major political decisions. And meanwhile, as it happens for my concerns here, it may be found that this support of memory is not merely a warning but an enrichment of the life of communities, certainly for those that commit themselves to democratic faith and practice.

The problem for any civil society is to establish a role for conscience and responsibility to it. The recited narrative of the Holocaust fosters the idea of responsibility, the victims being human in the relations of human beings. We are all implicated in it. As a human event, it was one in which many shared direct responsibility, and all shared general responsibility. This is only emphasized by the ways in which the Nazis covered their crimes with conceptualizations of racial law, or what they called the laws of existence and nature. They reduced murder to a bureaucratic and technological procedure with such unprecedented success that bureaucratic government, industrial technology, and even science may never really recover from the world's suspicion and dread.

The first function of totalitarian dictatorships was to offer a release from responsibility, their first incitement a liberation from moral anxiety. They could do this under the cover of collective discipline and the authority of a supramoral faith in racial or class destiny. The great historic paradox is that these systems, which believed primarily in power and the methods of naked enforcement, also could promise a liberation from force and oppression, achieving utopias of resolved conflict whether through racial or class conquest. Marx, for instance, prophesied that "communism [would be] the complete return of man to himself as a *social* (i.e. human) being."[35] Engels, writing for them both in the polemical essays against Eugen Duhring, described ethics as the possession of postrevolutionary man. "A really human morality, which transcends class antagonisms and their legacies in thought, becomes possible only at a stage of society which has not only overcome class contradictions but has even forgotten them in practical life."[36] Less persuasive in every respect, and even while implying an eternity of conflict as the law of nature, Nazism did promise the eugenic redemp-

tion of man through racial purification, even if it meant that the world
would then be populated by only one race.

•

There are thinkers today who debate myth and cultural subjectivity to the
point where any present or future report on the Holocaust is vulnerable to
the distortions of "point of view." We become convinced that we live from
birth in the private or group worlds of "point of view," and the only world
we might share is that of debatable fact and deconstructable judgment, not
a world at all but only the pivot upon which all possible worlds turn. As for
the Holocaust, that great dramatic last truth in millions of lives, revisionist
historians challenge documents and facts, some to the absurd extent of
denying that it occurred at all. It did not take place or, if something of
dreadfulness did, it can mean anything one chooses to make it mean. One
bias opposes another. Explanations are myths, though there may be good
or bad myths, right or wrong myths. You choose the illusion you wish to
live under; if you do not make room for God's revelation of purpose, you
find room for a philosophy of history driven by the economic interest of
class, the biological power interest of race or gender. What interest is served
by teaching the facts of the Holocaust? Do we wish to say the interests of
the Jews, Slavs, and Gypsies who survived? But in the context of its true
horror, that is paltry. Here no one wants anything but enlarged witness,
witness for the ages. We know also that truth has a moral function, is a
moral necessity; that a hard truth, a terrible truth, has redemptive value if
it brings us out of "myth" onto the ground we must share and into what
Jean Améry called "moral reality."

The secular faith in human rights, now more awake in the world than
ever before, just possibly could become the base of a valid world order.
Internationalist doctrine correctly opposes itself to nationalisms that are
exponents of the creed of competitive power. International democracy implies that a loyalty to human rights is the basis in fact for peace. What else
can act as umpire between conflicting interests, and what but the assent to
rights can act as substitute for the conflict of power? Political pragmatists
say that interests must be expressed, interests must be reconciled. What is
an "interest"? My profit, your loss, my survival, your extinction? Interests
can be prevented from approaching violence in only one way, through the
rule of higher right and consent under law. It is certain that most people
are more compelled by interests regarded as rights than by interests as such.
It is injustice that arouses the strongest political passions and which leads

men to fight. The deadening mistake, a form of moral suicide, is for the political process to deal always in the language of interests and power. If we believe it then it is so, and thus it gives implicit assent to the manipulations of power mongers. In that context, civic debate merely legitimizes deceit and hypocrisy as last steps before submitting to the realism of power and necessity. There is really only one weapon against force, not a counterforce but an antiforce, which expresses itself in the rule of right and the belief in it. It was vulgar and even malicious reduction to call the rule of law (in a human rights context) the rule of power and masked interest.

The Holocaust was the product of the political religions or myths of the twentieth century, and any redemptive value it may have must enter through those secular faiths and moralities of our time. Certainly the Holocaust will abruptly, brutally, clarify the moral base of political thought and political action. A great mystification in the name of truth was accomplished in the nineteenth century when it forced the moral rationale for behavior to hide behind other codes of language—historic process, biology, racial conflict, the laws of existence and survival, all sanctions of cosmic inevitability. But these metaphysical edicts cannot be the ground for political or moral action. It is fatal to make them that, except in one respect. Every antithesis to the Holocaust begins with the right to live. For humanity that becomes an ontological starting point. For instance, in the Holocaust we understand that free speech, the right of dissent, meant the right to defend existential humanity in each person. Free information and communication meant the right to know what threatens or supports personal existence. Freedom of choice and movement meant the right to share power over life. Mass death, mass murder, define a polity based on the absolute denial of that right. The Holocaust teaches that essential democracy, in its commitment to human rights, is a moral claim on existence itself which cannot be concealed or abrogated. Most pertinently, however, it is a collective commitment, so that all share responsibility when that basic right is denied.

•

There are many humanisms, and the task of judgment becomes one of discrimination. If Marx wrote that "communism, as fully developed naturalism, equals humanism, and as fully developed humanism equals naturalism," one lesson of the Holocaust, as I have tried to make my argument, refutes that scientist premise. A true humanism distinguishes itself from nature at every important point where the ethical consciousness can function. Where naturalism applies itself most stringently in human affairs is in the definition of species, or subcategories of the human. A humanism, in its own intrinsic character, gives first account to individuals in relationships that have moral immediacy. Marxist thought produced a valuable concept in "reification," the process whereby human beings are translated into commodities, things of use. Modern political humanism is following a parallel theme in opposing a process of abstraction or bureaucratization, where human beings are translated into their group membership, are subsumed in types, classes, races, and genders, and treated as such.

Emmanuel Levinas writes his philosophy with implicit attention, I believe, to what the Holocaust violated in the humanist ethos considered this way. He grounds his thought in moral immediacy, as when he says that the beginning text is the command against murder. But this is a direct message from the Other, who expresses it in the confrontation of face and eyes, not with words, and it becomes the basis of an ethical ontology, placed in concrete existence, not in abstraction. Levinas makes this clear in the added stress on the "face," the personal command, when "he names Hegel and Heidegger, charging them with 'exalting an obedience that no face commands'"[37] The powerful excitement in Levinas's thought lies in this basis of a critique for all forms of institutional, philosophic, and political "commands," including the commanded philosophic "presence" of Being in Heidegger's construction, something which "no face commands."

Levinas's preoccupation with the charge against murder gains large moral logic when he argues that the right to exist is entailed completely with that of one's neighbor. "One has to respond to one's right to be, not by referring to some abstract and anonymous law, or judicial entity, but because of one's fear for the Other." (The marked significance of Levinas's thought is in this reversal of the Hobbesian rule, fear *for* not *of*.) Humanity is morally enveloped on this basis, and the right to exist and all rights stem from this right of the Other, my putative victim. The passage needs fuller quotation:

In its mortality, the face before me summons me, calls for me, begs for me, as if the invisible death that must be faced by the Other, pure Otherness, separated, in some way, from any whole, were my business. . . . The other man's death calls me into question, as if, by my possible future indifference, I had become the accomplice of the death to which the other, who cannot see it, is exposed; and as if, even before vowing myself to him, I had to answer for this death of the other, and to accompany the Other in his mortal solitude. The Other becomes my neighbour precisely through the way the face summons me, calls for me, begs for me, and in so doing recalls my responsibility, and calls me into question.[38]

The language has spiritual depth but takes secular human rights to a level of appropriate moral dignity. It may be here that those writers and historians who pronounce the Holocaust meaningless, seeming to abjure ethics, politics, and history as well as religious eschatology for explanation, may have an answer. In their frustration they were really most ambitious for meaning and essentially making Job's challenge. And Levinas may, therefore, have risen to the profoundest level of Job's comfort. To pursue meaning is not to end with the meaningless, though one approaches that margin. It is really the margin of that "invisible death that must be faced by the Other" and which "calls me into question." Levinas says it "recalls my responsibility" which is a meaning that survives death and which we send, as we can, after those Others—those millions—in their "mortal solitude."

Elie Wiesel's story *Dawn* (to which I have referred above) has a perfect clarity in demonstrating the humanism of immediate experience, quite in the vein of Levinas's thinking. Elisha, survivor of the Nazi death camps, and now a member of a Jewish terrorist group fighting the British rule in Palestine, has been chosen by lot to be the executioner of a captured British officer, in direct retaliation for the execution of a captured member of his group. In Wiesel's story, the dead of the Holocaust, his own dead, appear before Elisha, the executioner, in the tense moments which precede the killing of the British officer. They act the role of the Furies upon his conscience, and he is almost nothing but conscience, quivering in agony as he approaches his victim. Strangely, the "dead" do not insist on a reprieve from the order, simply that he bring the condemned man food. It is notable also that Elisha finally accepts the curious duty, urged upon him by his comrades, of visiting with the victim before the act of execution, instead of emerging at the last moment with pistol ready. Elisha brings him food, for as the ghosts of his dead repeat, the man is hungry and must be fed. They seem to be instructing him, not against killing but in the life which is coexistence with his. This is one relief from the cold abstraction of murder. Another is that the two men do speak in those final minutes, not in many words but in Levinas's sense, face to face, and the last word of John Dawson is the name of his executioner, Elisha.

Wiesel has gathered together this lesson like a Chasidic fable that reports the essence of faith. Its revelation speaks most acutely at the margin between life and death, and in the ultimate kinship on the two sides of life and death. Know me, said the dying man, Dawson, "I want to tell you a story," and Elisha does know him, not in a remotely symbolic way but under the urgency of a sentence of death in which he is the executioner. If this is a religious fable, it says the following: to judge and cut off a life is to cut off a member of all common life. Six million people were given the extreme of death within death, a peculiar genocidal death, by their executioners, the Nazis. They were to have suffered the death that cuts off membership in memory; the genocidal judgment was against their original right of existence as well as the last right to an exchanged and empathic human consciousness. But even in an execution one might absurdly, desperately, confirm that right to shared being. Dawson draws Elisha down with him by calling his name. Elisha offers food and makes it a communion. Both are making longing gestures against the negation of a mutual fate. And those gestures are on behalf of a community of being which shapes meaningful existence.

Suspending consideration of the justice of Elisha's cause or the necessity of the execution, the story confronts the harsh urgency of political violence and terror with a moral sensibility that rings as if it were Wiesel's task to supply what the Nazis were incapable of feeling. In dealing death to another man, a totality of response is aroused and challenged to produce meaning. The last moments of life must be, we think, a testimonial to meaning. If the killer himself feels this, as in Wiesel's story, something has already begun to happen to change the nature of murder. What we appreciate in the dead is the fullness of their living as that presents itself to memory, tremendously charged and signified by its closure. All moral values begin with regard for the life in each other. Multiply six million deaths that killed that regard, prevented consideration and mourning; multiply the knowledge of that quantity of exclusion, in exile from meaning, and our response might be that of a self-obliterating nihilism. But it might be also, in refusal of all acts of extinction, an intense distillation of restored memory, restored affinity and kinship, proportionate to the magnitude of loss.

Notes

Introduction

1. Emmanuel Levinas, *Ethics and Infinity* (Pittsburgh: Duquesne University Press, 1985), 115.

2. Elias Canetti, *The Human Province* (New York: Seabury Press, 1978), 9.

3. Yehuda Bauer and Nathan Rotenstreich, eds., *The Holocaust as Historical Experience* (New York: Holmes & Meier Publishers, 1981), 251.

4. Non-Jews were of course also victims of the Nazis, and some, as in the case of homosexuals and Gypsies, in more or less the same province of death administered to Jews. One might accept the usage of Jean-Francois Lyotard in referring to victims in the lower case as "jews," or André Neher's description of the "universal character of the disaster of Auschwitz" in terms of "the meta-Jewish participation" in its death. It is likely, however, that only the deaths of Gypsies correspond exactly with the genocidal death of Jews. But even here, Lucy Dawidowicz points out that Himmler explicitly exempted Gypsies of settled residence in communities, and only nomadic Gypsies were destroyed. The "crime against humanity" is not expressed in generalized slaughter but in the specific extraction of a group from membership in humanity and in attack on its right to exist (Jean-Francois Lyotard, *Heidegger and "the jews"* [Minneapolis: University of Minnesota Press, 1990]; André Neher, *The Exile of the Word*, trans. David Maisel (Philadelphia: Jewish Publication Society, 1981), 144.

5. Simon Leys, in *New York Review of Books*, October 12, 1989.

6. Neher, *The Exile of the Word*, 143.

Chapter One

1. Lucy S. Dawidowicz, *The Holocaust and the Historians* (Cambridge, Mass: Harvard University Press, 1981), 15.

2. As one of the most articulate and morally sensible of Holocaust survivors, Jean Améry writes how he felt as a young student in Vienna, half-Jewish, and reading the Nuremberg Laws of 1935. "If the sentence that society had passed on me had a tangible meaning, it could only be that henceforth I was a quarry of Death . . . I do not believe that I am inadmissably projecting Auschwitz and the Final Solution back to 1935 when I advance these thoughts today. Rather, I am certain that in that year, at that moment when I read the Laws, I did indeed already hear the death threat—better, the death sentence—. . ." (Améry, *At the Mind's Limits* [Bloomington: Indiana University Press, 1980], 85).

3. This is the summary observation of his translator, Sidney Rosenfeld, writing the "Afterword" of *At the Mind's Limits* (111).

4. Michael Marrus, *The Holocaust in History* (Hanover and London: University Press of New England, 1987), 24.

5. Geoffrey Eley, in *London Review of Books,* March 3–17, 1982, 6. Theodor Adorno suggested that special attention to Jewish suffering in the Holocaust helped segregate them as a group and thus conceded too much ground to anti-Semitism. It may be unfair to conclude that this thought and Eley's both urge silence on the subject, the same silence and for similar reasons that affected many during the actual Holocaust (*Bitburg in Moral and Political Perspective,* ed. Geoffrey H. Hartman (Bloomington: Indiana University Press, 1986), 114–29.

6. "The Uniqueness and the Universality of the Holocaust," in *Holocaust: Religious and Philosophical Implications,* ed. John K. Roth & Michael Berenbaum (New York: Paragon House, 1989), 90–92.

7. Chaim A. Kaplan, *The Warsaw Diary of Chaim A. Kaplan* (New York: Macmillan Co., 1965), 284.

8. Philip Roth interviewing Aharon Appelfeld, *New York Times Book Review,* February 28, 1988, 28.

9. Arthur Cohen, *The Tremendum* (New York: Crossroad Publishing Co., 1988), 79.

10. Jean Améry, *Radical Humanism,* trans. Sidney and Stella P. Rosenfeld (Bloomington: Indiana University Press, 1984), 35.

11. Elie Wiesel, "The Holocaust as Literary Imperative," in *Dimensions of the Holocaust* (Evanston, Ill.: Northwestern University Press, 1977), 5.

12. Améry, *Radical Humanism,* 36.

13. Aharon Appelfeld, in *New York Times Book Review,* February 28, 1988, 31.

14. Alvin H. Rosenfeld, in *Bitburg in Moral and Political Perspective,* 97.

15. Wiesel, in *Dimensions of the Holocaust,* 57, 15.

16. Alice & Roy Eckardt, "How German Thinkers View the Holocaust," *Christian Century* 93, March 17, 1976, 249–52.

17. Quoted and translated by David Carroll in "Foreword" to Jean-Francois Lyotard, *Heidegger and "the jews,"* xxvii n.12.

18. George Steiner, *Language and Silence* (New York: Atheneum, 1966), 123, 160.

19. Lawrence L. Langer, in his critical treatment of Holocaust literature, refers to Theodor Adorno to suggest that through the principle of "esthetic stylization" the inconceivable fate of the victims appears to have had some sense after all, that a transfiguration occurs, that some of the horror of the events is removed. He quotes Adorno: "The prospect of art denying what it seeks to affirm, (the hideous chaos of dehumanization during the Holocaust) raises a spectre of paradox for the critic, the reader, and the artist himself, that is not easily circumvented" (Langer, *The Holocaust and the Literary Imagination* (New Haven: Yale University Press, 1975), 2. Langer pursues the subject in his recent book, *Holocaust Testimonies* (New Haven: Yale University Press, 1991) (which I examine at greater length below, Chap. 7), criticizing the teleological form and closure that written narratives inevitably produce. On the other side, Berel Lang, who gives extended treatment of the limits and barriers for imaginative representation of the Holocaust, says, "Literary agency is characteristically individual; thus, where what is crucial in the literary subject is

the impersonality of its causes and reasons, to aestheticize or individualize those sources is to falsify or misrepresent the subject" (*Act and Idea in the Nazi Genocide* [Chicago: University of Chicago Press, 1991], 146).

20. Berel Lang in his extended review of the Holocaust as ethical testimony cites the Passover Haggadah and the requirement of its recitation as the model of the serial "retelling" of the Holocaust, in all its versions of multiple and limited interpretation. To emphasize his point of moral education for individuals and not for official publics, Lang writes that "each Jew should tell the story of the genocide as though he or she had passed through it." This he urges as a function of moral discourse and thus not an experience limited to Jews and writers. I take his meaning as exactly relevant and supportive of my own (ibid., xiii).

21. Joachim C. Fest, *The Face of the Third Reich* (New York: Pantheon Books, 1970), 291.

22. Adolph Hitler, *Mein Kampf,* trans. Ralph Manheim (Boston: Houghton Mifflin Co. 1943), 339.

23. Bruno Bettelheim, *Surviving and Other Essays* (New York: Alfred A. Knopf, 1979), 93.

24. Raul Hilberg, *The Destruction of the European Jews* (New York: Holmes and Meier, 1985), 3:1118n22.

25. Améry, *At the Mind's Limits,* 72–78. In contrasting mood, George Steiner writes, "If totalitarian rule is so effective as to break all chances of denunciation, of satire, then let the poet cease—and let the scholar cease from editing the classics a few miles down the road from the death camp. Precisely because it is the signature of his humanity, . . . the word should have no natural life, no neutral sanctuary, in the places and season of bestiality. Silence is an alternative" (*Language and Silence,* 54). No one, however, speaks of a "neutral sanctuary"; rather they talk of "revolt" in the existential sense used by Jean Améry.

26. *Language and Silence,* ix, 149.

27. *New York Review of Books* (Winter 1989).

28. *Language and Silence,* ix.

29. "Indeed, if we ask ourselves what will happen to a humanity where every group is striving more eagerly than ever to feel conscious of its own particular interests, and makes its moralists tell it that it is sublime to the extent that it knows no law but this interest—a child can give the answer. This humanity is heading for the greatest and most perfect war ever seen in the world. . . . The logical end of the 'integral realism' professed by humanity today is the organized slaughter of nations and classes" (Julien Benda, *La trahison des clercs* (1927), published in English as *The Betrayal of the Intellectuals* [New York: William Morrow & Co., 1928], 145, 162).

30. Améry, *At the Mind's Limits,* 11–12.

Chapter Two

1. Emphasizing the point, Theodor W. Adorno has written, "The administrative murder of millions made of death a thing one had never yet to fear in just this fashion. There is no chance any more for death to come into the individual's empir-

ical life as somehow conformable with the course of that life. The last, the poorest
possession left to the individual is expropriated. That in the concentration camps
it was no longer an individual who died, but a specimen" (Adorno, *Negative Dialectics* [New York: Continuum, 1973], 362).

2. Lucy S. Dawidowicz, *The War against the Jews* (New York: Holt, Rinehart &
Winston, 1975), 350.

3. Adam Czerniakow, *The Warsaw Diary of Adam Czerniakow,* ed. Raul Hilberg
et al. (New York: Stein & Day, 1979), 90.

4. Améry, *Radical Humanism,* 29–30.

5. Primo Levi, *The Drowned and the Saved* (New York: Summit Books, 1988),
113–14.

6. Canetti, *The Human Province,* 12.

7. Chaim A. Kaplan, *The Warsaw Diary of . . . ,* 44.

8. Emmanuel Ringelblum, *Notes from the Warsaw Ghetto* (New York: McGraw
Hill, 1959), 24, 39, 109.

9. Ibid., 331, 232.

10. Ibid., 146.

11. Améry, *At the Mind's Limits,* 35, 31.

12. Emil Fackenheim, *To Mend the World* (New York: Schocken Books, 1982),
200.

13. Robert Jay Lifton, *The Nazi Doctors* (New York: Basic Books, 1986).

14. "Abstract," in my use here and elsewhere, is a generic term to describe moral
distancing and the reduction of agents in events to functions, or data, or generalized concepts.

15. Heinrich Himmler, speech in April 1943, *Nazi Conspiracy and Aggression,*
International Military Tribunal at Nurnberg (Washington, D.C.: Goverment Print-
ing Office, 1946), vol. 4, Document 1919-PS, 574.

16. Ringelblum, *Notes from the Warsaw Ghetto,* 17.

17. Peter Loewenberg reports details of the conference of Nazi leaders shortly
after Kristallnacht in November 1938. The conference was held to consider the
Kristallnacht consequences and further measures against the Jews. Present were
Goering, Goebbels, Heydrich, Funk, and Frick, among others. "At this point the
Nazi leadership was more interested in how to humiliate Jews than in other issues.
The conference lasted 3 1/2 hours detailing fantasies of sadistic humiliation . . . it is
evident that the most relevant and neglected element in German anti-Jewish policy
in 1938 is the heightened emotional tone of depreciation, of narcissistic devalua-
tion, and of personal humiliation of Jews under Nazi power" (Loewenberg, "The
Kristallnacht as Degradation Ritual," in *Leo Baeck Institute Yearbook,* (London,
New York: Secker and Warburg, 1987) 320).

18. Maimonides: *His Wisdom for Our Time,* ed. Gilbert S. Rosenthal (New York:
Funk & Wagnalls, 1969), 34.

19. Terrence Des Pres, *The Survivor* (New York: Oxford University Press, 1976),
55 and chap. 3.

20. Fackenheim, *To Mend the World,* 209.

21. Améry, *At the Mind's Limits,* 27, 28, 29.

22. Primo Levi, *Survival at Auschwitz* (New York: Summit Books, 1986), 171–72.

23. Ibid., 150.

24. Ringelblum, *Notes from the Warsaw Ghetto,* 263.

25. Primo Levi, *Survival at Auschwitz,* 52.

26. Ringelblum, *Notes from the Warsaw Ghetto,* 266.

27. Rudolf Hoess, *Commandant of Auschwitz* (London: Weidenfeld & Nicolson, 1960), 142.

28. Saul Friedlander, *Kurt Gerstein: The Ambiguity of Good* (New York: Alfred A. Knopf, 1969), 108.

29. Chaim A. Kaplan, *The Warsaw Diary of . . . ,* 70, 63.

30. René Girard, *Violence and the Sacred* (Baltimore and London: The Johns Hopkins University Press, 1977), chap. 1.

31. Chaim A. Kaplan, *The Warsaw Diary of . . . ,* 120.

32. Vasily Grossman, *Life and Fate* (London: Collins Harvill, 1985).

33. "Muselman," a word of uncertain derivation, was the term used in the camps for people who had surrendered and were ready to die, moving like limp shadows until they dropped in their places.

34. At that extreme of thought, the philosopher Robert Nozick judged that the Holocaust replaces the mythical Fall, that truly now "mankind has fallen . . . Humanity has lost its claim to continue" (*The Examined Life* [New York: Simon & Schuster, 1989], 238).

35. Bettelheim, *Surviving and Other Essays,* 90–93.

36. Primo Levi, *The Drowned and the Saved,* 136.

37. "Those who "trade blows" with the entire world achieve dignity but pay a very high price for it because they are sure to be defeated. Améry's suicide, . . . like other suicides admits of a cloud of explanations, but, in hindsight, that episode of defying the Pole offers one interpretation" (Primo Levi, *The Drowned and the Saved,* 136).

38. Ibid., 25.

39. Des Pres, *The Survivor,* 3.

40. Pelagia Lewinska, *Twenty Months at Auschwitz,* 141ff., 150, quoted by Fackenheim, in *To Mend the World,* 217.

41. Améry, *At the Mind's Limits,* 172.

Chapter Three

1. The duality in totalitarian thinking is suggested by an insightful remark made years ago by Lewis S. Feuer in the preface to his anthology of the writings of Marx and Engels: "In Marxism we find for the first time a combination of the language of science and the language of myth—a union of mysticism and logic" (*Marx and Engels: Basic Writings* [New York: Doubleday & Co., 1959], x).

2. Gerald Fleming, *Hitler and the Final Solution* (Berkeley: University of California Press, 1984), 52.

3. *The Secret Conferences of Dr. Goebbels,* ed. Willi A. Boelcke (New York: E. P. Dutton & Co., 1970), 309.

4. *Eichmann Interrogated,* ed. Jochen von Lang (New York: Farrar, Straus & Giroux, 1983), 147.

5. George Steiner, *Martin Heidegger* (New York: Viking Press, 1979), 118.

6. Hermann Rauschning, *The Voice of Destruction* (New York: G. P. Putnam's Sons, 1940), 223.

7. Arno Mayer makes a case for saying that even the genocide, not to mention the war and the general program of Nazism, was based on targeting "Judaeo-Bolshevism." Without attempting to argue the point here, there is room certainly for allowing an alliance in Hitler's mind between such products of the Enlightenment as Weimar democracy and the Bolshevik Revolution. I would cite the two images of Chamberlain and Stalin in Hitler's perspective. One was of a civilization about to decay from within and be destroyed, the other the actual powerful rival to his Thousand Year Reich. The Jewish poison could work in both, and propaganda could make the point, but evidence suggests that in Hitler's mind the Jewish power was more directly effective with Roosevelt's legions than with Stalin's (Arno Mayer, *Why Did the Heavens Not Darken* [New York: Pantheon Books, 1988]).

8. In his memoir, Rudolf Hoess, commandant at Auschwitz, describes being struck by this. Among much relevant elucidation by Raul Hilberg, he reports the similar reaction of the killing group, Einsatzgruppe C, in the early invasion of Russia (Hilberg, *The Destruction of the European Jews,* 127).

9. Rauschning, *The Voice of Destruction,* 25.

10. Alan Bullock, *Hitler: A Study in Tyranny* (New York: Harper & Row, 1962), 397.

11. Georg Wilhelm Friedrich Hegel, *The Philosophy of History,* trans. J. Sibree (New York: Dover Publications, 1956), 29–32.

12. Bullock, *Hitler: A Study in Tyranny,* 384.

13. On the general subject, in Germany and the West, see Karl Dietrich Bracher, *The German Dictatorship* (New York: Holt, Rinehard & Winston, 1970); Jeffrey Herf, *Reactionary Modernism* (Cambridge and New York: Cambridge University Press, 1984); James D. Wilkinson, *The Intellectual Resistance* (Cambridge, Mass.: Harvard University Press, 1981).

14. Perhaps in reaction the world learned the value of passive disobedience; Gandhi, though he gave some discouraging advice to the Jews of the Holocaust, achieved historic insight in promoting resistance to apparent fate and real power.

15. Isaiah Trunk, *Jewish Responses to Nazi Persecution* (New York: Stein & Day, 1979), 24.

16. Hegel, *The Philosophy of History,* 30. The passage in Hegel continues in shocking forecast of "made" history: "For that Spirit which had taken this fresh step in history is the inmost soul of all individuals; but in a state of unconsciousness which the great men in question aroused. Their fellows, therefore, follow these soul-leaders; for they feel the irresistible power of their own inner Spirit thus embodied."

17. Lyotard, *Heidegger and "the jews,"* 72 (passage quoted by Lyotard from Débat [184–85]).

18. Steiner, *Martin Heidegger,* 113.

19. Peter Viereck, *Metapolitics* (New York: Alfred A. Knopf, 1941), 194, quoted and trans. from Fichte, *Reden an deutsche Nation.*

20. Saul Friedlander, *Pius XII and the Third Reich* (New York: Alfred A. Knopf), 91.

21. Lifton, *The Nazi Doctors,* 196.

22. Canetti, *The Human Province,* 24–25.

23. Observing writers under Stalinist regimes choosing among ideas and principles, Milosz observed, "He weighs his chances and concludes it is unwise to align himself with the side that has been damned by the Being which has taken the place of God in this century i.e. history" (Milosz, *The Captive Mind* [New York: Alfred A. Knopf, 1953], 15, 31).

24. Lyotard, *Heidegger and "the jews,"* 68–69.

25. Steiner, *Martin Heidegger,* 113, 83, 119.

26. Hegel, *The Philosophy of History,* 66–67.

27. Rauschning, *The Voice of Destruction,* 39.

28. Ibid., 17.

29. Ibid., 41, 107.

Chapter Four

1. Von Lang, ed., *Eichmann Interrogated,* 91.

2. Ibid., 91.

3. Boelcke, ed., *The Secret Conferences of Dr. Goebbels,* 254.

4. Von Lang, ed., *Eichmann Interrogated,* 131.

5. Hannah Arendt, *Eichmann in Jerusalem* (New York: Viking Press, 1963). Perhaps ultimately Arendt meant that the Nazis had reduced murder to bureaucratic banality as a device for limiting consciousness in themselves, their victims, and the host of peoples, German and foreign, who gave passive assent to the slaughter. But that was strategy and bureaucratic practice; the motive for murder can never be banal.

6. Von Lang, ed., *Eichmann Interrogated,* 233.

7. Fleming, *Hitler and the Final Solution,* 27 (quoting from *Monologe im Führerhauptquartier: 1941–1944,* ed. W. Jochmann [Hamburg, 1980], 76).

8. George Steiner, *The Portage to San Cristobal of A. H.* (London: Faber & Faber, 1983), 115, 117.

9. Rauschning, *The Voice of Destruction,* 252.

10. Leon Poliakov, *Harvest of Hate* (New York: Holocaust Library, 1979), 5.

11. Rauschning, *The Voice of Destruction,* 237.

12. H. R. Trevor-Roper, *The Last Days of Hitler* (New York: Macmillan Co., 1947), 79.

13. Arad et al., *Documents on the Holocaust* ed. Yitzhak Arad, Yisrael Gutman,

Abraham Margaliot. (Jerusalem: Yad Vashem, and KTAV Publishing, 1981), 162.

14. *Hitler's Secret Conversations,* trans. Norman Cameron and R. H. Stevens (The Martin Bormann notes) (New York: Farrar, Straus & Young, 1953), 116.

15. Ibid., 116, 119.

16. Saul Friedlander, "AntiSemitism to Extermination," in *Unanswerable Questions,* ed. Francois Furet (New York: Schocken Books, 1989), 329n.

17. It has been more frequently called a political religion, as I have in these pages. There is no real inconsistency; the common dimension is what may be called the "metaphysicalization" of modern politics, or its irresistible tendency to become a "metapolitics."

18. Zygmunt Bauman, *Modernity and the Holocaust* (Ithaca, N.Y.: Cornell University Press, 1989).

19. Hitler, *Mein Kampf,* trans. Ralph Manheim (Boston: Houghton Mifflin Co., 1943), 394.

20. Bauman, *Modernity and the Holocaust,* 72.

21. Lifton, *The Nazi Doctors,* 17.

22. Ibid., 22–44.

23. Ibid., 31, 377.

24. The ripe conclusion of biological politics is illustrated in a remark by Werner Best, Heydrich's deputy and Himmler's legal aide, who identified the "political principle of totalitarianism" with the "ideological principle of the organically indivisible national community," and "any attempt to . . . uphold different political ideas will be ruthlessly dealt with, as the symptom of an illness which threatens the healthy unity of the indivisible national organism . . ." (Martin Broszat "The Concentration Camps 1933–45," in Helmut Krausnick et al., *Anatomy of the SS State* [New York: Walker 1968], 426–27).

25. Lifton, *The Nazi Doctors,* 178, 44.

26. Stephen Jay Gould, letter to the *New York Review of Books,* January 19, 1989, 60.

27. The analogy is with Freud's use of "metapsychology." Jean-Francois Lyotard defines what he meant this way: "They are the elements of a metaphysics that is inherent in all modern physics in which under the name of metapsychology Freud directs toward the determination of the state of the soul itself, which has, ever since, been considered a system of forces . . . a topics, a dynamics, and an economy that deal respectively with the instances, the forces and conflicts of force (attraction and repulsion) and the results (effects) assessed quantitatively" (11). The style is elliptical and abstract, but the statement will do as a basis for defining "metapolitics" (Lyotard, *Heidegger and "the jews";* see Freud, *Metapsychologie* [1915–17] [Paris: Gallimard, 1952]).

28. Viereck, *Metapolitics,* 4 (quote from Constantin Franz letter printed in *Bayreuther Blatter* 1, no. 6 [June 1878], 169).

29. Levinas, *Ethics and Infinity,* 89–90.

30. Nazism: *A History in Documents,* ed. J. Noakes and G. Pridham (New York: Schocken Books, 1988), 1199–20.

31. Rauschning, *The Voice of Destruction,* 225.

32. Viereck, *Metapolitics,* 301.

33. Lifton, *The Nazi Doctors,* 324.

34. Ibid., 324.

35. Jacob L. Talmon, *The Unique and the Universal,* (New York: George Braziller, 1966), 128.

36. *Karl Marx: Early Writings,* trans. and ed. T. B. Bottomore (New York: McGraw-Hill Book Co., 1963), "On the Jewish Question," 1–40.

37. Interview with Claude Lévi-Strauss, *New York Times,* December 21, 1987.

38. Karl Marx, *The Economic and Philosophic Manuscripts of 1844,* ed. Dirk J. Struik (New York: International Publishers, 1964), 169. Another passage from Marx's early writings is even more fundamental in drawing a distinction between his version of communism and Hitler's Fascism. In it he describes communism as the overcoming of "human self-estrangement" and as "the real appropriation of the human essence by and for man; communism therefore as the complete return of man to himself as a social (i.e., human) being—a return become conscious, and accomplished within the entire wealth of previous development. Thus communism, as fully developed naturalism, equals humanism, and as fully developed humanism equals naturalism; it is the genuine resolution of the conflict between man and nature and between man and man—the true resolution of the strife between existence and essence, between objectification and self-confirmation, between freedom and necessity, the individual and the species. Communism is the riddle of history solved, and knows itself to be this solution." Today, in the context of the Gulag as well as the Holocaust, this passage leaves one breathless, though admiring the moral passion under the philosophical burden of Marx's dialectic (135).

39. Cohen, *The Tremendum,* 10.

40. Michael A. Musmanno, *The Eichmann Commandos* (London: Peter Davies, 1961), 99.

Chapter Five

1. Reichstag speech of January 30, 1939: "During the time of my struggle for power it was in the first instance only the Jewish race that received my prophecies with laughter when I said that I would one day take over the leadership of the State, and with it that of the whole nation, and that I would then among other things settle the Jewish problem. Their laughter was uproarious, but I think that for some time now they have been laughing on the other side of their face." This was the speech where Hitler first threatened the Jews with annihilation (*The Speeches of Adolf Hitler, April 1922–August 1939,* ed. Norman H. Baynes (London: Oxford University Press, 1942), 2:740–41).

2. H. R. Trevor-Roper, *The Last Days of Hitler* (New York: Macmillan Co., 1947), 234.

3. Ibid., xiv, 232.

4. Fest quotes Himmler speaking in the memoirs of Felix Kersten, Himmler's Swedish masseur: "How can you find pleasure, Herr Kersten, in shooting from behind cover at poor creatures browsing on the edge of a wood, innocent, defenceless, and unsuspecting? It's really pure murder. Nature is so marvelously beautiful and every animal has a right to live." One must add to this the report of his "heart-

felt emotion, which overcame him at the sight of blond children" (Fest, *The Face of the Third Reich*, 121).

5. Von Lang, *Eichmann Interrogated*, 81.

6. At a time when it seemed almost certain that the Germans had lost the war, Goebbels said to his immediate followers, "The Fuhrer is happy over my report that the Jews have for the most part been evacuated from Berlin. He is right in saying that the war has made possible for us the solution of a whole series of problems that could never have been solved in normal times. The Jews will certainly be the losers in this war, come what may" (*The Goebbels Diaries* (1942–43), ed. Louis F. Lochner [New York: Doubleday & Co., 1948], 314). This was their victory in principle, their moral gain, and how casual the means—"one way or another"—and thus "the Fuhrer is happy."

7. Ibid., 80–81.

8. Ibid., 198.

9. *Hitler's Secret Conversations*, 72. Gerald Fleming translates this passage as follows: "It is good that we are preceded by an aura of terror for our plans to exterminate Jewry" (*Hitler and the Final Solution*, 2).

10. Fleming (2) quotes from *Adolf Hitler: Monologe im Fuhrerhauptquartier 1941–44*, ed. Werner Jochman (Hamburg, 1980, 99, 421). The early English version (*Hitler's Secret Conversations* [New York, 1953] 65) reads with less emphasis and bears mistakes.

11. Lifton, *The Nazi Doctors*, 469. (Refers to Ronald Gray's book, *The German Tradition in Literature* [Cambridge: Cambridge University Press, 1965], 48–49.)

12. Saul Friedlander, *Reflections of Nazism* (New York: Harper Row, 1984), 19, 136.

13. Trevor-Roper, *The Last Days of Hitler*, 72

14. Hugh Trevor-Roper describes how near the end of the war Goebbels sounded the "authentic voice of Nazism uninhibited." "It was the doctrine of class war, of permanent revolution." For the German press Goebbels wrote: "Under the debris of our shattered cities the last so-called achievements of the middle-class nineteenth century have been finally buried." "There is no end to revolution," cried his Radio Werewolf. "A revolution is only doomed to failure if those who make it cease to be revolutionaries. . . . Now that everything is in ruins, we are forced to rebuild Europe" (Trevor-Roper, *The Last Days of Hitler*, 50–51).

15. Emil Fackenheim sees Nazi power in that relentlessly reductive aspect. "The Third Reich made much use of Nietzschean phrases. However, it revealed itself not as a Will-to-Power but rather as a Will-to-Destruction which, being universal, was a Will-to-Self-destruction as well." But nothing phrased as the "Will-to-Power" can escape being at the same time a "Will-to-Destruction" (*To Mend the World*, 264).

16. Hitler never forgot his original ambitions in art which developed toward grandiose projects reported by Albert Speer. He had the vision of himself as *Kunstpolitiker* and the Thousand Year Reich as a *Gesamtkunstwerk* (total work of art) (Steven A. Luel and Paul Marcus, eds., *Psychoanalytic Reflections on the Holocaust* [New York: KTAV Publishing House, 1984], 40).

17. So Hitler observed in speaking for Rauschning's record: "The world can only be ruled by fear. . . . The people need wholesome fear. They *want* to fear some-

thing. They want someone to frighten them and make them shudderingly submissive." And speaking of his political enemies, "the beaten ones are the first to join the party as new members" (Rauschning, *The Voice of Destruction*, 81, 83).

18. Ibid., 281.

19. Ibid., 192.

20. Bullock, *Hitler: A Study in Tyranny*, 14.

21. Elias Canetti, *Crowds and Power*, (New York, The Viking Press, 1962) 227, 228.

22. Améry, *At the Mind's Limits*, 35, 36.

23. Musmanno, *The Eichmann Commandos*, 173.

24. Rauschning, *The Voice of Destruction*, 279, 40.

25. Hitler memorandum of 1936, in *Documents on the Holocaust*, 89.

26. Robert Conquest, *The Great Terror* (New York: Oxford University Press, 1990), 112; ref.: Boris Souvarine, *Stalin* (London, 1949), 362–63.

27. Conquest, 112; ref.: Boris I. Nicolaevsky, *Power and the Soviet Elite* (New York, 1965), 25.

28. Ibid., 110,111.

29. Ibid., 113.

30. Bukharin, after denouncing Stalin's insane ambitions, when asked why the oppositionists had surrendered to him (this was in 1935) replied, "You don't understand. . . . It is not him we trust but the man in whom the Party has reposed its confidence. It just so happened that he has become a sort of symbol of the Party (Conquest, 112; ref.: Raphael R. Abramovitch, *The Soviet Revolution* [London, 1962], 416).

31. Rauschning, 282. Such is the doctrine given to Machiavelli in the "Dialogue in Hell" featured in the introduction to the Protocols of Zion.

32. Fest, *The Face of the Third Reich*, 103.

33. Rauschning, *The Voice of Destruction*, 18. Bullock and Fest show the specific rivalry with revolutionary Communists and the left in the early days of the Nazi party when Hitler was influenced by the group of White Russian anti-Semitic émigrés, led by Lanz von Liebenfels, who published the Ostara pamphlets Hitler obtained and read (Bullock, *Hitler: A Study in Tyranny*, 79; Fest, *The Face of the Third Reich*, 36).

34. The thesis of Arno Mayer's recent book, *Why Did the Heavens Not Darken* (New York: Pantheon Books, 1988), is that Hitler's anti-Semitism was founded on his anti-Bolshevism and took second place to it. But the evidence suggests that he was much more sincere and consistent in his hatred of Jews. Witness his almost admiring references to Stalin and the Soviets during the height of the Russian campaign and even when it was beginning to go badly (see *Hitler's Secret Conversations*). Stalin was master of a power he could envy and emulate. It is likely that the Jew was more closely identified in his mind with democracy, not Bolshevism, as well as with internationalism or "cosmopolitanism," liberalism, and pacifism. But in the end, one must consider in the case of the Nazis that all forms of ideological hatred took second place to the thrust of violence and the struggle for power.

35. Rauschning, *The Voice of Destruction*, 11, 10, 192.

36. Otto Strasser, *Hitler and I* (Boston: Houghton Mifflin, 1940), 107.

37. Rauschning *The Voice of Destruction*, 175.

38. Ibid., 237.

39. "I found these Protocols [of Zion] enormously instructive." Asked what he took from the Protocols, Hitler answered, "Political intrigue, the technique of conspiracy, revolutionary subversion, prevarication, deception, organization" (*The Voice of Destruction*, 241).

40. Ibid., 239, 232.

41. Helmut Krausnick et al., *Anatomy of the SS State*, 338.

42. Hilberg, *The Destruction of the European Jews*, 3:989.

43. Christopher R. Browning, *The Final Solution and the German Foreign Office* (New York: Holmes & Meier, 1978), 86.

44. Oswald Spengler, *The Decline of the West* (New York: Alfred A. Knopf, 1926), 2:545–46.

45. James D. Wilkinson, *The Intellectual Resistance*, 156.

46. Ibid ., 157. Wilkinson's succinct phrasing points to the nub of the issue for posttotalitarian politics where it might be assumed that power and ethics are always in some form of tension or conflict. Additional reference to the theme can be found in Georg G. Iggers, *The German Conception of History*, (Middletown, Conn: Wesleyan University Press, 1968), 118; Friedrich Meinecke, *The German Catastrophe*, (Cambridge, Mass: Harvard University Press, 1950), 338; and, of course, Hegel.

47. Goebbels's statement of party mission, quoted by Viereck (124).

48. Hilberg, *The Destruction of the European Jews*, 3:1021.

49. Bullock, *Hitler: A Study in Tyranny*, 527. One result we know is that "of more than five million Russian soldiers captured by the Germans during the war, two million are known to have died in captivity (mostly of hunger, cold, neglected disease) and another million are unaccounted for" (Alexander Dallin, *German Rule in Russia, 1941–45*, 426–27).

50. Heinrich Himmler, speech in April 1943, International Military Tribunal at Nurnberg, Document 1919-PS vol. 4 (578).

51. Michel Foucault, "Prison Talk," in *Power/Knowledge*, ed. Colin Gordon (New York: Pantheon Books, 1980), 53.

52. "Prison Talk," 52, and "Body/Power," 55, in ibid.

53. "Body/Power," 57, and "Two Lectures," 89 and 90, in ibid.

54. "Two Lectures," 90, in ibid.

55. Ibid.

56. The subject which interests me most is Foucault's division between two schemas for the analysis of power, and it is a subject I take up in the last chapter of this book. But here is Foucault's own phrasing of the important opposition: "Thus we have two schemes for the analysis of power. The contract-oppression schema, which is the juridical one, and the domination-repression or war-repression schema for which the pertinent opposition is not between the legitimate and illegitimate, as in the first schema, but between struggle and submission." It should be observed that Foucault, in this lecture summarizing his life's work, ends by admitting some self-questioning reservations: "It is obvious that all my work in recent years has been couched in the schema of struggle-repression, and it is this—which I have

hitherto been attempting to apply—which I have now been forced to reconsider, both because it is still insufficiently elaborated at a whole number of points, and because I believe that these two notions of repression and war must themselves be considerably modified if not ultimately abandoned" (Foucault, "Two Lectures," 92).

57. Chaim A. Kaplan, *The Warsaw Diary of . . .*, 284.

58. Améry, *At the Mind's Limits*, 70.

59. Elias Canetti, *Crowds and Power*, 210.

60. Ibid.

61. As noted earlier, it is possible that Hitler drew his own dialectic of power-reality and conscience from the Protocols of Zion (which he knew in his formative years through his friend and follower Dietrich Eckart). The text presents an original scene, a "Dialogue in Hell," between Machiavelli and Montesquieu, one representing the policy of force and the latter the policy of justice (see Herman Bernstein, *The Truth about "The Protocols of Zion"* [New York: KTAV Publishing House, 1971], 16).

62. Lifton, 434.

Chapter Six

1. Ringelblum and Kaplan describe how German soldiers or SS would cruise the ghettos in their cars and randomly select passersby for victimization, jumping out to beat them and sometimes shoot them, always with the shock of surprise and without apparent cause. In hindsight we can see that these were not merely sadistic exercises but part of a psychological campaign to reduce their victims to the paralysis of fear.

2. *A Holocaust Reader*, ed. Lucy S. Dawidowicz (New York: Behrman House, 1976), 305.

3. Ibid., 303.

4. Ibid., 307.

5. Ibid., 311.

6. Raul Hilberg proposes the historic precedents for the response of Jews to persecution and pogrom, following ghetto-diaspora psychology: alleviation, evasion (escape), paralysis, compliance. The heaviest reliance was always on alleviation and compliance as instruments of survival. In his view this led to total disaster (*The Destruction of the European Jews*, 1:22–28).

7. "The perpetrators are the Holocaust; the victims stand apart. In this distinct sense, I would deny that the Holocaust belongs to the Jews. It belongs to the history and culture of the oppressors; it is theirs. It is German universities and churches that should be holding Holocaust conferences. And no Jew need or ought to be present" (Berel Lang, ed., *Writing and the Holocaust* (New York: Holmes & Meier, 1988), 284).

8. Adolph Hitler, Speech given January 30, 1939, in *Documents on the Holocaust*, (Jerusalem: Yad Vashem, 1981), 132.

9. Bracher in *The German Dictatorship* speaks of Nazi racism as biological anthropology. The Jewish stereotype changed from religious and moral to the racist-

biological, where, one can speculate, it remained the subversive antithesis to naturalist divinity.

10. Ibid., 37.

11. Everyone knows the useless cruel argument over the guilt of Jewish leaders or Jewish police, or the *sonderkommandos* in the death camps who helped operate the death machine. The crime was not *their* inability to choose heroic doomed resistance, or to choose suicide, like Czerniakow, leader of the Warsaw ghetto. The crime to focus on is the imposition of terms for survival, or the survival of a remnant, which entailed a moral destruction in advance of physical death. There is great punishment in the feeling of shame. Emmanuel Ringelblum was one who earned to right to protest Jewish nonresistance at the *Umschlagplatz,* the Warsaw railroad gathering place for transport to Treblinka. "This will be an eternal mystery—this passivity of the Jewish populace even toward its own police. Now that the populace has calmed down somewhat . . . they are becoming ashamed of having put up no resistance at all" (Ringelblum, 333).

12. Etty Hillesum, *Letters from Westerbork* (London: Jonathan Cape, 1987), 81.

13. Ibid., 87, 89.

14. Ibid., 126.

15. Ibid., 128.

16. Ibid., 124.

17. Isaiah Trunk, in his exhaustive account of victim responses, describes the following among reasons for the apparent "passivity" of most victims. "The Jews might also have actually wondered whether it was worth fighting for one's life in a world where the human beast could rule undisturbed amid the passive silence of the entire civilized world." He adds, "And if you find this unconvincing, read the reports below," referring to the detailed eyewitness testimonies he published in his book (*Jewish Responses to the Holocaust,* 55).

18. Etty Hillesum, *An Interrupted Life* (New York: Pantheon Books, 1983), 152.

19. Ibid., 153.

20. Hillesum, *Letters . . . ,* 77–78.

21. Hillesum, *An Interrupted Life,* 157ff.

22. Hillesum, *Letters . . . ,* 132.

23. Hillesum, *An Interrupted Life,* 130.

24. Ibid., 146–147.

25. George M. Kren and Leon Rappoport suggest "the fallacy of innocence" which explained the victims' inability to resist or escape, and which weakened the energy for survival. Seeing no rational basis for their abuse, feeling innocent of any wrong or of being a war problem for the Germans, they assumed abuse proceeded from a mistake or a temporary lapse of rationality. Thus the flaw might be corrected if understood, or at least moderated. Elie Cohen points out that "guilty" camp victims, that is, politicals resisting the Germans, survived better than the others (Kren and Rappoport, *The Holocaust and the Crisis of Human Behavior* [New York: Holmes & Meier Publishers, 1980], 74).

26. Helen Fein concisely observed, "Only if one were convinced that the Germans intended the death of all Jews was rebellion rational," and the possibility of

rebellion was of a sort in which "one enhanced one's life chances by increasing another's death chances" (*Accounting for Genocide* [New York: Free Press, 1979], 319–320).

27. Hillesum, *Letters from Westerbork,* p. 98.

28. *Language and Silence,* 141.

29. Ibid., 148.

30. Ibid., 141.

31. *The Kovno Ghetto Diary* (Cambridge, Mass.: Harvard University Press, 1990), 155 (entries for November 18 and 19, 1942).

32. Avraham Tory, "Surviving the Holocaust," in *The Kovno Ghetto Diary,* 5 (entries for June 23–July 7, 1941).

33. Saul Friedlander, *Kurt Gerstein, The Ambiguity of the Good,* 159.

34. Hans Mommsen, "Anti-Jewish Politics," in *The Challenge of the Third Reich,* ed. Hedley Bull (Oxford University Press, 1986), 121.

35. Lacoue-Labarthe belongs to a group of modern French thinkers, close to the thought of Martin Heidegger, who in participating in the debate over Heidegger's connection with Nazism have produced a rich discussion of issues pertaining to the Holocaust itself. Among them are Jean-Francois Lyotard (cited below and elsewhere in this text), Luc Ferry, Alain Renaut, and Victor Farias. The latter's book on Heidegger provoked much of the debate and induced a significant response from Jacques Derrida.

36. Phillippe Lacoue-Labarthe, *Heidegger, Art and Politics* (Oxford and Cambridge: Basil Blackwell, 1990), 36–37.

37. Lyotard, *Heidegger and "the jews,"* 22.

38. Hitler favorably quoted his mentor, Dietrich Eckart, who told him that in his life he had known only one "decent" Jew, Otto Weininger, a fanatically self-hating German Jew who committed suicide on that explicit basis [*Hitler's Secret Conversations, 1941–44,* 116.

39. Lifton, *The Nazi Doctors,* 371.

40. *The Lodz Ghetto Diary,* 425, 431.

41. Canetti, *The Human Province,* 71.

42. "The expectation of help, the certainty of help, is indeed one of the fundamental experiences of human beings, and probably also of animals . . . as much a constitutional psychic element as the struggle for existence" (Améry, *At the Mind's Limits,* 28).

43. Christopher Browning, *Ordinary Men* (New York: HarperCollins, 1992). Subsequent page references in text.

44. Three of the men reported seeing Trapp weep in ordering the first action at Jozefow. Together with allowing those who wished to withdraw from the action, this was highly unusual in the record of officer behavior. As for the tears, one would need to assign that to a deeper psychological study than the record makes possible. Only one other officer objected and successfully sustained resistance to further participation. Major Trapp continued to lead the battalion in almost all of its killing actions, efficiently obeying orders. He with two others from the battalion were later executed in Poland for war crimes. Those initial tears seem as difficult to reach as the actual thoughts of his victims at the point of death.

45. One officer had colitis, thought to be related to killings. But evidence led to this conclusion: "If mass murder was giving Hoffman stomach pains, it was a fact he was deeply ashamed of and sought to overcome to the best of his ability" (120).

46. Langer, *Holocaust Testimonies*. Subsequent page references in text.

47. Alvin A. Rosenfeld, *A Double Dying* (Bloomington: Indiana University Press, 1980).

48. See my reference to Lyotard's point in the following pages.

49. Primo Levi, *The Drowned and the Saved*, 148.

50. See fuller reference, 43–44.

51. Fackenheim, *To Mend the World*, 217.

52. Améry, *At the Mind's Limits*, 172.

53. See earlier references, 41–42.

54. Améry, *At the Mind's Limits*, 11–12.

55. Primo Levi, *The Drowned and the Saved*, 25.

56. Ibid., 85.

Chapter Seven

1. *Language and Silence*, 54, 123.

2. Lyotard, *Heidegger and "the jews,"* 25–26.

3. Chaim A. Kaplan, *The Warsaw Diary of . . .*, 85.

4. Cohen, *The Tremendum*, 37, 41.

5. Chaim A. Kaplan, *The Warsaw Diary of . . .*, January 16, 1940, 104.

6. "The Holocaust as Literary Imperative," *Dimensions of the Holocaust*, 5.

7. *Poems*, trans. Michael Hamburger (New York: Persea Books, 1989).

8. Lang, *Writing and the Holocaust*, 274.

9. Fackenheim, *To Mend the World*, 292, 293, 255.

10. Ibid., 293–94 (note refers to Johann Baptist Metz, *Gott nach Auschwitz* [Freiburg: Herder, 1979]), 121–44.

11. Ibid., 299.

12. Ibid., 302.

13. Ibid., 303.

14. Adorno later amended his meaning but only by going to a further extreme: "Perennial suffering has as much right to expression as a tortured man has to scream; hence it may have been wrong to say that after Auschwitz you could no longer write poems. But it is not wrong to raise the less cultural question whether after Auschwitz you can go on living—especially whether one who escaped by accident, one who by rights should have been killed, may go on living" (Theodor Adorno, *Negative Dialectics* [New York: Continuum Publishing Co., 1973], 362).

15. Kren and Rappaport, *The Holocaust and the Crisis of Human Behavior*, 132.

16. Erich Kahler, *The Tower and the Abyss* (New York: George Braziller, 1957), 151.

17. Charles S. Maier, *The Unmastered Past* (Cambridge, Mass: Harvard University Press, 1988). See reference to Nolte, 15.

18. Nolte was in part protesting the obsession with German guilt and writes that the current debate over judgment might be resolved if all regarded the universal

issues of guilt and responsibility toward human rights. The crime is an injunction against future behavior, not a rehearsal for punishment. One agrees, but with an important difference, for the distinctness of the crime, its uniqueness as expressed in the moral and political system of the Nazis, is the essential basis of its future moral relevance.

19. Berel Lang, ed., *Writing and the Holocaust* (Roundtable Discussion), 278–87, see also 279n.7.

20. Ibid., 198. Howe was not present at the Albany Conference, but his essay, originally published in the *New Republic* was reproduced in the volume collection of documents and statements.

21. *Writing and the Holocaust*, 287.

22. Ibid., 282, 284; and Norma Rosen "The Second Life of Holocaust Imagery," *Midstream* (April 1987).

23. It is remarkable how in the literature of the Holocaust the reference is made to the "Jewish question" by Jews and non-Jews alike, as if the fact of a "question" were self-evident.

24. Des Pres, *The Survivor*, 49.

25. Rauschning, *The Voice of Destruction*, 78.

26. Des Pres, *The Survivor*, 46, 47.

27. Levinas, *Ethics and Infinity*, 118–19.

28. Ibid., 115, 96.

29. Ibid., 96.

Chapter Eight

1. Friedrich Engels, "Socialism: Utopian and Scientific," in *Marx and Engels: Basic Writings*, ed. Lewis S. Feuer (New York: Doubleday & Co., 1959), 109.

2. Lucy S. Dawidowicz, *The War Against the Jews 1933–1945*, 188.

3. Rauschning, *The Voice of Destruction*, 223.

4. Ibid., 225.

5. Ibid., 97.

6. Lacoue-Labarthe, *Heidegger, Art and Politics*, 21.

7. To reorient ourselves with what was at stake, let us refer to an anecdote from Thomas Mann's memoirs. He was recalling his first visit to Roosevelt in 1935: "When I left the White House after my first visit (on June 30, 1935), I knew Hitler was lost." Later he writes, "I passionately longed for war against Hitler and 'agitated' for it; and I shall be eternally grateful to Roosevelt, the born and conscious enemy of *L'infame* for having maneuvered his all-important country into it with consummate skill." The author who quotes this, Robert E. Hertzstein, points out that Churchill was praising and envying Hitler in that same year—1935—whereas Roosevelt loathed and opposed him (in the geopolitical sense as well) as early as 1933. Few would question the judgment that Hitler and Roosevelt saw each other as "born and conscious enemies" (Hertzstein, *Roosevelt & Hitler* [New York: Paragon House, 1989], 413.

8. *Bitburg in Moral and Political Perspective*, 114–29. In calling for "a mature political pedagogy," Adorno writes, "Essentially, it is a matter of the *way* in which

the past is called up and made present: whether one stops at sheer reproach, or whether one endures the horror through a certain strength that comprehends even the incomprehensible" (126).

9. Trans. Charles Maier, *The Unmastered Past*, 45.

10. Jürgen Habermas, "Defusing the Past," in *Bitburg in Moral and Political Perspective*, 42–49.

11. Chaim A. Kaplan, *The Warsaw Diary of . . .* , 362.

12. Adolf Hitler, *Mein Kampf*, 64.

13. Lyotard, *Heidegger and "the jews,"* 26.

14. Adorno, *Negative Dialectics*, 361, 365.

15. Levinas, *Ethics and Infinity*, 117.

16. Chaim A. Kaplan, *The Warsaw Diary of . . .* , 92.

17. Ibid., 104.

18. Fackenheim, *To Mend the World*, 237.

19. Bullock, *Hitler: A Study in Tyranny*, 401–2.

20. *Aden, Arabie,* quoted by Wilkinson, 265.

21. Wilkinson, *The Intellectual Resistance*, 266.

22. The doctrine from which Nazism drew was specific. As Paul de Lagarde, a German anti-Semite writing in 1884, said, "We have to break with the idea of humanity" and associated humanitarianism. He was a neo-Darwinian who believed in natural selection as justification for killing inferior individuals and species (*The Catastrophe of European Jewry* [Jerusalem: Yad Vashem, 1976], 255.

23. Richard L. Rubenstein, *After Auschwitz* (New York: Macmillan Publishing Co. 1966), 118.

24. Hannah Arendt, *The Origins of Totalitarianism* (New York: Harcourt, Brace & Co., 1951), 277ff.

25. Richard Rubenstein, "Some Perspectives on Religious Faith after Auschwitz," *The German Church Struggle and the Holocaust* (Detroit: Wayne State University Press, 1974), 264–65.

26. *Basic Writings of Marx and Engels*, 34.

27. Lewis Feuer writes understandingly about Marxism in this aphoristic remark: "Ethics repressed returned as pseudoscience" (*Basic Writings of Marx and Engels*, xiii).

28. Currently the topic of humanism has reached high visibility in French intellectual debate, brought to a focus on the issue of Heidegger's involvement with Nazi ideology and politics (see Luc Ferry and Alain Renaut, *Heidegger and Modernity*, trans. Franklin Phillip [Chicago: University of Chicago Press, 1990], 81–108; and their *French Philosophy of the Sixties: An Essay on Anti-Humanism*, trans. Mary H. S. Cattani [Amherst: University of Massachusetts Press, 1990]).

29. Isaiah Berlin, *New York Review of Books*, Serial issues of October 1990. Now available in book form: *The Crooked Timber of Humanity* (New York: Alfred A. Knopf, 1991).

30. Isaiah Berlin, *New York Review of Books*, October 25, 1990, 65.

31. Foucault, "Two Lectures," 95.

32. Ibid., 96.

33. Karl Marx, *"A Contribution to the Critique of Political Economy,* from *Basic*

Writings: Marx and Engels, ed. Lewis S. Feuer (New York: Doubleday & Co. 1959), 43.

34. In fact, the Bomb, in its total destructiveness, illustrates the self-defeat of the power thesis in Foucault's argument. The power that when unleashed destroys everything is a power that must be contained by something other than itself, a priority resistant to power embodied in conscience and law. One hopes that this may be founded in societies and nations on a principle larger than self-preservation, and it must, for self-preservation is only the backside of the thrust for power.

35. In fuller excerpt Marx wrote: "This communism, as fully developed naturalism, equals humanism, and as full developed humanism equals naturalism; it is the *genuine* resolution of the conflict between man and nature and between man and man—the true resolution of the strife between existence and essence, between objectification and self-confirmation, between freedom and necessity, between the individual and the species. Communism is the riddle of history solved, and it knows itself to be this solution" (Marx, "Private Property and Communism," in *The Economic and Philosophic Manuscripts of 1844,* ed. Dirk J. Struik [New York: International Publishers, 1964], 135). Obviously, my argument is not with Marxist theory except indirectly, and my focus here is on what might be called the degenerate philosophy of redemption in the power-conflict theory of Nazism, but Marx with these words was making his own apocalyptic "final solution" to the "riddle of history." In Marx's phrasing, however, the dialectical terms—naturalism-humanism, necessity-freedom, the individual-the species—still posed their riddle. What was done to force them into resolution became the issue in the historic critique and defeat of communism.

36. "Excerpts from Herr Eugen Duhring's Revolution in Science," in Feuer, *Basic Writings,* 272.

37. Robert Bernasconi, "Levinas and Derrida" (in *Face to Face with Levinas,* ed. Richard A. Cohen [Albany: State University of New York Press, 1986], 181–202) is a valuable introduction to Levinas's primary ideas (see Levinas, *Totality and Infinity* [Pittsburgh: Duquesne University Press, 1969]), 173, 199.

38. Levinas, *Justification de l'ethique* (Bruxelles: Edition de l'Universite de Bruxelles, 1984) 41–51; trans. and republished as "Ethics as First Philosophy," *The Levinas Reader,* ed. Sean Hand (Oxford: Basil Blackwell Ltd., 1989), 82, 83.

Index

Adorno, Theodor, xi, xvi, 7, 19, 142, 150, 170, 174, 190nn.5, 19, 191n.1, 204n.14, 206n.8

Albany Holocaust Conference, 153, 205n.20

Amery, Jean, xvi, 2, 4, 20, 24, 31, 95, 131, 189n.2, 191n.25, 193n.37, 203n.42; suicide, xii, 41–43, 140, 174; moral reality, 17, 44, 107, 139, 184; on history and power, 19; on the antihuman, 26

Anti-Communism, 62, 100, 170

Anti-Semitism, xiii, 1, 26, 114, 128, 146, 190n.5; Christian, 75, 116, 127, 149; German, 172; Hitler's, 12, 173, 199n.34, 203n.38; naturalist, 75–76, 173; Nazi, 117, 126, 155–57; White Russian, 199n.33

Appelfeld, Aharon, 3, 5, 6

Arendt, Hannah, 64, 84, 124, 128–29, 141, 178–79, 195n.5

Aron, Raymond, 170

Baeck, Leo, 23

Bakunin, Mikhail, 103

Bangladesh, 2

Barbie trial, 13, 23

Bataille, Georges, 26

Bauman, Zygmunt, 69–70; *Modernity and the Holocaust,* 180

Benda, Julien, 19, 191n.29

Berenbaum, Michael, 3

Berlin, Isaiah, 180–81

Best, Werner, 196n.24

Bettelheim, Bruno, 14, 15, 73

Bible, ix, x, 175; Genesis, 140; Job, 18, 20, 147, 187; Old Testament, 116

Bitburg, 171

Bolshevism, 51–55 passim, 66, 69, 172; and Nazism, 62; and Hitler, 96, 146, 169, 171, 199n.34; and Jews, 64, 117, 147. *See also* Judeo-Bolshevism

Bracher, Karl, 117, 201n.9

Brecht, Berthold, 56, 87

Browning, Christopher, 102; *Ordinary Men,* 132–35

Budapest Jews, 86

Buddhism, 122

Bukharin, Nikolai, 97, 199n.30

Bullock, Alan, 54, 146, 199n.33

Bundists, 57

Bureaucratization, 61

Cambodia, 126

Camus, Albert, xii

Canetti, Elias, xi, xvi, 25, 59, 83, 130; *Crowds and Power,* 93–95, 107–8

Catholic Church, 101

Celan, Paul, 42, 145–46

Chamberlain, Neville, 91, 171, 194n.7

Chaplin, Charles, 83

Christ, 19, 40, 116, 128

Christian: ethic, 4; Gospel, 128; theology, 148–49

Christianity, 57, 59, 116–17, 122, 150, 155–56; Hitler and, 54, 101; and Nazis, 75–76, 126

Churchill, Winston, 205n.7

Clausewitz, Karl von, 67, 105

Cohen, Arthur, xvi, 4, 6, 9, 79, 85, 144, 150

Cold War, 171

Communism, 55, 87, 172, 183, 185, 197n.38

Communist(s), 27, 50, 55, 57, 62, 79; anthem, xiii; Manifesto, 55, 179; party, 97–99, 199n.30; Russia, 171

Conquest, Robert, 47, 98

Craig, Gordon, 18

Crane, Stephen, 162

Crime against humanity, xii, 12–15, 26–27, 34, 67, 189n.4

Crucifixion, ix, x, 57, 128

Czerniakow, Adam, 24, 40, 111, 202n.11

Dadaist, 102

Daladier, Edouard, 91

DATE DUE